BASIC Program Conversions

How to Convert Programs from One Computer to Another

Includes:
IBM PC & PCjr, COMMODORE 64, APPLE IIe & II+,
TRS-80 MODELS III & IV, TRS-80 COLOR COMPUTER

Computer Skill Builders
Bill Crider, Managing Editor
in consultation with Chuck Steele, David Byrum, David Lovelock,
Ignacio Mendivil, Joseph Rotello

HPBooks®

Publisher: Rick Bailey
Editorial Director: Theodore DiSante
Art Director: Don Burton
Book Design: Leslie Sinclair
Typography: Cindy Coatsworth, Michelle Carter
Director of Manufacturing: Anthony B. Narducci

Published by HPBooks, Inc., P.O. Box 5367, Tucson, AZ 85703 602/888-2150
ISBN: 0-89586-297-2   Library of Congress Catalog No. 84-80558
©1984 HPBooks, Inc.   Printed in USA
4th Printing

Table of Contents

Introduction

A computer can do amazing things if it is given logical instructions. But the instructions must be in the appropriate dialect of the appropriate language. If you thought any computer running BASIC would run any BASIC program, you have by now discovered that you were sadly mistaken.

Like French people who will accept only "French French" and openly scorn "Franglais," your computer won't accept BASIC programs not written in its specific dialect. For example, you will find that Apple BASIC will not run on an IBM PC, TRS-80 Model IV, Commodore 64, or TRS-80 Color Computer.

THREE SCENARIOS

This can be a real problem. Consider the plight of the following individuals:

Sue the Teacher—Sue knew that she would be using her school's microcomputers to teach arithmetic in the fall. She assumed that she would be using the TRS-80 in the school library. Because her nearby Radio Shack store was offering a BASIC programming class for teachers at a reduced rate, she eagerly enrolled.

After learning programming, she spent her whole summer writing a math program for her students. The first day of school she was greeted by her principal at the door. "Good news, Sue," the principal beamed, "The PTA has donated two Commodore computers to the school, and we are going to put one in your class. You won't have to share the TRS-80 with the science teacher."

Chuck the Manager—Chuck, an up-and-coming manager in a prospering company, felt that his company could control inventory better with a microcomputer. But his boss was opposed to the idea. "We've managed our inventory on 3x5 cards for 15 years. Why should we change now?" the boss scowled.

Not easily intimidated, Chuck decided to take matters into his own hands. He bought an Apple. Not finding any inventory programs he liked, he spent all his evenings for the next month writing a program. When his boss saw it, he was impressed. "There's only one problem," he pointed out. "An Apple doesn't have enough disk space to put all our inventory on one disk. We will buy an IBM PC." You can guess what happened next. Chuck's program wouldn't run on the PC!

Joe the Gamesman—Joe had a great idea for a new game that was interesting and exciting. He spent many hours programming it in TRS-80 Color Computer BASIC. When it was perfected, he made an appointment with a software publisher. The publisher was also excited, and offered him a sizable royalty for the program. There was only one hitch. "Joe, we offer only programs that run on at least three popular machines," the publisher informed him. "Which other machines do you have this running on?"

WHAT TO DO?

If one of these scenarios describes your situation, you have only three possible means of obtaining software for your computer:

Solution 1—Purchase, or otherwise obtain, only that software written for your computer.

Solution 2—Write your own software.

Solution 3—Convert existing software to your computer's dialect.

You may decide to take Solution 1 and purchase only that software already written for your machine. Or, obtain it by other means, such as through your users-group's public domain library. This is certainly the easiest method of solving the problem, but also the most expensive.

Solution 2, writing your own software, is only a solution if you are an experienced programmer and have plenty of time. Very few people are in this category.

Solution 3, converting existing software, combines the best features of 1 and 2. You save the money you would spend on new software, and you don't need as much time to develop it. If you are converting a program you or your associates have already been using on a different machine, you will save the training time involved with a new program. You will also avoid the bugs and limitations inherent in new software. However, you may possibly put in a few bugs of your own.

Modifying an existing BASIC program from one machine to another is not difficult. In fact, it is both fun and interesting. It is also one of the easiest ways to learn the BASIC dialect of the second machine if you do not already know it.

For the most part, the various computers actually share basic terms and keywords. The only difference is that some BASIC functions may be known by another name on another machine.

1 How To Start Converting Programs

We'll start by looking at some elementary concepts of program conversion. Let's call the machine the program was originally written for the *source*. The machine you want it to run on is the *target*.

LEVELS OF CONVERSION

There are many different levels of converting BASIC programs from source to target.

First Level—Little or no conversion may be required. For example, a program written for the TRS-80 may run on an IBM PC with no changes. If this is the case, you are either very lucky or working with a very simple program! You can just type in the program and run it.

Usually, many of the words in the target program will be the same as in the source program, but not all of them.

Second Level—The source and target languages may have the same function, but different words are used. For example, CLS on a TRS-80 will do the same thing as HOME on an Apple. All you have to do in this case is substitute the target word for the source word.

Third Level—It's possible that a word used in the source language means something entirely different in the target language. This requires more ingenuity than the first and second levels. If you do not translate the word—having mistaken it for a first-level conversion—you will not get expected results. In this case you may have to write a subroutine (or use one from this book) that simulates the source word for the target computer.

An example of this is RND. In TRS-80 BASIC, RND(n) will generate a random integer between 0 and n, inclusive. In Applesoft BASIC, RND(n) generates a random number between 0 and 1, non-inclusive. You would therefore have to replace the TRS-80 command with a subroutine in Applesoft BASIC. You could use this:

```
INT(RND(1)*n+.5)
```

to get the same results in a program converted from a TRS-80 to an Apple computer.

Fourth Level—In this case the word in the source language has no equivalent in the target language. Translation at this level is more demanding. Typically, you must write a subroutine to approximate the effect of the source word.

For example, in IBM BASIC

```
A$=STRING$(B,C)
```

assigns to A$ the value of B characters having the ASCII value of C.

```
10 A$=STRING$(5,42)
20 PRINT A$
```

would print

```
* * * * *
```

because the ASCII value of an asterisk is 42. Commodore BASIC does not have this function. You would have to use the program line

```
PRINT "* * * * *"
```

to simulate it. In this case, $*$ is the character you want to print.

This example also illustrates another possible pitfall in conversion. The expressions STR$, STRIG and STRING$ all look similar, but have radically different meanings. Watch your spelling and typing, and never assume that a command means what you expect it to mean. Look it up if you are not sure.

Another fourth-level possibility applies to machine language and PEEKs and POKEs. If the source program calls a machine language routine, you may have to write a subroutine that emulates the machine code. Rewriting machine language routines into BASIC almost always slows the program down. If the source code uses PEEKs and POKEs, you will have to determine their equivalents for your machine or write an equivalent subroutine.

You can recognize machine language by such words as CALL, SYS, USR and BLOAD (in some cases). Another clue is a loop that reads a series of DATA statements and POKEs the values into consecutive memory locations.

Fifth Level—It's possible that an entire expression, line or subroutine in the source language may be emulated in the target language with a single word. This is just the opposite of Level 3. Actually, Level 5 is easier than Level 3 or Level 4, but requires a sharp eye to catch.

Here's an example:

```
130 RA=1/AR
140 FOR I=X-R TO X+R
150 H=I:V=Y+SQR((R^2)-(H-X)^2)*AR
160 HPLOT H,V
170 H=I:V=Y-SQR((R^2)-(H-X)^2)*AR
180 HPLOT H,V
190 NEXT I
200 FOR I=Y-R*AR TO Y+R*AR
210 V=I:H=X+SQR((R^2)-(RA*(V-Y))^2)
220 HPLOT H,V
230 V=I:H=X-SQR((R^2)-(RA*(V-Y))^2)
240 HPLOT H,V
250 NEXT I
```

That Apple routine draws a circle. The whole routine could be replaced in a program for the IBM PC with just one statement:

```
10 CIRCLE (X,Y),R
```

The key is to identify what a routine does within the program. Usually this means running it. Then determine if the target computer allows an easier way.

Sixth Level—This is not a level at all, but a statement of impossibility. That is, some programs or commands simply may not be translated into the target language. This is most likely to occur in graphics, PEEKs and POKEs and machine-language parts of a program.

If you have a color program designed to run on a high-resolution Apple screen, for example, you will never be able to convert it exactly into TRS-80 Model III BASIC. This is because the TRS-80 Model III does not have high-resolution or color. There is no way to even simulate the Applesoft

COLOR commmand. You must either greatly modify the program—if the particular graphics are not necessary—or abandon the project.

Another example concerns memory. If the source program uses 64K RAM and your machine has only 48K RAM, the program won't fit.

Another impossiblity would be to translate from compiler BASIC on the source to interpreter BASIC on the target—and in some cases vice-versa. It is unlikely, however, that you will have access to the source code of a program written in compiler BASIC. The programs you find in magazines, books, electronic bulletin boards and users groups are usually interpreter BASIC.

CONVERSION STRATEGY

If you convert programs with a hit-or-miss technique, you will find it slow and frustrating. Even so, this is exactly what many programmers do. A typical unplanned session goes like this:

The programmer types in a program from a magazine or other similar source. When he tries to run the program, it crashes. The programmer looks at the line number of the error message, and edits that line. Run again, crash again.

This time the line number leads the programmer to what might as well be Greek. He has never seen these words before. Nor does the computer's reference manual list the words, so he deletes the line with the offending syntax.

When he runs the program again, it seems to work for a while, but then the screen fills with gibberish—yet no error messages. Finally, he gives up.

There is a better way!

What You Need—You should have at least an elementary working knowledge of the target BASIC. If you know no programming at all, you may be able to translate simple programs with the help of this book, but it is easy to get in over your head. Start simple and work your way up.

You should also have this book. You will find it irreplaceable for cross-referencing the most popular BASICs. The programming hints in it will save you hours of work.

A printout of the source program is essential. You could possibly work with just the program in memory and on the screen, but you will soon see that this is not the best method.

The printout may take many forms. Perhaps you have a book of BASIC programs in a "generic" BASIC or one that is written for a different computer. Possibly you are looking at a magazine article with the listing. Or best of all, you have a printout from a computer. If you can, specify a double-spaced printout on wide paper that has room for margin notes.

You must have the target computer. Otherwise, what's the point of converting? Even if you did make the conversion, how would you know it ran correctly? Debugging is essential to any program conversion.

The BASIC documentation for the target computer is also necessary. It helps with syntax and vocabulary. Some may have translation tips, too.

Useful But Not Essential—Having the source computer is convenient. If you can run the program on the source computer you will gain invaluable insight into what the program is *supposed* to do. This will help you when debugging the program on the target computer. It's especially useful when writing graphics routines.

The BASIC documentation for the source machine will help determine if the word on the source is really the same as for the target. If it has a memory map, you may even be able to translate the PEEKs and POKEs.

With a good word processor you can convert a program more easily. The "search-and-replace" feature makes overall fixes efficient. In addition, a word processor usually allows full-screen editing.

Some users groups and electronic bulletin boards actually have programs designed to convert programs from one machine to another. Typically, these make simple search-and-replace changes and alert you to lines requiring further attention. Such programs will speed you along in the early stages of the project, but will not do it all. They can't follow program logic and cannot handle most graphics displays. Even so, they are helpful if available. Check with some of the "old-timers" in your users group to see if a conversion program is available.

Multicolored, felt-tipped highlighting pens will make the job easier by allowing you to mark up your printout. Use different colors to indicate different sections or conversion problems. You will be able to refer to your marked-up printout more quickly and better remember significant portions.

Find a roomy area to work in. Typically, computers seem to leave little space on a desk for printouts, books and notepads. If you can, make room for your references and printouts around the computer. We have found it helpful to have a small, four-wheeled cart with space underneath for disks and pens and a flat top for notepads and printouts. A typing stand is nice for setting books next to the computer.

UNDERSTAND THE PROGRAM LOGIC

Learn the logical flow of the program. This is the most important step in converting a program from one machine to another. Don't pass it by. The sample program we will use—PICK UP STICKS—is short, but the principles illustrated become even more valuable as you translate longer programs.

How To Do It—If you have the source machine available, run the program several times, using all possible options. Take notes on what happens in what order. Sketch the menu screens and especially the graphics screens.

If the source computer has "screen-dump" utility, use it to print out different screen displays on hardcopy. Does the program use color? Animation? Scrolling? Number your sketches or screen printouts and give them titles, such as *Main Menu, Option Menu #1,* or *Graphics Screen #3*. If you have a camera, take color photos of any particularly intricate screen displays. An instant-developing Polaroid or Kodak camera is very useful for this purpose.

Be sure you thoroughly understand program operation before you move on to the next step.

Determine Memory Used by Program—As mentioned earlier, this can be important. In fact, you may discover at this stage that you can't make a conversion.

Use the FRE or MEM command as explained in Chapter 3. If the program uses more memory than available on the target machine, you cannot convert. In fact, if it uses more than about 75% of the target memory, you may have difficulty running it unless you modify it to use less RAM. You may have to break a large program into modules—called *overlays* in some documentation—to get the program into memory a little at a time.

Using Pens and Printout—Using the source-program printout and highlighting pens, determine the logical flow of the program. Mark logical sections and subroutines. Label them with appropriate titles. Use expressions such as *Input Routine, Error-Trapping Routine* or *Disk-I/O Routine*.

You may want to develop a flowchart of the program and tape it to the wall near your computer. Write notes to yourself in the printout margins as you go through it. Figure 1-1 on the next page shows what a simple game program might look like after it has been marked up.

Write in Pseudocode—This is merely an explanation in English of what each program section does or is supposed to do.

This allows you to break the overall project into small, manageable tasks rather than approaching it as one monstrous endeavor.

Don't make your pseudocode too detailed. Go for the "big picture." A pseudocode description of the game in Figure 1-1 is shown in Figure 1-2.

You will refer to the pseudocode repeatedly when you encounter GOTO and GOSUB statements. This saves you from searching through printouts or screens of information when you are converting a large program.

```
100     REM * * * * * * * * * * * * * * * * * *
110     REM PICK - UP - STICKS GAME
120     REM * * * * * * * * * * * * * * * * * *
130     PRINT "THE OBJECT OF THIS GAME IS ";
140     PRINT "TO PICK UP STICKS IN SUCH ";
150     PRINT "A WAY THAT YOU ARE NOT THE ";
160     PRINT "ONE TO PICK UP THE LAST ";
170     PRINT "STICK. WE WILL START WITH ";
180     PRINT "21 STICKS AND YOU WILL ";
190     PRINT "HAVE THE FIRST TURN. YOU ";
200     PRINT "MAY PICK UP EITHER 1 , 2 , 3 , ";
210     PRINT " OR 4 STICKS PER TURN. " : PRINT
220     S=21
230     PRINT "HOW MANY STICKS DO YOU WISH ";
240     INPUT "TO PICK UP"; P
250     IF P <> INT (P) THEN 600
260     IF P < 1 OR P > 4 THEN 700
270     S=S-5
280     PRINT "I WILL PICK UP "; 5 - P; ". ";
290     PRINT "THAT LEAVES "; S; " STICKS. "
300     IF S > 1 THEN 230
310     PRINT "YOU MUST PICK UP THE LAST ";
320     PRINT "STICK, SO I WIN. " : PRINT
330     INPUT "SHALL WE PLAY AGAIN (Y/N)"; A$
340     IF A$ = "Y" THEN 220
350     END
600     PRINT "YOU CAN'T PICK UP A ";
610     PRINT "FRACTION OF A STICK! " : PRINT
620     GOTO 230
700     PRINT "THE RULES SAY YOU MAY ONLY ";
710     PRINT "PICK UP 1 , 2 , 3 OR 4 STICKS. "
720     GOTO 230
```

Handwritten annotations:
- INSTRUCTIONS (lines 130–210)
- # OF STICKS (line 220)
- INPUT ROUTINE (lines 230–240)
- # STICKS (line 240)
- FRACTION CHOSEN (line 250)
- WRONG NUMBER CHOSEN (line 260)
- KEY TO GAME! (line 270)
- PLAY AGAIN UNTIL ONE STICK LEFT (line 300)
- 230-300 MAIN SECTION OF PROGRAM
- COMPUTER ALWAYS WINS!! (lines 310–350)
- ERROR TRAP FOR 250 (lines 600–620)
- ERROR TRAP FOR 260 (lines 700–720)

Fig. 1-1/Begin by making notes to yourself on a printout of the program you want to convert. This way, you will understand program flow and make the task of converting more efficient.

Program Lines	What They Do
100-210	Instructions
220	Initialize variables
230-240	Input routine
250-260	Catch errors
270-300	Computer's turn; go back to input
310-350	End of game; start another
600-720	Error-trapping routines

Fig. 1-2/A pseudocode explanation of the PICK-UP-STICKS program clarifies its major segments.

Handling Variables—Make a list of the variables, their names and how they are used. This will be a very important reference if your program is long. If you have a *cross-reference utility,* now is the time to use it.

This is a program that reads a file and compiles useful information from it. Usually a cross-reference utility constructs lists of variables and the lines where they are found, lists of lines that call other line numbers (GOSUBs, GOTOs, etc.) and the lines they call, and sometimes lists of variable values at each line.

Figure 1-3 on the next page shows how a cross-reference listing for PICK UP STICKS might look.

Also, review the reserve words of the target computer and the acceptable format for its variables. Are all the variables of the source language compatible with the target language? Are the variable-name rules the same on both computers? If not, note those that you will have to rename. (The rules for naming variables for each computer are listed in Chapter 2 under *Data Types.*) Post the list next to the flowchart.

Handling Machine Language—Highlight any PEEKs and POKEs or machine-language routines. Look up the PEEK and POKE equivalents in the target documentation and write them in the printout margin. If there are no equivalents on the target machine, note it in the margin.

Try to determine what the original programmer was doing, and ask yourself "What other method could I use to achieve the same effect?"

Syntax Considerations—If your printout does not differentiate between the letter O and the number zero (0), go through the printout and mark all zeros by putting a slash through them. If it is difficult to distinguish between the number 1, the letter l and the letter I, mark them somehow.

As you are going through the printout, be alert for other syntax considerations. If the source differs from what you expect, doublecheck to see if the target will accept it. If not, note in the margin what requires changing.

Arrays—Note any arrays in the program. Did the programmer DIMension them at the beginning? Do the current dimensions make the best possible use of memory? Eliminate any doubts by DIMensioning them yourself.

```
Variable Locations
P appears in 240, 250, 260, 280
S appears in 220, 270, 290, 300
A$ appears in 330, 340

Line Calls
220 is called by 340
230 is called by 300, 620, 720
600 is called by 250
700 is called by 260

Running Variable Values For Sample Run
at 220 S=21
at 240 P=3
at 270 S=16
at 240 P=4
at 270 S=11
at 240 P=1
at 270 S=6
at 240 P=3
at 270 S=1
at 330 A$=N
```

Fig. 1-3/A sample printout from a cross-reference utility shows the variable locations, line calls and running variable values.

RUN THE PROGRAM ON THE TARGET MACHINE

Now that you understand the program and what it should do, load it into your computer. If you already have it on a medium your computer can read, you are a step ahead. If not, type it in.

If you are typing the program lines into your computer, you will be tempted to make many changes. If so, observe the following general rules:

Variables—Change those variable names that are inappropriate. But be careful to change them consistently! For example, don't call a variable TITLE in one place and TI in another place.

Statements—Change only those statements you are *sure* should be changed.

Syntax—Don't change syntax yet.

Renumbering—Don't renumber the lines yet. If you do, you will run into problems with GOSUBs, GOTOs and IF-THEN statements.

REM—Add any REM statements that will help you later when debugging.

Indent—Use indentation to make loops easier to read. For example, a FOR-NEXT loop might be indented this way:

```
10 FOR A=1 TO 10
20    PRINT "A LOOP #",A
30    FOR B=1 TO 5
40      PRINT "THIS IS A TEST"
50    NEXT B
60 NEXT A
```

See how easy it is to read that the B loop occurs completely within the A loop? This type of indentation will assist you when you are not sure what is going on within a loop. If the machine you're using does not allow leading blanks in statements, you can usually indent by using colons—as with the Commodore 64, for example.

Typing and Proofing—Type very carefully and proofread at least twice—once on the screen, and again from a printout after you have typed in the program.

Using Conversion Aids—You may have various conversion aids not previously discussed. One of the most useful—but probably also the most imperfect—is a *Conversion Program.* This is an advanced type of special-application word processor. It reads in a file in one BASIC language and outputs it as a file in the target language.

Conversion programs are limited for several reasons. First, they cannot take into account all the possible permutations of the BASIC language. Second, they cannot correct syntax. Third, they cannot translate PEEKs, POKEs, machine language routines or screen displays. Fourth, and most important, they do not know what a program is supposed to do. They cannot verify that the product is running correctly.

In spite of these limitations, conversion programs can help. They serve primarily as a search-and-replace tool. Where commands have a direct equivalent (Level 2), they can take the tedium out of the task. They may also identify areas requiring further intervention on your part.

If you have a conversion program, use it, but don't expect it to work perfectly.

Word Processor—If you haven't already been using it to enter the program, now is the time to load the word-processor or programmer's-aid program. You should first use it to do any search-and-replace tasks you have identified. All the words with a direct equivalent in the target language can be replaced this way.

As you are doing this, you may wish to use some particular character—such as the asterisk—to mark those places requiring special attention. Instead of marking them within the line, set them off with remark lines. This way you can find them again easily. Here is an example:

```
300 REM*******The next 5 lines need attention
```

This will add a few lines to the program, but you can delete them when you work on the routine in question.

If your word processor has a spelling checker, you may want to use it. But be aware that it is going to find a large number of "misspelled" words, namely the variables and almost all the reserve words.

If your spelling checker can build a custom dictionary, add all your reserve words to it as you come across them. Don't add the variables, though. Even if your spelling checker identifies most of the words as "misspelled," it is useful in that it brings each one to your attention. You may find problems you would have otherwise overlooked.

Renumbering—It's possible that your program is getting cluttered by this time. If that is the case, you may wish to use the RENUMBER command to give you more working space. You can do this at any time, but keep in mind that you will have to run your cross-reference utility again when the line numbers change. And you should note the changes on your psuedocode listing.

Also, because you have been working with the program already, you probably have some idea of where each routine is located within it. You will have to "relearn" the line numbers if you renumber them.

Another way to resolve the numbering problem and create some working space between the lines is to simply add a 0 to each line number with your word processor. Line 12 becomes line 120; line 30 becomes line 300, and so forth. This will not affect your previously prepared reference aids and will give you 99 lines to work with between each of the old lines. Remember that your highest line number can't be greater than 65535. (63999 for Applesoft and Commodore 64 BASIC.)

When you are completely finished debugging the converted program, it makes sense to use the RENUMBER command to make it more readable. There is really no need to renumber before then.

ABOUT EQUIPMENT DISCUSSED IN THIS BOOK

There are hundreds of microcomputers on the market today, and each computer may be able to use multiple dialects of BASIC. It would be impossible to cover even half of the total possibilities in the space available. Therefore, this book is limited to the five brands that comprise at least 90% of computers in use.

Of these brands we cover one model extensively and may discuss a second model only if it differs from the first. In each case, we limit the discussion to one BASIC for each brand, and comment if the second machine differs.

Remember that just because a computer may have 64K RAM, it is not necessarily true that a 64K program will run on it. The computer must also have memory available for the BASIC interpreter itself. Typically, a 64K machine will not run a program that is longer than 40K. The actual length of program that your computer will run depends not only on memory, but also on the size of the BASIC interpreter, the amount of variable storage space needed by the program and the amount of work space needed by that particular program.

APPLE PRIMARY DISCUSSION
Model: Apple IIe
Memory: 64K RAM
Monitor: Color
Storage: Disk Drive(s)
DOS: Apple DOS 3.3
BASIC: Applesoft BASIC

APPLE SECONDARY DISCUSSION
Model: Apple II+
Memory: 48K RAM
Monitor: Color
Storage: Disk Drive(s)
DOS: Apple DOS 3.3
BASIC: Applesoft BASIC

COMMODORE 64 DISCUSSION
Model: Commodore 64
Memory: 64K RAM
Monitor: Color
Storage: Disk Drive(s)
DOS: DOS 2.6
BASIC: PET BASIC 2.0

IBM PRIMARY DISCUSSION
Model: IBM PC or XT
Memory: 64K RAM
Monitor: Color
Storage: Disk Drive(s)
DOS: 2.0
BASIC: 2.0

IBM SECONDARY DISCUSSION
Model: IBM PCjr
Memory: 128K RAM
Monitor: Color
Storage: Disk Drive, BASIC Cartridge
DOS: 2.1
BASIC: Cartridge BASIC

RADIO SHACK TRS-80 PRIMARY DISCUSSION
Model: Model IV
Memory: 64K RAM
Monitor: Monochrome
Storage: Disk Drive(s)
DOS: TRS-DOS 6.0.0
BASIC: TRS-DOS 6.0.0 BASIC

RADIO SHACK TRS-80 SECONDARY DISCUSSION
Model: Model III
Memory: 48K RAM
Monitor: Monochrome
Storage: Disk Drive(s)
DOS: TRS-DOS 1.3
BASIC: TRS-DOS 1.3 BASIC

RADIO SHACK TRS-80 COLOR COMPUTER (COCO)
Model: Color Computer
Memory: 48K RAM
Monitor: Color
Storage: Disk Drive(s)
BASIC: Disk Extended Color BASIC 1.0

USING THIS BOOK

By now you're probably wondering when you were going to get to use this book. Now is the time! At this point you should be very close to having a program that will run. Now you need to get down to details of the various routines that present translation difficulties.

First, identify what a word or routine is supposed to do. Then refer to the alphabetic listing in this book, Chapter 3. Look up that word. Read the text portion at the beginning of the chapter to gain a better understanding of what is involved in translating that type of command. Then look at the command specifically.

Sometimes you will be given an alternate command, sometimes a suggested subroutine. If you must add lines to insert a subroutine, be careful not to renumber any lines that may be called from another routine. If you must use a long routine—or if the routine must be used more than once—consider using a GOSUB instruction.

Make sure you haven't used the variable names in the subroutine in some other way elsewhere in your program. If you have used them, rename them in the subroutine.

FINAL DEBUGGING

When you have completed all the substitutions, you will be ready for the final debugging. Load the program into your computer and try running it. If it runs the first time, give yourself a big pat on the back! Chances are it will not run perfectly. In this case you are ready to endure the programming ritual called *debugging*.

Each time the program crashes it should give you an error message. Refer to the computer's documentation to determine what the message means. Use your editor or word processor to correct the offending program line. Save the corrected version on disk and try again.

If your computer has a TRACE or TRON function, use it. There are also commercial programs available that allow you to view your program in special ways as you run it. If you have one of these available, you may wish to use it.

You will probably spend very little time "tweaking" the program if you have followed the systematic approach advocated here. If you find you are spending more time debugging than in previous stages, you probably failed to grasp the overall flow and logic of the program before starting. Go back and start over!

When you have finished debugging the program, you should look over it again to be sure you have optimized memory usage. You may wish to delete most of your REMs now. And you may find that combining some lines make it run faster. Like a living organism, a program should be in a constant state of change and improvement.

LEGAL CONSIDERATIONS

Converting programs from one computer to another may present some complicated legal problems. Guidelines discussed here are general and may or may not apply to your specific case. If you have any doubt at all, seek legal counsel.

If a program is in the public domain, you can usually do whatever you wish with it—convert it, use it or sell it. The problem is being certain of a program's status. A program is public domain if the author has allowed it to be so. Generally the programs on electronic bulletin boards and in club libraries are in the public domain. If they have a copyright notice anywhere in the listing they are probably *not* in the public domain.

Programs found in books and magazines are usually *not* in the public domain. Although they may not have a copyright notice in the listing, they are covered by the copyright notice at the beginning of the book or magazine. If you are just using the program on your computer and are not making any profit on it, the right to copy it from a magazine or book is implied. But check with your lawyer if you have any doubts or want to make money from the program.

Programs purchased in local computer stores or through the mail are also not generally in the public domain. There are a few exceptions. If you wish to convert a program that you are reasonably certain is not in the public domain, you must have the written permission of the copyright holder to copy it, convert it, use it on multiple machines, or especially to sell it.

If you wish to convert it to another machine and are willing to give the converted version to the copyright holder, you will usually find the owner very helpful. This is because having multiple versions of a program makes it more salable.

If you plan to use the converted program on multiple machines, the copyright owner will likely grant you permission, but may ask for an additional license fee. If you plan to convert it and sell the converted version, the owner will probably either deny permission or allow you to do it only if you pay a royalty.

WHERE DO YOU FIND PROGRAMS?

You can find programs to convert in a variety of places. Some possibilities follow:
1) Programs you have written.
2) Programs your friends or business associates have written.
3) A users-group library.
4) Electronic bulletin boards.
5) Computer magazines.
6) Computer books.
7) Trade journals in your field.
8) Programs you have purchased.

Again we emphasize: *Check the copyright status of a program before you convert it.*

2 About BASIC Commands and Programs

The various things you can do with BASIC commands vary little from machine to machine. But how you implement those actions with BASIC syntax and program structure vary greatly.

This chapter discusses the various actions, giving you the commands that cause them. Chapter 3 lists the specific commands in alphabetical order, explaining the parameters included with them and comparing their usage on each machine.

Computing has three stages—input, processing and output. Each stage can be broken down into sub-stages. Looking at it this way fragments the explanation—such as splitting up file handling into two steps—but provides a logical way to understand this chapter.

USING THE NEXT CHAPTER

It would be impossible to detail every possible usage of every BASIC command on each of the computers discussed in this book. Therefore, we didn't try to do that!

Instead, each command has been explained in sufficient detail for you to understand what it does, what the syntax is, what parameters or switches are needed, and in some cases what the common program structure is. If you still need help, refer to the documentation that came with the target computer. Let it be the final arbiter of any doubts you have about syntax or legal parameter values.

If we couldn't simulate the command in less than 15 lines of BASIC code, without machine-language code, or without hardware modification, then simulation was considered beyond the scope of this book. You'll see something like *Not available. Cannot be simulated.* In these cases we mean that it can't be simulated within these limitations. If you are an experienced programmer, you may wish to attempt simulation if the command is essential to your program.

In a few cases machine-language routines or extensive PEEKs and POKEs were used where necessary.

ABOUT TERMINOLOGY

In this book, an *instruction* is any BASIC *key word* or *reserved word.* For example, commands and statements are both instructions.

If an instruction has no line number before it, it is called a *command* because it is issued from the command mode. It is sometimes called the *immediate* mode.

If a line number precedes an instruction, it is called a *statement.* Therefore

```
RUN
```

is a command, but

```
10 RUN
```

is a statement. Despite this distinction, the terms *instruction, command* and *statement* are used interchangeably in most computer literature—including this book.

An *algorithm* is a series of instructions. For example, a program is an algorithm. A program may consist of one statement, or many statements. Usually a portion of a program—or a small program that does a specific task and is inserted into a larger program—is called a *routine.* If a routine is accessed by a GOSUB statement, it is called a *subroutine.*

All or part of a program may also be generically called *code,* because an algorithm is just a series of codes the computer understands.

ABOUT SYNTAX

The syntax of a command has been indicated using symbols and conventions compatible with the IBM PC BASIC 2.0 documentation. Some of the conventions will seem strange to programmers familiar only with Apple, Commodore or TRS-80 documentation. Here is what the conventions mean.

COMMAND

A word in all capital letters is a *key word.* It is usually the command under discussion.

variable

A word or letter in lowercase is a *variable* or *constant* that must be supplied by the programmer.

filename

The words *file* and *filename* are used to denote a valid filename, whether variable or constant. This implies all the data associated with or required by the computer in use. This may include a drive or device designator, a filename of the correct length and an extension. In IBM BASIC 2.0 it may also be a path.

[ ]

Items enclosed in brackets are optional. They are not required for correct program execution. For example, **PRINT #1, a[,b]** means that you can have more than one variable printed to a file. In addition to *a*, you could also include *b*.

...

An ellipsis (three dots) indicates a list based on a pattern. For example, **PRINT #1, a[,b]...** means you may have more variables PRINTed to the file than just *a* and *b*. You could also have *c*, *d* and others.

( )

If parentheses are indicated, they *must be* included. Also be sure to include all punctuation and to differentiate between 1 (one) and l (the letter l), as well as between 0 (zero) and O (the letter *oh*).

INPUT

Before your computer can do any useful work, it must have some data. Getting this data is called *input*. It can come from a number of locations—keyboard or joysticks, storage devices such as a disk drive or cassette player, or from another external communication device such as a modem, graphics table, A/D converter or host computer. In addition, data may be accessed either serially or randomly.

**KEYBOARD, JOYSTICKS
AND LIGHT PENS**

The Apple computer normally gets its input from the keyboard. Input may be redirected to files using PR#, thus rendering the keyboard ineffective until input is directed back to it. No keyboard buffer is used—only one character can be sent at a time. Apple normally uses up to three paddles instead of joysticks, but some companies have released joysticks as well. Unlike other computers, Apple reads a resistance value from the paddles rather than an x,y coordinate.

The IBM PC has a unique keyboard. Key assignments are all under software control. Some keys can be "event trapped." The keyboard has a 15-character buffer, which can be accessed from BASIC. In addition to the shift and control keys, it has an ALT key—the PCjr has a FN key. They work the same way. Four joysticks are supported. A light pen will work, too. You can open the keyboard as a file for input.

The keyboard on the Commodore 64 also has many unique features. It includes a 10-key buffer—accessible from BASIC—known as the *dynamic keyboard*. In addition to four function keys, each key is addressable as a command or graphics character using the shift or Commodore key. You can open the keyboard as a file for input. Two joysticks are supported.

The keyboards on Radio Shack computers are "economy" models. They have no control key and no buffer. Models III and IV do not support joysticks. On the Color Computer, the keyboard may be opened as an input file. Two joysticks are supported.

Keyboard and Joystick Commands—Those relating to keyboard or joystick usage are in the box on the next page.

```
┌─────────────────────────────────────────────────┐
│          KEYBOARD AND JOYSTICK VOCABULARY         │
│                                                   │
│   CMD        INPUT#      LINEINPUT      PR#        │
│   GET        INPUT$      LINE INPUT#    READ       │
│   GET#       INPUTLINE   PDL           READ#      │
│   IN#        JOYSTK      PEN            STICK      │
│   INKEY$     KEY         PEEK           STRIG      │
│   INPUT      KEY$        POKE                      │
└─────────────────────────────────────────────────┘
```

STORAGE

This part of program operation is critical if you want to retrieve information, programs or data for re-use. These commands get information from a disk drive or cassette recorder.

Cassette—All computers discussed in this book—except the TRS-80 Model IV—are capable of using cassette-based programs and files. The Model IV uses cassettes only in the Model III mode or for downloading from the Model 100. The file structure for sequential access files is similar for each of them, but the syntax of the command for opening and closing the files differs. The Apple is the only one that cannot turn the cassette motor on and off under program control.

The TRS-80 Color Computer, IBM PCjr and Commodore 64 can use cartridge-based software. Cartridges are not compatible among machines.

Sequential Access—Converting sequential-access, disk-file-handling routines from one computer to another is not difficult. Although the commands have different syntax, usage is very similar. Apple is somewhat different from the others. It uses a syntax that accesses the DOS disk routines. Here's the general syntax:

```
10 PRINT CHR$(4);"OPEN filename"
20 PRINT CHR$(4);"READ filename"
30 INPUT A$
```

Thereafter, all input words will receive data from the disk file instead of the keyboard. Because Apple does not keep track of the number of records in the file and does not have an end-of-file marker, the program should also keep track of those items. The general procedure for other computers is:

```
10 OPEN "I",1,"filename"
20 INPUT#1, A$
```

The specific syntax will vary, but you can have multiple files open, and send output to or get input from each. Simply specify the number of the file buffer.

Random File Access—The syntax of random-file-access routines varies greatly among computers, but there are only two general methods of actual data handling. Apple and Commodore have a method that differs from other computers. They handle each record as one long string, without breaking it up into fields. Accessing a specific item in a record requires positioning the pointer at the specific byte, or reading the entire record and breaking it up with string functions. Conversely, IBM and Radio Shack computers define a record as a number of fields of specific length in a random file. Each field may be accessed individually.

Disk—The TRS-80 Color Computer and the Commodore 64 allow accessing information directly from a specified sector of a disk from within a BASIC program—a task handled by DOS on other computers. Commodore also allows direct access to the routines controlling the disk drive, via MEMORY commands.

Disk and Tape Input Commands—Those relating to reading disk or tape files are in the following box.

DISK AND TAPE-FILE VOCABULARY

APPEND	CSAVEM	INPUT	PR#
AUDIO	DCLOSE	INPUT#	PRINT#
B-A:	DELETE	INPUT$	PRINT#USING
B-F:	DIR	KILL	PRINT
B-P:	DIRECTORY	LINEINPUT	PRINT USING
B-R:	DLOAD	LINE INPUT#	PUT
B-W:	DLOADM	LOAD	PUT#
BACKUP	DOPEN	LOADM	READ
BLOAD	DRIVE	LOF	READ#
BLOCK-READ:	DSAVE	LPOS	RECALL
BLOCK-WRITE:	DSKINI	M-E:	RECORD
BLOCK-ALLOCATE:	DSKI$	M-R:	RESTORE
BLOCK-EXECUTE:	DSKO$	M-W:	RMDIR
BLOCK-FREE:	EOF	MEMORY-EXECUTE:	RUN
BUFFER-POINTER	ERASE	MEMORY-READ:	SAVE
BSAVE	FIELD	MEMORY-WRITE:	SAVEM
CATALOG	FILE	MERGE	SCRATCH
CHAIN	FILES	MKDIR	SHLOAD
CHDIR	FORMAT	MOTOR	SKIPF
CLOAD	FRE	NAME	ST
CLOADM	FREE	NEW	STATUS
CLOSE	GET#	OPEN	STORE
CMD	GET	OUT	UNLOAD
COPY	IN#	OUTPUT	WRITE
CSAVE	INP	POINTER	WRITE#

EXTERNAL COMMUNICATIONS

Computers receive input from peripherals—such as the display, modem, printer and A/D converters—in diverse ways. The IBM has the richest BASIC vocabulary for external input. Other computers may require machine-language programming. Because IBM OPENs the COM port like a file, all file input commands apply. Other commands relating to external input include the following words.

EXTERNAL-INPUT VOCABULARY

COM	IN	POINT	ST
CMD	INP	POSN	STATUS
CSRLIN	LPOS	PPOINT	WAIT
IN#	PEEK	SCREEN	

PROCESSING

This category includes commands dealing with program flow, functions, operators, data types, and memory and machine interfacing.

PROGRAM FLOW

Commands for program flow are almost identical for all computers discussed in this book. You should note that some of the computers do not include the ELSE command, and some do not include WHILE—WEND loops

---

PROGRAM-FLOW VOCABULARY

AUTO	GOSUB	ONERR	SHELL
BUFFER-POINTER	GOTO	POINTER	SKIPF
CHAIN	IF	REM	SPEED=
CHDIR	IF-THEN	REN	STOP
CMD	IF-THEN-ELSE	RENAME	THEN
DATA	KILL	RENUM	TO
DELETE	LIST	RENUMBER	TRACE OFF
ELSE	LLIST	RESTORE	TRACE ON
END	M-E	RESUME	TRACE
ERASE	MEMORY-EXECUTE	RESUME NEXT	TROFF
ERL	MKDIR	RETURN	TRON
ERR	NEXT	RMDIR	WAIT
ERROR	NOTRACE	RUN	WEND
ERRS$	ON ERR GOTO	SCRATCH	WHILE
FOR	ON ERROR GOTO		

FUNCTIONS

Numeric functions, such as SIN, SQRT and VAL, are used nearly the same way on all the computers discussed here. One exception is RND.

String functions are also very similar, with a few exceptions. For example, MID$ and SCREEN as statements have radically different definitions from those they have when used as functions.

FUNCTION VOCABULARY

ABS	EOF	LEFT$	MKS$
ASC	ERL	LOC	OCT$
ATN	ERR	LOF	PDL
CDBL	ERRS$	LOG	PEEK
CHR$	EXP	LPOS	PEN
CINT	FIX	M-R:	POINT
COS	FRE	MEM	POS
CSRLIN	HEX$	MEMORY-READ:	PPOINT
CVD	INKEY$	MID$	RIGHT$
CVI	INP	MKD$	RND
CVN	INPUT$	MKI$	ROW
CVS	JOYSTK	MKN$	SCREEN

(Continued at top of next page.)

```
┌─────────────────────────────────────────────────┐
│          FUNCTION VOCABULARY (cont.)             │
│   SGN          SQR          STRIG        TIME$    │
│   SIN          STATUS       STRING$      VAL      │
│   SPACE$       STICK        TAN          VARPTR   │
│   SPC(         STR$         TI$          VARPTR$  │
└─────────────────────────────────────────────────┘
```

OPERATORS

Few differences exist among numeric operators used on the various computers. Not all systems will perform modulo arithmetic or integer division, for example. But all systems provide the same exponentiation, negation, addition, subtraction, multiplication and division operators.

Relational operators are the same on all computers. Logical operators NOT, AND and OR are included on all systems, but not all use XOR, EQV and IMP. Apple, however, does not allow bitwise manipulation with the logical operators, as the others do. Some differences exist in the priority order of operations, so doublecheck if you are experiencing unexpected results from operations.

```
┌───────────────────────────────────────┐
│           BASIC OPERATORS             │
│                                       │
│    ^      Exponentiation              │
│    –      Negation                    │
│    *      Multiplication              │
│    /      Floating-Point Division     │
│    \      Integer Division            │
│    MOD    Modulo Arithmetic           │
│    +      Addition                    │
│    –      Subtraction                 │
│    =      Equality                    │
│    <      Less Than                   │
│    >      Greater Than                │
│    NOT                                │
│    AND                                │
│    OR                                 │
│    XOR                                │
│    EQV                                │
│    IMP                                │
│                                       │
└───────────────────────────────────────┘
```

DATA TYPES

This section includes constants, variables, strings, numerics and arrays. Variable names must always begin with a letter.

Apple uses floating-point numbers with nine digits of precision. Though you can use INT to get an integer, it will still be stored as a floating point. Variable names may be any length, but only the first two digits are significant, and they may not contain embedded key words.

IBM uses integers, single-precision numbers (seven or fewer digits of precision), and double-precision numbers (17 digits of precision, of which 16 are printed). Variable names may be any length, of which only the first 40 characters are significant.

The Commodore 64 uses floating-point numbers with nine digits of precision. Though you can use INT to get an integer, it will still be stored as a floating point. Variable names may be any length, but only the first two digits are significant, and they may not contain embedded key words.

The TRS-80 Model IV uses integers, single-precision numbers (seven or fewer digits of precision), and double-precision numbers (17 digits of precision, of which 16 are printed). Variable names may be 40 characters long, and each character is significant.

The TRS-80 Model III and TRS-80 Color Computer use integers, single-precision numbers (seven or fewer digits of precision), and double-precision numbers (17 digits of precision, of which 16 are printed). Variable names may be any length, of which only the first two characters are significant.

VARIABLE-TYPE VOCABULARY

CDBL	CVS	FIX	OCT$
CHR$	DATA	HEX$	OPTION BASE
CINT	DEFDBL	INT	STR$
COMMON	DEFFN	LET	STRING$
CONCAT	DEFINT	MKD$	SWAP
CSNG	DEFSNG	MKI$	VAL
CVD	DEFSTR	MKN$	VARPTR
CVI	DIM	MKS$	VARPTR$
CVN			

MACHINE AND MEMORY INTERFACE

The interface to the machine and memory is necessarily different on the computers. Some words used, such as PEEK and POKE, perform the same function but require completely different addresses. Some machines don't allow USR(n). Some reserved words are unique to the individual machine, such as MEMORY-EXECUTE on the Commodore 64.

In fact, you may not be able to translate a program that depends heavily on a machine or memory interface. In such cases it may be easier to rewrite the program.

MACHINE AND MEMORY-INTERFACE VOCABULARY

B-A:	BSAVE	MEMORY-EXECUTE:	SAVEM
B-F:	CALL	MEMORY-READ:	SHLOAD
B-P:	DEF SEG	MEMORY-WRITE:	SPEED=
B-R:	FRE	OUT	STATUS
B-W:	HIMEM:	PCLEAR	SYS
BLOAD	INP	PCLS	SYSTEM
BLOCK-READ:	LOADM	PCOPY	UNLOAD
BLOCK-WRITE:	LOMEM:	PEEK	USER
BLOCK-ALLOCATE:	M-E:	PMODE	USR
BLOCK-EXECUTE:	M-R:	POKE	VARPTR
BLOCK-FREE:	M-W:	POP	VARPTR$
BUFFER-POINTER:	MEM	PR#	VERIFY

OUTPUT

This category includes commands dealing with display, sound, the printer, storage and external communications.

DISPLAY

Some of the greatest differences among the systems under discussion concern the screen display. Some differences exist in the way text and graphics are displayed in terms of the SYNTAX used, the modes available, colors available, and differences in the physical size and shape of the display screen.

The Apple allows monochrome text of 40 or 80 columns by 24 rows. Low-resolution graphics allows 40x48 pixels, with 16 colors available. High-resolution graphics offer 280x192 pixels, with six colors available. The shape table feature allows fast DRAWing and manipulation of predefined shapes.

The IBM PC provides both text and graphic modes. The text mode may be 40 or 80 columns by 25 rows, which may be displayed in any one of 16 foreground and eight background colors. Limited graphics are possible on the text screen by using a set of built-in character graphics. There are several graphics modes with various levels of resolution, but a graphics adapter card is required. A medium-resolution graphics mode allows text on the screen, and has a resolution of 320x200 pixels with six foreground colors available—three colors at a time—and 16 background colors. Only black and white are available in the highest resolution—640x200 pixels. Advanced graphics features include PAINT tiling, GETting and PUTting screen blocks, and a graphics language.

The IBM PCjr allows all of the same modes as the PC, with the addition of a 160x200 pixel low-resolution mode (15 foreground and 16 background colors), an additional four-color medium-resolution mode, a 16-color medium-resolution mode, and a four-color high-resolution mode. This means that there are seven modes on the PCjr, as opposed to three on the PC. The PCjr also allows PALETTE and PALETTE USING commands.

The Commodore 64 text mode has 24 rows of 40 columns each. Characters may be displayed in 16 colors. It has several combinations of graphics modes, including bit mapping the screen. Resolutions available are 160x200 and 320x200 pixels. Advanced capabilities include sprites and programmable character sets. Many of the graphics features require extensive PEEKing and POKEing.

The TRS-80 Model III allows either 32 or 64 columns by 16 lines on the text screen. The Model IV has 80 columns by 25 rows. The only graphics options available are block graphics characters, although individual graphics blocks may be turned on and off. Color is not available.

The TRS-80 Color Computer provides both text and graphic modes. The text mode is 32 columns by 16 rows, which is limited to one color. Several graphics resolutions are available, including 128x96, 128x192 and 256x192. Eight colors are available, depending on which resolution you choose. Advanced graphics features include GETting and PUTting screen blocks, and a graphics language.

Display Processing Commands—Those associated with display output include the following list.

DISPLAY-OUTPUT VOCABULARY

CIRCLE	FLASH	HLIN-AT	PAGE
CLS	GET	HPLOT	PAINT
CMD	GR	HTAB	PALETTE
COLOR	HCOLOR	INVERSE	PALETTE USING
COLOR=	HCOLOR=	KEY	PCLEAR
CSRLIN	HGR	LINE	PCLS
DRAW	HGR2	LOCATE	PCOPY
DRAWTO	HLIN	NORMAL	PEEK

(Continued at top of next page.)

PEN	PRINT	ROT=	VLIN-AT
PLOT	PRINT@	SCALE	VPOS
PMAP	PRINT#	SCALE=	VTAB
PMODE	PRINT#USING	SCREEN	WIDTH
POINT	PRINT AT	SCRN(	WINDOW
POINTER	PRINT USING	SET	WRITE
POKE	PSET	SHLOAD	WRITE#
PPOINT	PUT	VIEW	XDRAW
PR#	RESET	VLIN	XPLOT
PRESET			

SOUND

Although it has a built-in speaker, the Apple supports sound only with PEEKs and POKEs or machine-language programs.

The IBM PC supports extensive sound capabilities through the PLAY and SOUND commands. It too has a built-in speaker. You may also turn the cassette on and off via the cassette port, and thus generate sound. The IBM PCjr has even greater sound capabilities, including a three-voice music generator and a NOISE command.

The Commodore 64 supports up to four voices, but only by machine-language programming or PEEKs and POKEs.

The TRS-80 Model III and Model IV do not support sound, but you can turn the cassette on and off on the Model III.

The TRS-80 Color Computer supports extensive sound capabilities, including a music language used with the PLAY command. Another command, AUDIO, allows you to direct cassette output to the monitor speaker.

Sound Processing Commands—Instructions used with sound output are in the following box.

SOUND-OUTPUT VOCABULARY

AUDIO	MOTOR	PEEK	POKE
BEEP	NOISE	PLAY	SOUND

PRINTER

There are two fundamental ways computers deal with the printer—as a device or as a file.

Apple always treats it as a device. PR#1 usually sends output to the printer as well as to the screen.

IBM and the TRS-80 Color Computer will treat the printer either way. You can open it as a file or use commands such as LPRINT, which treat it as a device.

The Commodore 64 makes no distinction between devices and files as far as PRINTing to them is concerned.

The TRS-80 Model III and Model IV treat the printer only as a device, accessing it with commands such as LPRINT.

Printer Processing Commands—Those relating to the printer include all those that relate to file output—IBM, Commodore 64 and COCO—plus the following.

```
                    MORE PRINTER VOCABULARY
    CMD             POSN            PRINT#USING     TAB
    LLIST           PR#             PRINT USING     TAB(
    LPOS            PRINT           ST              WRITE
    LPRINT          PRINT@          STATUS          WRITE#
    LPRINT USING    PRINT#
```

STORAGE

Methods of outputting data to cassette or disk are similar to input methods.

Commodore allows you to write directly to a specified sector of the disk using the BLOCK and BUFFER commands. COCO allows you to do the same, but utilizes the DSK commands. In addition, both of these and the other computers handle disk output automatically through their DOS routines.

See the discussion of input above, or the discussions of the commands in chapter 3, for more details on the different file structures.

Output Storage Commands—Those relating to output to cassette and disk are in the following box.

```
                    OUTPUT VOCABULARY
    APPEND          CHDIR           DSKI$           PRINT USING
    B-A:            CLOSE           DSKO$           PUT
    B-F:            CMD             ERASE           PUT#
    B-P:            COLLECT         FIELD           RENAME
    B-R:            COPY            FILES           RMDIR
    B-W:            CSAVE           KILL            SAVE
    BACKUP          CSAVEM          LOF             SAVEM
    BLOCK-READ:     DCLOSE          MKDIR           SCRATCH
    BLOCK-WRITE:    DELETE          MOTOR           SYSTEM
    BLOCK-ALLOCATE: DIR             OPEN            TAB
    BLOCK-EXECUTE:  DIRECTORY       OUTPUT          TAB(
    BLOCK-FREE:     DOPEN           PR#             STORE
    BUFFER-POINTER  DRIVE           PRINT           UNLOAD
    BSAVE           DSAVE           PRINT#          WRITE
    CATALOG         DSKINI          PRINT#USING     WRITE#
```

EXTERNAL COMMUNICATIONS

Outputting methods to external devices, such as modems or relays, are very diverse. The IBM has the richest BASIC vocabulary for external output. Other computers may require machine-language programming.

Because the IBM OPENs the COM port as a file, all the file output commands apply. Other commands relating to external output include the following.

EXTERNAL-OUTPUT VOCABULARY

AUDIO	MOTOR	OUT	PR#
CMD	OFF	PEEK	WAIT
COM	ON	POKE	

RESERVED WORDS

Words in this list are used by various computers as *reserved* words. Apple and Commodore do not allow embedded reserved words in variable names. Therefore, you should avoid using these words in variable names.

Not all of these words are used on the machines covered in this book. But to get maximum portability from your software, you should avoid using them.

RESERVED WORDS

ABS	BLOCK-READ:	CLOG	CVT$F	DRIVE	FIELD
ACS	BLOCK-WRITE:	CLOSE	CVT%$	DS	FIF
ACSD	BLOCK-ALLOCATE:	CLR	CVTF$	DSAVE	FILE
ACSG	BLOCK-EXECUTE:	CLRDOT	DASH	DSKINI	FILES
ADR	BLOCK-FREE:	CLS	DAT	DSKI$	FILL
AND	BUFFER-POINTER	CMD	DATA	DSKO$	FIN
APPEND	BOLD	CO	DATE$	DSP	FIND
ARCOS	BPUT	CODE	DCLOSE	EDIT	FINPUT
ARCSIN	BREAK	COLLECT	DEBUG	ELSE	FIX
ARCTAN	BRIGHTNESS	COLOR	DEF	END	FLASH
ASC	BSAVE	COLOR=	DEFDBL	ENTER	FLOW
ASCII	BUTTON	COM	DEFFN	ENVIRON	FLT
ASN	BYE	COMMON	DEFINT	ENVIRON$	FMT
ASND	CALL	CON	DEF SEG	EOF	FN
ASNG	CATALOG	CONCAT	DEFSNG	EQ	FNEND
AT	CDBL	CONSOLE	DEFSTR	EQV	FONT
ATAN	CH	CONT	DEFUSR	ERASE	FOR
ATN	CHAIN	COPY	DEG	ERDEV	FORMAT
ATND	CHANGE	COS	DEGREE	ERDEV$	FOUT
ATNG	CHAR$	COSD	DEL	ERL	FPRINT
AUDIO	CHAR	COSG	DELETE	ERR	FPUT
AUTO	CHARSIZE	COSH	DET	ERRL	FRAC
AXIS	CHDIR	COUNT	DIGITS	ERRN	FRE
B-A:	CHR	CSAVE	DIM	ERROR	FREE
B-F:	CHR$	CSAVEM	DIR	ERRS$	FUNTIL
B-P:	CINT	CSH	DIRECTORY	EXAM	FUZZ
B-R:	CIRCLE	CSNG	DLOAD	EXCHANGE	GE
B-W:	CLEAR	CSRLIN	DLOADM	EXEC	GET#
BACKUP	CLG	CUR	DMS	EXIT	GET
BAPPEN	CLK$	CVD	DOPEN	EXP	GIN
BASE	CLK	CVI	DOS	EXT	GO
BEEP	CLOAD	CVN	DOT	FDIM	GO TO
BGET	CLOADM	CVS	DRAW	FETCH	GOODBYE
BLOAD	CLOCK	CVT$%	DRAWTO	FGET	GOSUB

(Continued at top of next page.)

RESERVED WORDS (cont.)

GOSUB-OF	LI	MONITOR	POSITION	SCALE	TAN
GOT	LIN	MOTOR	POSN	SCALE=	TAND
GOTO	LINE	MPY	PPOINT	SER	TANG
GOTO-OF	LINEINPUT	MTPACK	PR#	SCRATCH	TANH
GR	LINE INPUT#	NAME	PRECISION	SCREEN	TAPPEND
GRAD	LINK	NE	PRESET	SCRN	TEXT
GRAPHICS	LINPUT	NEW	PRI	SCRN(	THE
GT	LIS	NEX	PRINT	SECRET	THEN
HCOLOR	LIST	NEXT	PRINT@	SEG$	TI
HCOLOR=	LLIST	NOFLOW	PRINT#	SEG	TI$
HEADER	LN	NOISE	PRINT#USING	SET	TIM
HEX$	LOAD	NORMAL	PRINT AT	SETCOLOR	TIME$
HGR	LOADM	NOT	PRINT USING	SETDOT	TIME
HGR2	LOC	NOTE	PSET	SGET	TIMER
HIMEM:	LOCATE	NOTRACE	PTR	SGN	TLIST
HLIN	LOF	NULL	PTRIG	SHELL	TLOAD
HLIN-AT	LOG	NUM$	PUT	SHLOAD	TNH
HOME	LOG10	NUM	PUT#	SHUT	TO
HPLOT	LOGE	OCT$	RAD	SIN	TOP
HSCRN	LOMEM:	OFF	RADIAN	SIND	TRACE OFF
HTAB	LPOS	OLD	RAN	SING	TRACE ON
IF	LPRINT	ON	RANDOM	SINH	TRACE
IF-GOT	LPRINTUSING	ON ERR GOTO	RANDOMIZE	SKIPF	TRAP
IF-GOTO	LSET	ON ERROR GOTO	RBYTE	SLEEP	TROFF
IF-LET	LT	ONERR	RDRAW	SNH	TRON
IF-THE	M-E:	ON-GOSUB	REA	SORT	TSAVE
IF-THEN	M-R:	ON-GOT	READ	SOUND	TYP
IF-THEN-ELSE	M-W:	ON-GOTO	READ#	SPA	TYPE
IMAGE	MAN	OPEN	RECALL	SPACE$	UNLOAD
IMP	MARK	OPTION	RECORD	SPACE	UNTIL
IN#	MAT CON	OPTION BASE	REM	SPC	USER
INCH	MAT IDN	OR	REMARK	SPC(	USING
INCHAR	MAT INPUT	OUT	REN	SPEED=	USR
INDEX	MAT INV	OUTPUT	RENAME	SPUT	VAL
INIT	MAT PRINT	PADDLE	RENUM	SQR	VARPTR
INKEY$	MAT READ	PAGE	RENUMBER	SQRT	VARPTR$
INP	MAT TRN	PAINT	REP	ST	VERIFY
INPUT	MAT ZER	PALETTE	REPEAT$	STATUS	VIEW
INPUT#	MAT*	PALETTE USING	RES	STE	VIEWPORT
INPUT$	MAT+	PAUSE	RESET	STEP	VLIN
INPUT1	MAT-	PCLEAR	RESTORE	STICK	VLIN-AT
INPUTLINE	MAT=	PCLS	RESUME	STO	VPOS
INSTR	MAX	PCOPY	RESUME NEXT	STOP	VTAB
INT	MDD	PDL	RET	STORE	WAIT
INTER$	MEM	PEEK	RETURN	STR$	WBYTE
INVERSE	MEMORY-EXECUTE:	PEN	RIGHT$	STR	WEAVE
IOCTL	MEMORY-READ:	PI	RIGHT	STRIG	WEND
IOCTL$	MEMORY-WRITE:	PIN	RMDIR	STRING$	WHILE
JOYSTK	MERGE	PLAY	RMOVE	STRING	WIDTH
KEY	MID$	PLOT	RND	STUFF	WINDOW
KEY$	MID	PMAP	ROT=	SUB	WRITE
KILL	MIN	PMODE	ROTATE	SUBEND	WRITE#
LE	MKD$	POINT	ROW	SUM	XDRAW
LEFT	MKDIR	POINTER	RSET	SWAP	XIO
LEFT$	MKI$	POKE	RU	SYS	XOR
LEN	MKN$	POLL	RUN	SYSTEM	XPLOT
LET	MKS$	POP	SAVE	TAB	XRA
LGT	MOD	POS	SAVEM	TAB(	

3 Alphabetic Listing of BASIC Words

ABS

APPLE IIe & II+

ABS (x) returns the absolute value of x, where x is any numeric expression.

IBM PC & PCjr

Same.

COMMODORE 64

Same.

AND

APPLE IIe & II+

AND is a logical operator that returns a True (1) or False (0) value based on a bitwise computation. The truth table for AND follows:

x	y	x AND y
T	T	T
T	F	F
F	T	F
F	F	F

IBM PC & PCjr

AND is a logical operator that returns a True (1) or False (0) value based on a bitwise computation. The truth table for AND follows:

x	y	x AND y
T	T	T
T	F	F
F	T	F
F	F	F

AND may also be used to test for a particular bit pattern. See page 3-28 in the IBM BASIC documentation for a detailed explanation.

COMMODORE 64

AND is a logical operator that returns a True (−1) or False (0) value. The truth table for AND follows:

x	y	x AND y
T	T	T
T	F	F
F	T	F
F	F	F

CLEAR

APPLE IIe & II+	IBM PC & PCjr	COMMODORE 64	TRS-80 Models IV & III	TRS-80 Color Computer	COMMENTS
CLEAR clears variables and resets internal control stack.	CLEAR [,n] [,m] (BASIC 2.0) where n is the optional number of bytes you want for BASIC workspace, and m is the optional stack space you desire. Used alone, CLEAR frees all memory, erases all DIMs, DEFs and variable values, and sets any sound, PEN and STRIG values to OFF. CLEAR [,n] [,m] [,v] (Cartridge BASIC Only) clears memory, where n is the optional number of bytes you want for BASIC workspace, m is the optional stack space you desire, and v specifies the total number of bytes to set aside for video memory. Used alone, CLEAR frees all memory, erases all DIMs, DEFs and variable values, and sets any SOUND, PLAY, PEN and STRIG values to OFF.	CLR aborts all logical files that may be open, sets all nonreserved variables to zero, and releases all array space, but does not affect all BASIC program in memory.	CLEAR [,m] [,n] (Model IV) where m is an optional integer indicating the highest memory location available to BASIC, and n is a numeric constant, numeric variable or expression indicating the number of bytes to allocate for stack storage (default n=512). CLEAR eliminates all variables and closes all files. CLEAR n (Model III) where n is the amount of space to reserve for string storage. Default = 50 bytes. Note that this does not affect files.	CLEAR [n] [,m] where n is the amount of space to allocate for string storage—default=200 bytes—and m is the highest memory location available for BASIC. This command also initializes all variables. Note that this is the opposite order of TRS-80 Model IV	If it's available, you may wish to use ERASE to clear some memory if you don't want to lose the values stored in variables, arrays and DEF statements.

CLOAD

APPLE IIe & II+	IBM PC & PCjr	COMMODORE 64	TRS-80 Models IV & III	TRS-80 Color Computer	COMMENTS
LOAD causes the next program on the cassette to load. Note that the cassette must be ready!	LOAD cas:[filename][,R] loads the next program on the cassette, unless the optional filename is supplied. In this case it searches the cassette for the named file. If the R option is specified, the program is run as soon as loaded.	LOAD [filename][,device][,location] where filename is the name of the file you wish to load. Default on cassette is the next file, but the filename must be specified on disk. Device is the storage device—cassette=1; disk=8; default=1. Location is the type of load you wish to achieve—0 (the default) loads in at the start of BASIC, 1 loads in from where it is saved. Files saved on cassette with a non-relocatable LOAD—see SAVE—are LOADed back into the same location they came from. This ignores the location direction. Although LOAD closes all files when used as a statement within a program, it does not clear variables. Nor does it reset BASIC memory pointers. After the LOAD is complete, it automatically RUNs the BASIC program in memory. Be careful when using LOAD to chain BASIC programs. The first program that has the initial LOAD in it must be longer than any programs subsequently called. If you wish to LOAD and RUN a longer program from a shorter one, use the dynamic keyboard as in the following program	The Model IV operates from cassette only in the Model III or Model 100 mode. The Model 100 is not covered in this book. CLOAD [filename] (Model III) loads the next file on cassette into memory. If filename is specified, the computer searches for that file on cassette. CLOAD? compares the file in memory to the next file on the cassette. If the files do not match bit for bit, the word BAD is displayed on the screen.	CLOAD [filename] loads a program from cassette, where filename is a file on the cassette. If filename is omitted, the next program on the cassette is loaded. CLOADM "filename" [,n] loads the machine-language file filename, beginning at the optional memory location offset n.	Some computers close all files and re-initialize all variable values when asked to LOAD or CLOAD a program.

← COLUMN ENDS HERE

← COPY CONTINUES HERE

lines. Remember, though, that this technique clears all the variables.

```
10 PRINT CHR$(147) "LOAD"
   CHR$(34) "filename"
   CHR$(34) ".8"
20 POKE 214,4: PRINT: PRINT
   "RUN"
30 POKE 198,4: POKE 631,19
40 FOR I=2 TO 4: POKE
   630+I,13: NEXT
50 END
```

Sometimes, conversion information for a certain computer is so long and detailed that it won't fit in one column. When that happens, the column ends with a solid black bar. The copy continues under the next black bar in a column to the right—typically the next column. See the above illustration.

TRS-80 Models IV & III	TRS-80 Color Computer	COMMENTS
Same.	Same.	

TRS-80 Models IV & III	TRS-80 Color Computer	COMMENTS
AND is a logical operator that returns a True (1) or False (0) value. The truth table for AND follows:	**AND** is a logical operator that returns a True (1) or False (0) value. The truth table for AND follows:	

x	y	x AND y
T	T	T
T	F	F
F	T	F
F	F	F

x	y	x AND y
T	T	T
T	F	F
F	T	F
F	F	F

APPEND

APPLE IIe & II+

PRINT D$;"APPEND filename"** where **D$ is equal to CTRL-D or CHR$(4). Opens the sequential file **filename** and positions the pointer at the end of the file, so that data may be written to it.

IBM PC & PCjr

OPEN"filename" FOR APPEND AS #n opens the sequential data file **filename** as logical file **n**, and positions the pointer at the end of the file.

COMMODORE 64

Although there is no documented reference to APPEND in the Commodore Model 1541 disk drive manual, it is possible to simulate it on all current disk drives:

```
10 OPEN n, dv,
   sa, "filename, A"
```

where **n** is the logical file number to be written to, **dv** is the disk drive device number (usually 8), **sa** is the secondary address, and **filename** is the name of the file. When the file is then written to, the new data will be inserted at the end of the file.

ASC

APPLE IIe & II+

ASC(n$) returns the ASCII value of the first character of **n$**, where **n$** is any string expression except a null. This is the reverse of CHR$.

IBM PC & PCjr

Same.

COMMODORE 64

Same.

ATN

APPLE IIe & II+

ATN(x) returns the angle whose tangent is **x**. The value returned is single precision, and is measured in radians in the range $-\pi/2$ to $\pi/2$.

IBM PC & PCjr

Same.

COMMODORE 64

Same.

TRS-80 Models IV & III

OPEN "E", b, filename [,r1] where **"E"** is required for the extend ("append") mode, **b** is the number of the buffer in the range 1-15, **filename** is the name of the file, and **r1** is the optional record length of the data fields in **filename**. This file OPENing method will cause data written to the file to be appended to the end. Also see **OPEN** for other uses of this command.

TRS-80 Color Computer

Because COCO does not have an APPEND mode, you must use program lines similar to the following to append to a file. This renames the file with the name "TEMP.DAT", OPENs the file, reads it into the new file to move the pointer to the end, and returns you to the main program. You can then write your data to the file. **F$** is the variable reserved for the filename, which you must assign before calling this routine. You must also be sure to close the file. And, it's a good idea to KILL TEMP.DAT when you're finished.

```
1000 RENAME F$ TO "TEMP.DAT"
1010 OPEN "I",1,"TEMP.DAT"
1020 OPEN "O",2,F$
1030 IF EOF(1) GOTO 1070
1040 LINE INPUT #1,T$
1050 PRINT #2,T$
1060 GOTO 1030
1070 CLOSE #1
1080 RETURN
```

To simulate APPEND on cassette, the entire data file must be read into memory. Add the data to the file—be sure to increase the record counter if there is one—and write the file back out to cassette.

COMMENTS

See **OPEN FOR APPEND**. Note that some other BASICs not covered in this book use APPEND as a form of MERGE, loading a program into memory rather than adding data to the end of a file.

TRS-80 Models IV & III
Same.

TRS-80 Color Computer
Same.

COMMENTS

TRS-80 Models IV & III
Same.

TRS-80 Color Computer
Same.

COMMENTS

To convert degrees (D) to radians (R), use the following formula:

$R=D*3.141593/180$

Also note that AT is used within other commands by Apple and TRS-80, so it should not be assigned as a variable.

AUDIO

APPLE IIe & II+

There is no way to control starting and stopping of the cassette on the Apple. Simulating AUDIO would be impossible without hardware modification. If this function is desired, you need an interface with the RS232 port.

IBM PC & PCjr

If you wish to hear audio from a cassette, such as a tutorial tape, under program control, you can leave the earplug jack out of the cassette. Then use the following program lines to operate the cassette for 60 seconds. Adjust the time period by altering line 1020:

```
1000 MOTOR ON
1010 A=TIMER
1020 WHILE TIMER<A+60
1030 WEND
1040 MOTOR OFF
1050 RETURN
```

COMMODORE 64

The Commodore cassette recorder does not allow audio recording. AUDIO cannot be simulated.

AUTO

turns on automatic line-numbering. It is not used within programs.

B-A (See BLOCK)

BACKUP

is a reserved word for the TRS-80 Color Computer. It is used to create backup disks, but is not used within BASIC programs. It would erase the program from memory.

BEEP

APPLE IIe & II+

PRINT CHR$(7) causes the speaker to sound 1000 Hz tone for .10 seconds.

PEEK (−16336) causes the speaker to emit a single click.

IBM PC & PCjr

BEEP
BEEP ON (Cartridge BASIC Only)
BASIC OFF (Cartridge BASIC Only) sounds the speaker at 800Hz for 1/4 second and is the equivalent of PRINT CHR$(7). In Cartridge BASIC, BEEP may be used with SOUND to select the active speaker:

SOUND OFF: BEEP OFF selects the internal speaker only.
SOUND ON: BEEP OFF selects the external speaker only.
SOUND OFF: BEEP ON selects both speakers (default setting).

COMMODORE 64

Although there is no BEEP command on the Commodore 64, the following program lines produce a similar effect. In this subroutine, **T** is the numeric value associated with the tone (range 0-255). **D** is a positive integer associated with tone duration.

```
1000 T=60: D=100: S=54273
1010 POKE S,T: POKE S+5,240
1020 POKE S+23,5: POKE S+3,17
1030 FOR A=1 TO D: NEXT
1040 POKE S+23,0: POKE S,0
1050 RETURN
```

B-F (See BLOCK)

TRS-80 Models IV & III

Because the Model IV does not use cassette (except in Model III mode), you cannot simulate AUDIO on it.

On the Model III, if you wish to hear audio from a cassette, such as a tutorial tape, you can leave the earplug jack out of the cassette. Then use the following program lines to operate the cassette. The cassette will continue to operate until a key is pressed and held for a few seconds.

```
1000 PRINT#-1,""
1010 I$=INKEY$ : IF I$="" THEN
     1000
1020 RETURN
```

TRS-80 Color Computer

AUDIO ON turns on cassette output to the tv speaker.

AUDIO OFF toggles it off. You must use **MOTOR ON** to start the cassette motor. Use **MOTOR OFF** to stop it.

COMMENTS

TRS-80 Models IV & III

Models IV and III have no sound capabilities without hardware modification or machine-language programming.

TRS-80 Color Computer

SOUND t,d where **t** is a numeric value relating to tone (range 1-255), and **d** is a numeric value relating to duration (range 1-128). You can simulate BEEP with a tone and duration of your choice. For example, **SOUND 200,2** is a fair representation of BEEP.

COMMENTS

BLOAD

APPLE IIe & II+

BLOAD filename [,An] [,Sm] [,Do] [,Vp] where **filename** is a binary file, and **n** is a memory address from 0-65535—for a 64K RAM machine—where the file is to be loaded. If **An** is omitted, the file is loaded into the memory address from which it was saved. Parameter **m** is a slot number (range 1-7) of the disk drive controller. Parameter **o** is 1 or 2, representing the desired disk drive. Parameter **p** is the volume number of the disk to be accessed. If omitted, volume number is ignored. BLOAD loads a binary file, such as a screen image or machine-language program, into memory.

IBM PC & PCjr

BLOAD d:filename [,offset] where **d:** is the name of a storage device, such as CAS1: or A:. **Filename** is the name of the file to be loaded. **Offset** is an optional offset from the memory location defined in the most recent DEF SEG. BLOAD loads a memory image file, such as a machine-language program or screen saved with the BSAVE instruction, into a specified memory location.

Note: Because you can easily load a program into any memory location, be careful not to overwrite a memory area currently used by BASIC.

COMMODORE 64

Be careful when loading a binary file, such as a machine-language program, from within a BASIC program. A LOAD from within a program causes that BASIC program in memory after the load to RUN. Consequently, the program may get into an infinite loop with a line like the following:

```
10 LOAD "filename",8,1
```

where **8** is the device number and **1** indicates a nonrelocatable load.

If you wish to simulate BLOAD where the file is to be loaded into the address from which it was saved, use one of the following routines:

```
10 IF A=0 THEN A=1:
   LOAD"filename",8,1
20 REM REST OF PROGRAM HERE
```

The above lines must be near the beginning of the BASIC program because the program will be reRUN after line 10 is executed once. Because LOAD does not clear variables, **A** has the value 1 on the second time around, so the rest of the line is not re-executed.

If it is necessary to LOAD a binary file from well within the BASIC program, then use the following lines:

```
1000 OPEN 8,8,8
     "filename,P,R"
1010 POKE 780,0
1020 SYS 65493
1030 CLOSE 8
1040 REM PROGRAM CONTINUES
     EXECUTING FROM HERE
```

To simulate BLOAD where the file is to be loaded into a memory address different from where it was saved (a relocatable load), use the following routine. **DV** is the device number, usually 8. **SA** is the decimal-starting address at which the file "filename" will be loaded.

```
10 NA$="filename":
   N=LEN(NA$)
20 DV=8: SA=32768
30 FOR I=1 TO N:
   M=ASC(MID$(NA$,I,1)):
   POKE 2023+I,M: NEXT
40 POKE 183,N: POKE
   187,232: POKE 188,7
50 SH=INT(SA/256):
   SL=SA-SH*256
```

TRS-80 Models IV & III

SYSTEM "LOAD[X] filename" (Model IV) loads the machine-language file **filename** into memory. If the **X** is included, it will load from a non-system disk. The default file extension is /CMD. Programs to be loaded must reside above address x'3000.

Note: Be careful to protect high memory at the MEMORY SIZE question when first entering BASIC to avoid overwriting your BASIC program. You should answer the MEMORY SIZE question with the highest address you want BASIC to use. This is one byte less than the location you intend to load your machine-language routine into. You can also protect high memory with the CLEAR command.

CMD"L",filename (Model III) where **filename** is a machine-language routine, normally created by the DUMP command.

Note: Be careful to protect high memory at the MEMORY SIZE question when first entering BASIC to avoid overwriting your BASIC program. You should answer the MEMORY SIZE question with the highest address you want BASIC to use. This is one byte less than the location you intend to load your machine-language routine into. You can also protect high memory with the CLEAR command.

An alternative scheme would be to avoid using DUMP to save the machine-language program. See **BSAVE**. Instead, you could PEEK the address you wish to save, convert it with CHR$(n), and PRINT it to a file. Simulating BLOAD would be accomplished with a routine that would OPEN that file for input, use INPUT# to get each value, convert it with ASC(n$), and then POKE it into the appropriate memory location.

```
60 POKE 186,DV: POKE 185,0:
   POKE 780,0
70 POKE 781,SL: POKE 782,SH
80 SYS 65493
```

TRS-80 Color Computer

CLOADM name [,offset] where **name** is a machine-language program to be loaded from cassette. If **offset** is omitted, the program will load as specified in the program itself. Otherwise, **offset** is added to the loading address.

LOADM filename [,offset] loads a machine-language program from disk. If an extension is not specified for the **filename**, BASIC uses /BIN. If the **offset** address is not specified, BASIC loads the program into the location specified within the program.

COMMENTS

BLOCK-ALLOCATE, BLOCK-FREE, BLOCK-READ,

APPLE IIe & II+

Not available. Cannot be simulated.

IBM PC & PCjr

Not available. Cannot be simulated.

COMMODORE 64

PRINT#f,"BLOCK-READ:"c,d,t,b
PRINT#f,"BLOCK-WRITE:"c,d,
t,b
PRINT#f,"BLOCK-ALLOCATE:
"d,t,b
PRINT#f,"BLOCK-FREE:"d,t,b
PRINT#f,"BUFFER-POINTER:
"c,1

These commands allow you to read (BLOCK-READ) and write (BLOCK-WRITE) data directly to disk, allocate space on a disk for data, logically free up space for data (by writing to the RAM, not actually erasing), and change the location of the data pointer.

Here, **f** is the number used to OPEN the file, **c** is the channel number, **d** is the drive number, **t** is the track number and **b** is the block number. To use these you must OPEN the command channel (#15) as well as the file buffer. These are often abbreviated with only their first letters (B-R, B-W, B-A, B-F and B-P). These commands may be used from BASIC, but are most useful when used with machine-language programs. They are very hazardous without careful syntax and program structure.

For a full discussion of their proper use, see the *1541 Disk Drive User's Manual,* pages 26 through 33.

B-R (See BLOCK)

BLOCK-WRITE, BUFFER-POINTER

TRS-80 Models IV & III

Not available. Cannot be simulated.

TRS-80 Color Computer

DSKI$ d,t,s,s1$,s2$
DSKO$ d,t,s,s1$,s2$
These commands allow you to read (DSKI$) and write (DSKO$) data directly to the disks, where **d** is the number of the disk drive, **t** is the track number, and **s** is the sector number. The strings to be input and output are represented by **s1$** (which will be read from or written to the first 128 bytes of the sector) and **s2$** (which relates to the last 128 bytes of the sector).

COMMENTS

Direct access to disk sectors is not available from BASIC on the other computers covered by this book. Data is written onto the disk under the control of the Disk Operating System.

BSAVE

APPLE IIe & II+

BSAVE filename ,An, Lq [,Sm] [,Do] [,Vp] where **filename** is a binary file, and **n** is a memory address from 0-65535—for a 64K RAM machine—where the first byte of the file is located. Parameter **q** is the number of bytes to be saved, range 0-32767. Parameter **m** is a slot number, range 1-7, of the disk drive controller. Parameter **o** is 1 or 2, representing the desired disk drive. Parameter **p** is the volume number of the disk to be accessed. If omitted, the volume number is ignored. BLOAD loads a binary file, such as a screen image or machine-language program, into memory.

IBM PC & PCjr

BSAVE d:filename, offset, length saves a memory-image file, where **d:** is the optional device name—default is currently logged disk drive. **Offset** is a numerical offset into the location specified in the most recent DEF SEG, and **length** is a numeric expression between 1 and 65535 indicating the length of the segment to be saved.

COMMODORE 64

The following program lines will simulate the BSAVE command on the Commodore 64. In it, **filename** is the name of the file, **SA** is the decimal memory location where the save is to start, and **EN** is the decimal memory location where the save is to end.

```
 10 SA=32768
 20 EN=33000: EN=EN+1
 30 SH=INT(SA/256):
    SL=SA-SH*256
 40 EH=INT(EN/256):
    EL=EN-EH*256
 50 POKE 2024,PEEK(43):
    POKE 2028,SL
 60 POKE 2025,PEEK(44):
    POKE 2029,SH
 70 POKE 2026,PEEK(45):
    POKE 2030,EL
 80 POKE 2027,PEEK(46):
    POKE 2031,EH
 90 POKE 43,PEEK(2028)
100 POKE 44,PEEK(2029)
110 POKE 45,PEEK(2030)
120 POKE 46,PEEK(2031)
130 SAVE "filename",8
140 POKE 43,PEEK(2024)
150 POKE 44,PEEK(2025)
160 POKE 45,PEEK(2026)
170 POKE 46,PEEK(2027)
```

BUFFER-POINTER (See BLOCK)

B-W (See BLOCK)

TRS-80 Models IV & III

SYSTEM "DUMP file$ (START = a1, END = a2, TRA = a3 [,ASCII,ETX= v]) " (Model IV) will DUMP a segment of memory top disk, where **file$** specifies the name of the file to be written. Parameter **a1** specifies the starting address of memory to be DUMPed, **a2** specifies the ending address, **a3** specifies the address where program execution will start. Using ASCII specifies that the DUMP is to an ASCII file. **ETX** is required when using ASCII and specifies that the character at the end of an ASCII file is equal to the hexadecimal value **v**. Control will return to your BASIC program after the DUMP is executed.

CMD"I" , "DUMP file$ (START = a1,END = a2, TRA = a3, RELO = a4)" (Model III) will DUMP a ment of memory to disk, where **file$** specifies the name of the file to be written. Parameter **a1** specifies the starting address of memory to be DUMPed, **a2** specifies the ending address, **a3** specifies the address where program execution will start. Parameter **a4** specifies the start address at which the program is to be reloaded. However, you will not return to BASIC after the DUMP is executed. You will be left in TRS-

TRS-80 Color Computer

CSAVEM **filename, start, end, offset** saves a machine-language program on cassette specified in the **filename**, starting at memory address **start** and ending at memory address **end**. **Offset** is the actual memory address at which execution will start.

SAVEM **filename, start, end, transfer** saves a machine-language program on the disk drive specified in the **filename**, starting at memory address **start** and ending at memory address **end**. **Offset** is the actual memory address at which execution will start.

DOS. Your BASIC program may or may not still be available using the BASIC* command.

An alternative scheme on either computer would be to avoid using DUMP to save the machine-language program. Instead, you could PEEK the addresses you wish to save by using a loop. Then convert the values returned with CHR$(n), and PRINT them to a file. Simulating BLOAD would be done with a routine that would OPEN that file for input. Use INPUT# to get each value, convert it with ASC(n$), and then POKE it into the appropriate memory location.

COMMENTS

CALL

APPLE IIe & II+

CALL n where n is a decimal numeric expression in the range of −65535-65535, representing a memory location. CALL causes execution of the machine-language routine at memory location n.

IBM PC & PCjr

CALL n[(x1 [,x2]...)] where n is the name of a numeric variable and x1, x2... are names of variables to be passed as arguments to a machine-language routine. CALL executes a machine-language subroutine at the location specified by the most recent DEF SEG and the offset defined by variable n.

COMMODORE 64

SYS n where n is decimal numeric expression the range 0-65535 representing a memory location. The command causes execution of the machine-language routine starting at memory location n.

MEMORY-EXECUTE calls machine-language code that is present in the 1541 disk drive's RAM or ROM. Because memory maps of the 1541's operating system are not widely available, this kind of code is rare. In the example below, SA is the start address in decimal of the machine-language code to be executed. L and H are the low and high bytes of SA when written in hexadecimal:

```
10 SA=60064:H=INT(SA/256)
   :L=SA-H*256
20 OPEN15,8,15
30 PRINT#15,
   "M-E"CHR$(L)CHR$(H)
40 CLOSE15
```

You can also use a MEMORY-WRITE command to write code to the 1541 RAM.

CATALOG

APPLE IIe & II+

CATALOG [,Ss][,Dd] where s specifies slot number 1-7 and d specifies drive 1 or 2. CATALOG will display the directory of the specified drive. It may be used in the programming mode when preceded by CHR$(4). If the drive number is omitted, the most recently selected drive will be used. The code format is:

```
10 PRINT CHR$(4);
   "CATALOG,S6,D2"
```

If the catalog listing is too long to fit on one screen, it will halt at the end of each screenful. Listing continues when the user presses any key.

IBM PC & PCjr

FILES [filename] lists the name of the file specified. If the optional filename is omitted, all files are listed. You can use the wildcards * and ? to obtain a list of all files that satisfy a particular pattern. You can also specify a drive other than the default. In BASIC 2.0 or Cartridge BASIC, FILES can also contain a path command, which cannot be simulated on any other machine.

Use of this command in Cartridge BASIC will result in an ILLEGAL FUNCTION CALL if DOS 2.1 is not present.

Command DIR is used in DOS only.

COMMODORE 64

Although there is no command in Commodore 64 BASIC to obtain a catalog (directory), the following program lines produce a similar effect. However, they will cause the directory to replace the current program in memory. If you need a program that reads the directory without destroying the program in memory, see the *1541 Disk Drive User's Manual,* page 47.

```
100 POKE 631,19: POKE
    632,13: POKE 633,13:
    POKE 198,3
110 PRINT CHR$(147) "LIST"
120 LOAD "$",8: END
```

TRS-80 Models IV & III

CALL n [,a [,b,...]] where **n** is a non-array variable specifying the beginning address of the machine-language subroutine being called, and **a, b,...** are variables representing parameters passed to the machine-language routine.

TRS-80 Color Computer

EXEC [n] transfers control to the machine-language program at memory location **n**. If **n** is omitted, it assumes the address specified at the last CLOAD.

COMMENTS

Also see the **USR** function and **VARPTR**.

The primary difference between **USR** and **CALL** is the ability to pass multiple arguments or parameters to the machine-language routine using CALL. In addition, CALL does not require POKEing the address of the routine, but rather specifies it in the CALL statement.

The method of passing parameters to the machine-language routine varies from machine to machine. IBM passes parameters through its stack, while TRS uses registers HL, DE and BC. Consult the manuals for a more detailed explanation.

TRS-80 Models IV & III

SYSTEM "DIR:d" (Model IV) will display the directory of disk drive **d**, then continue program execution. The drive number is not optional.

CMD"D:d" (Model III) will display the directory of drive **d**, then continue program execution. The drive number is not optional.

TRS-80 Color Computer

DIR [d] where **d** specifies the drive number to be accessed. The command will display the directory of the specified drive, then continue program execution.

COMMENTS

CDBL

APPLE IIe & II+

Because Apple allows up to nine digits of precision for floating-point numeric constants, CDBL is not available and cannot be simulated.

IBM PC & PCjr

CDBL(n) where n is any numeric expression. CDBL converts n to a double-precision number having 17 digits of precision, of which 16 are printed. Note that not all the digits will be accurate because not all were supplied with n.

COMMODORE 64

Because Commodore allows up to nine digits of precision for floating-point numeric constants, CDBL is not available and cannot be simulated.

CHAIN

APPLE IIe & II+

Applesoft BASIC does not use CHAIN. Simulate it with the following procedure:

Protect high memory by using the HIMEM instruction. Then POKE the common variables into the protected memory. Use RUN (or MERGE and then RUN) to start the new program. Then PEEK the variables back into the program out of high memory.

CHAIN filename [,Ss][,Dd][,Vv] (Integer BASIC Only) where filename is the name of the file, s is the number of the slot, d is the number of the disk drive, and v is the volume number of the disk. CHAIN loads and runs the specified program, maintaining the variables and arrays from the previous program.

IBM PC & PCjr

CHAIN filename [,line] [,ALL] causes the program filename to be run beginning with the line number specified, and with all variables the same as in the program currently in memory. If the line number is omitted, the execution begins with the first line of the new program. If ALL is omitted, then the original program must have a COMMON statement.

Use of this command in Cartridge BASIC will result in an ILLEGAL FUNCTION CALL if DOS 2.1 is not present.

CHAIN MERGE filename [,DELETE range] merges the new program with the current one, optionally DELETing some lines of the current one. This is different from MERGE in that it executes the program after merging it. The range option allows you to indicate which lines to delete, using the same format you would use with the LIST command. By using the MERGE option, the OPTION BASE setting and all user-defined functions and variable types—such as DEFINT, DEFSNG, DEFDBL, DEFSTR and DEF FN—are preserved. Otherwise, they would have to be restated. CHAIN also causes a RESTORE to be executed, so a READ statement will read the first data item, not the next one.

COMMODORE 64

LOAD [filename][,device][,location] where filename is the name of the file you wish to load. Default on cassette is the next file, but the file name must be specified on disk. Device is the storage device—cassette=1, disk=8, default=1. Location is the type of load you wish to achieve—0 (the default) loads in at the start of BASIC; 1 loads in from where it was saved.

Files saved on cassette with a non-relocatable load—see SAVE—are loaded back into the same location they came from and ignore the location direction. Although LOAD closes all files, when used as a statement within a program it does not clear variables. Nor does it reset the BASIC memory pointers.

After the load is complete, it automatically RUNs the BASIC program in memory. Be careful when using LOAD to chain BASIC programs. The first program that has the initial LOAD in it must be longer than any of the programs subsequently called. However, some variable declarations may be lost, so you should redeclare the variables in the chained program. With this in mind, you can use LOAD similarly to CHAIN.

TRS-80 Models IV & III

CDBL(n) where **n** is any numeric expression, CDBL converts **n** to a double-precision number having 17 digits of precision, of which 16 are printed. Note that not all the digits will be accurate because not all were supplied with **n**.

TRS-80 Color Computer

Because the COCO allows only up to nine digits of precision for floating-point numeric constants, CDBL is not available and cannot be simulated.

COMMENTS

TRS-80 Models IV & III

CHAIN filename [,line] [,ALL] (Model IV) causes the program **filename** to be run beginning with the **line** number specified, and with all variables the same as in the program currently in memory. If the **line** number is omitted, execution begins with the first line of the new program. If **ALL** is omitted, then the original program must have a COMMON statement.

CHAIN MERGE filename [,DELETE range] (Model IV) merges the new program with the current one, optionally DELETing some lines of the current one. This is different from MERGE in that it executes the program after merging it. The range option allows you to indicate which lines to delete, using the same format you'd use with the LIST command. By using the MERGE option, you preserve the OPTION BASE setting and all user-defined functions and variable types—such as DEFINT, DEFSNG, DEFDBL, DEFSTR and DEF FN. Otherwise, they would have to be restated. CHAIN also causes a RESTORE to be executed, so a READ statement will read the first data item, not the next one.

CHAIN is not available on the Model III, but can be simulated. First, protect high memory when you encounter the MEMORY SIZE question when entering BASIC. Then POKE the variables to be common into the protected memory. Use RUN (or MERGE and then RUN) to start the new program, then PEEK the variables back into the program out of high memory.

TRS-80 Color Computer

Not available on the COCO, but CHAIN can be simulated by protecting a portion of memory using the CLEAR command. Then POKE the variables to be common into the protected memory. Use RUN (or MERGE and then RUN) to start the new program. Then PEEK the variables back into the program out of protected memory.

COMMENTS

The CHAIN instruction leaves files open. Also see **MERGE**.

CHDIR

APPLE IIe & II+	IBM PC & PCjr	COMMODORE 64
Not available. Cannot be simulated.	**CHDIR path** where **path** is a string constant not more than 63 characters long specifying the new directory that becomes the current directory. CHDIR is used by IBM only—and only in DOS versions 2.0 and 2.1. Use of this command in Cartridge BASIC will result in an ILLEGAL FUNCTION CALL if DOS 2.1 is not present.	Not available. Cannot be simulated.

CHR$

APPLE IIe & II+	IBM PC & PCjr	COMMODORE 64
CHR$(n) where **n** is an ASCII code in the range 0-255. CHR$ returns the character represented by ASCII code **n**.	**CHR$(n)** where **n** is an ASCII code in the range 0-255. CHR$ returns the character represented by the ASCII code **n**.	**CHR$(n)** where **n** is an ASCII code in the range 0-255. CHR$ returns the character represented by the ASCII code **n**. Some non-standard CHR$ codes that occur frequently in Commodore 64 program listings are listed below:

COMMODORE 64 codes:

CHR$(14)	Switch to lower case
CHR$(17)	Move cursor down
CHR$(18)	Switch reverse on
CHR$(19)	Move cursor to home position
CHR$(20)	Delete a character
CHR$(29)	Move cursor right
CHR$(142)	Switch to upper case
CHR$(145)	Move cursor up
CHR$(146)	Switch reverse off
CHR$(147)	Clear screen and move cursor home
CHR$(148)	Insert a character
CHR$(133) to CHR$(140)	Refer to function keys f1 to f8
CHR$(96) to CHR$(127)	Refer to graphics characters
CHR$(161) to CHR$(191)	Refer to graphics characters

CINT

APPLE IIe & II+	IBM PC & PCjr	COMMODORE 64
Not available. Use **INT** instead.	**CINT (n)** where **n** is a numeric expression between −32768 and 32767. Converts **n** to an integer by rounding.	Not available. Use **INT** instead.

TRS-80 Models IV & III	TRS-80 Color Computer	COMMENTS
Not available. Cannot be simulated.	Not available. Cannot be simulated.	

TRS-80 Models IV & III	TRS-80 Color Computer	COMMENTS
CHR$(n) where **n** is an ASCII code in the range 0-255. CHR$ returns the character represented by the ASCII code **n**.	**CHR$(n)** where **n** is an ASCII code in the range 0-255. CHR$ returns the character represented by the ASCII code **n**.	

TRS-80 Models IV & III

CINT (n) where **n** is a numeric expression between −32768 and 32767. Converts **n** to an integer by rounding.

TRS-80 Color Computer

Not available. Use **INT** or **FIX** instead.

COMMENTS

	If n is positive	If n is negative
CINT	Rounds up	Rounds up
FIX	Truncates	Truncates
INT	Truncates	Rounds up (negatively)

CIRCLE

APPLE IIe & II+

Not available. Simulate it with the following routine. You must define the following variables before entering the routine:

X x coordinate of the center. Range 0-279.

Y y coordinate of the center. Range 0-159

R Radius of the circle measured in screen points.

C Color of the circle. Range 0-7.

AR Numeric expression affecting the aspect ratio. **AR**=3/4 is a circle. **AR**>3/4 draws an ellipse with the major axis axis in the y direction. **AR**<3/4 yields an ellipse with its major axis in the x direction.

You cannot specify a circle or arc that would lie outside the range of the screen, or you will get an ILLEGAL QUANTITY error. Get semicircles by manipulating the loops in lines 140 and 200. Get quarter circles by manipulating lines 150, 170, 210 and 230 along with the loops in lines 140 and 200.

```
130 HGR:HCOLOR=C:RA=1/AR
140 FOR I=X-R TO X+R
150 H=I:V=Y+SQR((R^2)-
    (H-X)^2)*AR
160 HPLOT H,V
170 H=I:V=Y-SQR((R^2)-
    (H-X)^2)*AR
180 HPLOT H,V
190 NEXT I
200 FOR I=Y-R*AR TO Y+R*AR
210 V=I:H=X+SQR(ABS((R^2)-
    (RA*(V-Y))^2))
220 HPLOT H,V
230 V=I:H=X-SQR(ABS((R^2)-
    (RA*(V-Y))^2))
240 HPLOT H,V
250 NEXT I
```

IBM PC & PCjr

CIRCLE(x,y),r[,color[,start,end[,aspect]]] draws a circle, arc or ellipse where **x** and **y** are the coordinates of the center of the circle or ellipse, and **r** is the radius measured in screen points. **Color** is a an optional number whose range depends on the screen chosen. See **COLOR**. **Start** and **end** are angles measured in radians in the range of $-2*\pi$ to $2*\pi$, which indicate the start and end of an arc.

Aspect is a numeric expression. If it is 5/6 in medium resolution or 5/12 in high resolution, a circle is drawn. If **aspect** is less than 1, then **r** is the x radius. If **aspect** is greater than 1, then **r** is the y radius.

COMMODORE 64

Not available. Simulate it with the following routine. You must define the following variables before entering the routine:

X x coordinate of the center. Range 0-319.

Y y coordinate of the center. Range 0-199

R Radius of the circle measured in screen points.

AR Numeric expression affecting the aspect ratio. **AR**=3/4 is a circle. **AR**>3/4 draws an ellipse with the major axis in the y direction. **AR**<3/4 yields an ellipse with its major axis in the x direction.

You must also call a high-resolution screen routine, such as the one listed at HGR. Subroutine 1000 should be a routine that will set individual points, such as those listed at HPOINT. Get semicircles by manipulating the loops in line 310 and 370. Get quarter circles by manipulating lines 320, 340, 370 and 400 along with loops in lines 310 and 370.

```
100 REM HIGH RES SCREEN
    LOADER GOES HERE (SEE
    HGR)
300 RA=1/AR:REM X,Y,R AND AR
    MUST BE LOADED BEFORE
    THIS LINE
310 FOR I=X-R TO X+R
320 H=I:V=Y+SQR((R↑2)-
    (H-X)↑2)*AR
330 GOSUB 1000
340 H=I:V=Y-SQR((R↑2)-
    (H-X)↑2)*AR
350 GOSUB 1000
360 NEXT I
370 FOR I=Y-R*AR TO Y+R*AR
380 V=I:H=X+SQR(ABS((R↑2)-
    (RA*(V-Y))↑2))
390 GOSUB 1000
400 V=I:H=X-SQR(ABS((R↑2)-
    (RA*(V-Y))↑2))
410 GOSUB 1000
420 NEXT I
430 REM PROGRAM CONTINUES
    HERE
1000 REM PLOTTING SUBROUTINE
     HERE (SEE HPOINT)
```

TRS-80 Models IV & III

Not available and cannot be easily simulated on the TRS-80 Models IV or III. They do not support high-resolution graphics.

TRS-80 Color Computer

CIRCLE   **(x,y),r[,c,hw,start,end]** draws an ellipse, circle or arc with a centerpoint at **(x,y)**. Parameter **x** has range of 0-255; **y** has range of 0-191. Parameter **r** is the radius of the circle measured in screen-position points. Parameter **c** is the optional color number in the range of 1-8, with the default as the current foreground color. Parameter **hw** is the optional height/width ratio and is a numeric expression in the range of 0-255 (default=1). **Start** and **end** are the optional starting and stopping points for an arc. The range for each is 0-1, with the default for **start** being 0 (the three o'clock position) and the default for **end** being 1 (also the three o'clock position).

COMMENTS

To convert degrees (D) to radians (R), use the following formula:

$$R=D*3.141593/180$$

CLEAR

APPLE IIe & II+

CLEAR clears variables and resets internal control stack.

IBM PC & PCjr

CLEAR [,[n] [,m]] (BASIC 2.0) where **n** is the optional number of bytes you want for BASIC workspace, and **m** is the optional stack space you desire. Used alone, CLEAR frees all memory, erases all DIMs, DEFs and variable values, and sets any sound, PEN and STRIG values to OFF.

CLEAR [,[n] [,m] [,v]] (Cartridge BASIC Only) clears memory, where **n** is the optional number of bytes you want for BASIC workspace, **m** is the optional stack space you desire, and **v** specifies the total number of bytes to set aside for video memory. Used alone, CLEAR frees all memory, erases all DIMs, DEFs and variable values, and sets any SOUND, PLAY, PEN and STRIG values to OFF.

COMMODORE 64

CLR aborts all logical files that may be open, sets all nonreserved variables to zero, and releases all array space, but does not affect the BASIC program in memory.

CLOAD

APPLE IIe & II+

LOAD causes the next program on the cassette to load. Note that the cassette must be ready!

IBM PC & PCjr

LOAD cas1:[filename][,R] loads the next program on the cassette, unless the optional **filename** is supplied. In this case it searches the cassette for the named file. If the **R** option is specified, the program is run as soon as loaded.

COMMODORE 64

LOAD [filename][,device][,location] where **filename** is the name of the file you wish to load. Default on cassette is the next file, but the **filename** must be specified on disk. **Device** is the storage device—cassette=1; disk=8; default=1. **Location** is the type of load you wish to achieve—0 (the default) loads in at the start of BASIC; 1 loads in from where it was saved. Files saved on cassette with a non-relocatable LOAD—see **SAVE**—are LOADed back into the same location they came from. This ignores the location direction.

Although LOAD closes all files when used as a statement within a program, it does not clear variables. Nor does it reset BASIC memory pointers. After the LOAD is complete, it automatically RUNs the BASIC program in memory.

Be careful when using LOAD to chain BASIC programs. The first program that has the initial LOAD in it must be longer than any programs subsequently called. If you wish to LOAD and RUN a longer program from a shorter one, use the dynamic keyboard as in the following program

TRS-80 Models IV & III

CLEAR [,m] [,n] (Model IV) where **m** is an optional integer indicating the highest memory location available to BASIC, and **n** is a numeric constant, numeric variable or expression indicating the number of bytes to allocate for stack storage (default n=512). CLEAR eliminates all variables and closes all files.

CLEAR n (Model III) where **n** is the amount of space to reserve for string storage. Default=50 bytes. Note that this does not affect files.

TRS-80 Color Computer

CLEAR [n] [,m] where **n** is the amount of space to allocate for string storage—default=200 bytes—and **m** is the highest memory location available for BASIC. This command also initializes all variables. Note that this is the opposite order of TRS-80 Model IV.

COMMENTS

If it's available, you may wish to use **ERASE** to clear some memory if you don't want to lose the values stored in variables, arrays and DEF statements.

TRS-80 Models IV & III

The Model IV operates from cassette only in the Model III or Model 100 mode. The Model 100 is not covered in this book.

CLOAD [filename] (Model III) loads the next file on cassette into memory. If **filename** is specified, the computer searches for that file on cassette.

CLOAD? compares the file in memory to the next file on the cassette. If the files do not match bit for bit, the word BAD is displayed on the screen.

TRS-80 Color Computer

CLOAD [filename] loads a program from cassette, where **filename** is a file on the cassette. If **filename** is omitted, the next program on the cassette is loaded.

CLOADM "filename" [,n] loads the machine-language file **filename**, beginning at the optional memory location offset **n**.

COMMENTS

Some computers close all files and re-initialize all variable values when asked to LOAD or CLOAD a program.

---

lines. Remember, though, that this technique clears all the variables.

```
10 PRINT CHR$(147)"LOAD"
   CHR$(34)"filename"
   CHR$(34)",8"
20 POKE 214,4: PRINT: PRINT
   "RUN"
30 POKE 198,4: POKE 631,19
40 FOR I=2 TO 4: POKE
   630+I,13: NEXT
50 END
```

CLOSE

APPLE IIe & II+

PRINT D$;"CLOSE filename" closes the sequential file **filename**, where **D$**=CHR$(4). Apple does not use file numbers as the other computers do.

IBM PC & PCjr

CLOSE [[#]file1[,[#]file2]...] where **file1, file2,...** are file numbers of files previously OPENed. If the optional file numbers are omitted, all files are closed. # signs are also optional. If any data is still stored in the file buffer, it is written to the file before the file is CLOSEd. END, NEW, RESET, SYSTEM or RUN without the R option will also close all files.

COMMODORE 64

CLOSE n where **n** is the number of a file or device previously OPENed. Any data stored in the buffer is written to the file before it is CLOSEd.

SYS 65511 closes all open files.

CLR (See CLEAR)

CLS

APPLE IIe & II+

HOME clears the text window—which may or may not be the entire screen—and moves the cursor to the upper-left corner.

IBM PC & PCjr

CLS clears the screen and moves the cursor to the home position. In text mode, home is the upper-left corner of the screen. In graphics mode, home is the center of the screen.

If you are using a viewport defined with the VIEW command, only the viewport will be affected, and the cursor will be centered in the viewport. To clear the whole screen in such a case, use VIEW without any parameters. Then use CLS.

COMMODORE 64

PRINT CHR$(147); clears the screen and moves the cursor to the upper-left corner.

CMD

APPLE IIe & II+

See **PR#.**

IBM PC & PCjr

See **LPRINT** or **LLIST.**

COMMODORE 64

CMDn redirects output to the previously OPENed device **n**—range 1-255—instead of to the monitor. It is deactivated by PRINT#n, a process called *unlistening* by Commodore. It is most commonly used to redirect output to the printer, device #4.

This effect is achieved on other computers by using PR# (Apple) or by using LPRINT or LLIST.

TRS-80 Models IV & III

CLOSE [n[,n...]] where **n** is a number of an open file range of 1-15. If **n** is omitted, all OPEN files are CLOSEd.

TRS-80 Color Computer

CLOSE [#n] closes all communications to buffer **n**. If **n** is omitted, all OPEN files are CLOSEd. The following are possible buffers:

n=1-15	File opened with that number
n=0	Screen or Keyboard
n=−1	Cassette
n=−2	Printer

COMMENTS

TRS-80 Models IV & III

CLS clears the screen and moves the cursor to the upper-left corner.

TRS-80 Color Computer

CLS [(n)] where **n** is a numeric expression (range 0-8) specifying screen color. Clears the screen to the specified color. Default is green. Possible values for **n** are listed below:

0	Black
1	Green
2	Yellow
3	Blue
4	Red
5	Buff
6	Cyan
7	Magenta
8	Orange

COMMENTS

TRS-80 Models IV & III

Not available on the Model IV. Output can be redirected to the printer with LLIST or LPRINT.

CMD"A" (Model III) causes the computer to return to DOS and display the message OPERATION ABORTED. This is similar to SYSTEM on most other computers.

CMD"B","switch" (Model III) where **switch** is either "ON" or "OFF"—switch must be enclosed in quotation marks. CMD"B" toggles the break key on or off. BASIC program execution will continue after using CMD"B". There is no com-

TRS-80 Color Computer

Not available. Cannot be simulated.

mand to achieve this on other computers, but might be possible with POKEs if you can determine the location to POKE for your computer. For example, CTRL-BREAK is disabled on the IBM PC with the following:

```
10 DEF SEG=0: POKE
   &H6C,&H53: POKE
   &H6D,&HFF: POKE
   &H6E,&H00: POKE
   &H6F,&HF0: DEF SEG
```

CMD"C"[,option] (Model III) where **option** is either "R" (to remove remarks only) or "S" (to remove spaces only). If **option** is omitted, both remarks and spaces will be removed from the BASIC program in memory. BASIC program execution will continue after using CMD"C". This command cannot be easily simulated from within a BASIC program on other computers. But there are commercial utilities available for most other computers that will do this from outside the program.

CMD (cont.)

TRS-80 Models IV & III

CMD"D:d" (Model III) where parameter **d** specifies a currently connected disk drive number, CMD"D:d" will display the directory of the specified drive. Note that the drive specification is not optional. BASIC program execution will continue after using CMD"D". See **CATALOG**, **DIR** and **FILES** for explanations of how this is accomplished on other computers.

CMD"I",command (Model III) where **command** is a legal DOS command or a Z-80 program name, CMD"I" will exit BASIC and execute the specified command. If the command does not overlay BASIC, you will be returned BASIC. Otherwise, you will remain in DOS.

This instruction is similar to SYSTEM on the TRS-80 Model IV; to PRINT CHR$(4);"command" on the Apple; to POKEing the keyboard buffer on the IBM PC; or to using the dynamic keyboard of the Commodore 64. Any disk-operating commands may be issued from a BASIC program on the COCO, but the program may or may not be left in memory afterward, depending on the command.

CMD"J",s,d (Model III) where **s** specifies the source date, and **d** specifies the destination date. This command converts Julian dates to standard dates and vice-versa. The source date must be in the form mm/dd/yy for standard-to-Julian conversion, or -yy/ddd for Julian-to-standard conversion. Note that specification of a Julian date requires a leading hyphen. BASIC program execution will continue after using CMD"J".

Other computers covered in this book have no equivalent to CMD"J". However, a program could be written to do the same thing.

CMD"L",filename (Model III) where **filename** is a machine-language routine or program. This command will load the specified file into memory. If the loaded file does not overlay BASIC or TRSDOS, control will be returned to BASIC. See **BLOAD** for a discussion of how this is accomplished on other computers.

CMD"O",n,array(start) (Model III) will sort an array, where **n** specifies the number of items to be sorted, **array** is the variable name of the array to be sorted, and **start** specifies the array element to be the first element sorted. BASIC program execution will continue after using CMD"O".

The other computers covered in this book do not have built-in sort routines. There are many possible ways of writing sort routines for each of them.

CMD"P",status (Model III) returns information about the printer, where **status** is a string variable that will receive the returned status from the printer. CMD"P" will return different values for different printers. The string variable status may be examined by the program for an expected value, such as a value representing "printer ready." BASIC program execution will continue after using CMD"P".

CMD"R" (Model III) causes the real-time clock to be displayed in the upper-right corner of the screen and updated every second. The clock is turned off by the command CMD"T". BASIC program execution will continue after using CMD"R". There is no way to easily simulate this as a background task from BASIC on any other computer, but there are utilities commercially available that do this on the IBM PC.

CMD"S" (Model III) causes the computer to exit BASIC and return to DOS. This is similar to SYSTEM on other computers. See **SYSTEM**.

CMD"T" (Model III) turns off the clock display. See **CMD"R"**. BASIC program execution will continue after using CMD"T".

CMD"X",target (Model III) cross-references the program in memory, listing all occurrences of the **target** variable. If the **target** variable is a reserved word—such as INPUT—it must not be enclosed in quotation marks. If the **target** variable is a literal string, it must be enclosed in quotation marks. No other computers covered in this book have this as a resident command, nor can it be simulated without extensive code. Most computers have commercially available utilities that do this.

CMD"Z","switch" (Model III) where **switch** is either "ON" or "OFF"—which must be enclosed in quotation marks. CMD"Z","ON" causes all output going to the screen to also go to the printer, and vice-versa. CMD"Z","OFF" causes this echoing to stop. BASIC program execution continues after using CMD"Z".

On the Apple, you can have simultaneous output to the screen and the printer by specifying PR#n, where n is the number of the slot where the printer card resides—usually #1. Echoing is disabled by PR#0.

You can redirect output to other devices on the Commodore 64 with the CMDn command, but simultaneous output is not available on it or the TRS-80 Models IV or III.

DYNAMIC KEYBOARDS

The Commodore 64 has a keyboard buffer that can be loaded with characters from within a program. When the program ends, these characters are printed on the screen and can be used to execute commands not usually available from within a program. You can get some very unusual and sophisticated effects this way. Some include programs that create or destroy their own lines while running, and programs that exit to the command level, then return to the program.

(Continued at top of next page.)

The memory locations usually used by this technique are 198 (which contains the number of characters in the keyboard buffer) and 631 to 641 (the keyboard buffer that contains the ASCII codes of the keys to be printed). Here is a very simple example to demonstrate using this technique.

```
10   REM THIS LINE WILL BE DELETED
20   PRINT CHR$ (147) "10":REM CLEARS SCREEN AND PRINTS 10 AT HOME
     POSITION
30   POKE 198,2: POKE 631,19: POKE 632,13
40   END
```

When this program is RUN the screen is cleared, and the number 10 is printed in the home position. Two characters—"move cursor to home" and a carriage return—are then placed in the keyboard buffer. When the program ends, these characters are printed on the screen, which causes the cursor to be moved over the 10 already there. When the program is LISTed, line 10 will be gone!

The IBM PC also allows access to the keyboard buffer. You can read or change the status of several important keys, clear the buffer, or plug values into the buffer. The values you plug into the buffer will be retrieved the next time you allow keyboard access, such as when using INKEY$ or when returning to the command mode.

The following PEEKs and POKEs let you toggle the keys as indicated. You must declare DEF SEG=64 before using them.

```
POKE 23, (PEEK(23) OR 64) turns CAPS LOCK on
POKE 23, (PEEK(23) AND 191) turns CAPS LOCK off
POKE 23, (PEEK(23) OR 32) turns NUM LOCK on
POKE 23, (PEEK(23) AND 223) turns NUM LOCK off
POKE 23, (PEEK(23) OR 16) turns SCROLL LOCK on
POKE 23, (PEEK(23) AND 239) turns SCROLL LOCK off
POKE 23, (PEEK(23) OR 128) turns INS on
POKE 23, (PEEK(23) AND 127) turns INS off
POKE 23, (PEEK(23) OR 8) turns ALT on
POKE 23, (PEEK(23) AND 247) turns ALT off
POKE 23, (PEEK(23) OR 4) turns CTRL on
POKE 23, (PEEK(23) AND 251) turns CTRL off
POKE 23, (PEEK(23) OR 2) turns LEFT SHIFT on
POKE 23, (PEEK(23) AND 253) turns LEFT SHIFT off
POKE 23, (PEEK(23) OR 1) turns RIGHT SHIFT on
POKE 23, (PEEK(23) AND 254) turns RIGHT SHIFT off
POKE 26, (PEEK(28)) Clears the keyboard buffer
```

You can send characters to the keyboard buffer with the following code:

```
1000   REM SUBROUTINE TO PUT CHARACTERS INTO KEYBOARD BUFFER
1010   DEF SEG=0
1020   X=LEN(a$): REM a$ SHOULD BE DEFINED BEFORE THIS ROUTINE. IT IS WHAT
       YOU ARE GOING TO SEND TO THE BUFFER
1030   POKE 1050,30: POKE 1052,30+(X*2): REM TELLS BUFFER HOW MANY
       CHARACTERS TO EXPECT
1040   FOR I=1 TO X*2 STEP 2
1050   POKE 1053+I,ASC(MID$(a$,(I+1)/2,1))
1060   NEXT I
1070   RETURN
```

If you want the buffer to include a carriage return, you should include this line:

```
1015   a$=a$+CHR$(13)
```

If you know exactly what you wish to put in—instead of using a$—you could greatly simplify the routine. In the example below, the command RUN followed by a carriage return is sent to the buffer.

```
1000   REM SUBROUTINE TO PUT RUN AND CARRIAGE RETURN INTO THE BUFFER
1010   DEF SEG=0: POKE 1050,30: POKE 1052,38
1020   POKE 1054,82: POKE 1056,85: POKE 1058,78: POKE 1060,13
1030   RETURN
```

COLOR, COLOR=

APPLE IIe & II+

COLOR=n sets the color for plotting in low-resolution graphics. Parameter n is a numeric expression in the range 0-255 modulo 16. If n is a real number, it is converted to an integer before the modulo arithmetic is performed. Possible values for n are as follows:

0	Black	8	Brown
1	Magenta	9	Orange
2	Dark blue	10	Grey
3	Purple	11	Pink
4	Dark green	12	Green
5	Gray	13	Yellow
6	Medium blue	14	Aqua
7	Light blue	15	White

Parameter n is set to 0 by the GR command. When in TEXT mode, COLOR assists in determining which character will be affected by the PLOT command. COLOR is ignored when in the high-resolution graphics mode.

HCOLOR=n where n is a numeric expression in the range 0-7. Sets the color plotted in the high-resolution graphics mode. Color assignments for n are given below. Note that if n=3, the dot will be blue if the x coordinate is even, green if the x coordinate is odd, and white only if (x,y) and (x+1,y) are both plotted.

0	Black 1	5	Depends on monitor
1	Green		
2	Blue	6	Depends on monitor
3	White 1		
4	Black 2	7	White 2

IBM PC & PCjr

COLOR [fg] [,[bg][,bd]] sets the screen colors in the TEXT mode, where fg is the foreground color represented by a numeric expression in the range 0-31. Default=7 or the most recently stated value. Parameter bg is the background color in the range 0-7. Default=0 or the most recently stated value. And bd is the border color in the range 0-15. Default=0 or the most recently stated value.

Following are color-parameter values for foreground and border with the color graphics adapter:

0	Black	9	Light Blue
1	Blue	10	Light Green
2	Green	11	Light Cyan
3	Cyan	12	Light Red
4	Red	13	Light Magenta
5	Magenta		
6	Brown	14	Yellow
7	White	15	High-intensity White
8	Grey		

A foreground color of 16-31 will produce the same colors as the above table, but in blinking mode. For example, 16 produces blinking black and 31 produces blinking high-intensity white.

The background color numbers are the same, but limited to the range 0-7.

On the PCjr you can use the PALETTE and PALETTE USING commands to obtain any color combination for foreground, background and border.

With the monochrome adapter (not available on the PCjr), the color parameter values are below:

0	Black
1	Underline
2-7	White

As with the color-graphics adapter, adding 8 to the foreground will produce a high-intensity color. For example, COLOR 15 will produce high-intensity white, COLOR 9 will produce high-intensity white, underlined. Adding 16 to the foreground will produce a blinking foreground.

The background parameters with the

COMMODORE 64

To set the color of the screen, border or cursor on the Commodore 64, use one of the following POKEs, with N selected out of the following table:

POKE 53280,N   Colors BORDER
POKE 53281,N   Colors SCREEN
POKE 646,N   Colors CURSOR

The value of N must be an integer in the range of 0-15, and produces the result indicated in the following table:

0	Black	8	Orange
1	White	9	Brown
2	Red	10	Light Red
3	Cyan	11	Gray 1
4	Purple	12	Gray 2
5	Green	13	Light Green
6	Blue	14	Light Blue
7	Yellow	15	Gray 3

See HGR for a further discussion of COLOR on the Commodore 64.

monochrome display (not available on the PCjr) are below:

0-6	Black
7	White

COLOR [bg][,[p]] in the Screen 1 medium-resolution graphics mode, which requires the color-graphics adapter, where bg is the background color in the range 0-15 (default=7 or the most recently named value), using the above table. Parameter p is the numeric expression in the range 0-255, indicating which palette to use. If p is even, palette 0 is selected, which includes the attributes green, red and brown. If p is odd, palette 1 is chosen, which includes the attributes cyan, magenta and white. The attribute used is determined when giving a graphics command, such as PSET, PRESET, LINE, CIRCLE, PAINT or DRAW.

Using COLOR in the Screen 2 high-resolution graphics mode will result in an ILLEGAL FUNCTION CALL error.

TRS-80 Models IV & III

Cannot be simulated on the TRS-80 Models IV or III.

TRS-80 Color Computer

COLOR (fg,bg) sets the color of the display, where **fg** is the color for the foreground, and **bg** is the color of the background. Depending upon the PMODE selected, the range of **fg** and **bg** may be 1-2, 1-4 or 1-8, with the actual color-number correspondence varying.

SET (x,y,c) determines the color of an individual screen point, where **x** and **y** are screen coordinates and **c** is a numeric expression associated with the color. Possible values for **c** follow:

0	Black	5	Buff
1	Green	6	Cyan
2	Yellow	7	Magenta
3	Blue	8	Orange
4	Red		

COLOR [fg][,[bg]] (Cartridge BASIC Only) in the Screen 3 low-resolution graphics mode, Screens 4 and 5 medium-resolution graphics mode, and Screen 6 high-resolution graphics mode this command selects the foreground attribute and background color. Parameter **fg** is the foreground attribute; range 1-15 for Screen 3, range 1-3 for Screen 4, range 1-15 for Screen 5, and range 1-3 for Screen 6. Parameter **bg** is the background color, range 0-15. The colors associated with the numeric values are the same as in the above table. The exception is that on Screen 4 and 6 the default colors for foreground attributes 1, 2 and 3 are cyan, magenta and white. You can change these defaults with the PALETTE and PALETTE USING commands.

In any of the COLOR commands you may omit a parameter by including a comma before the following parameters. In this case, the old value is considered to be still in effect.

COMMENTS

COM

APPLE IIe & II+

Not available. Cannot be simulated.

IBM PC & PCjr

ON COM (n) GOSUB x enables event trapping for a COM port, where **n** is a numeric expression representing communications adapter 1 or 2, and **x** is a line number of a subroutine. ON COM enables trapping of activity for the specified COM port if followed by a COM ON instruction, unless **x** represents line 0. In this case, trapping is disabled.

COM (n) ON where **n** is a numeric expression representing communications adapter 1 or 2. This instruction initiates checking for activity at the specified adapter each time BASIC starts a new statement. If characters have come into the adapter, BASIC branches immediately to the line number specified in the ON COM(n) GOSUB x instruction.

COM (n) OFF where **n** is a numeric expression representing communications adapter 1 or 2. This instruction causes trapping for the specified adapter to cease. If any characters come into the adapter, they are not remembered.

COM (n) STOP where **n** is a numeric expression representing communications adapter 1 or 2. This instruction causes trapping for the specified adapter to cease, but any characters coming into the adapter are remembered—until the buffer overflows—and an immediate trap takes place when a COM (n) ON command is reached.

When a trap occurs during COM (n) ON status, a COM (n) STOP is immediately executed. A RETURN from a trap immediately executes a COM (n) ON unless a COM (n) OFF is used within the routine. All COM commands are disabled when error trapping occurs as the result of an ON ERROR GOTO command.

COMMODORE 64

WAIT n,m[,p] where **n** is a memory location (range 0-65535), **m** and **p** are in the range 0-255 with the optional **p** defaulting to 0. WAIT is not the same as COM, but can be used to roughly approximate its action. WAIT causes program execution to halt until the value of the bit at memory location **n** changes in a specific way dictated by the other two parameters. Parameter **n** is exclusively ORed with **p**, then the result is ANDed with **m**, continuing until the final result is non-zero. It is seldom used.

TRS-80 Models IV & III

Not available. Cannot be simulated on TRS-80 Models IV and III without machine-language routines.

TRS-80 Color Computer

Not available. Cannot be simulated on COCO without machine-language routines.

COMMENTS

COMMON

APPLE IIe & II+

Not available. Simulate it by protecting a portion of memory with HIMEM. POKE the value of the variables into the protected memory, RUN the new program, then PEEK the values of the variables you wish to use in the second program out of memory.

IBM PC & PCjr

COMMON v1[,v2...] where **v1, v2,...** are variables passed to the chained program. COMMON passes the named variables to a program chained with the CHAIN command. Array variables must have ( ) appended to the variable name. If the ALL option is invoked with the CHAIN command, COMMON is not necessary. It is also not necessary to reDIMension any arrays when using the CHAIN command. You can use any number of COMMON statements, but the same variable cannot appear twice.

COMMODORE 64

Not needed on the Commodore 64 if you just LOAD the new program from within the currently running program, and the currently running program is longer than the new program. The new program automatically RUNs. Variables are not cleared, although any open files are CLOSEd. Also see **LOAD.**

CONT

is not available within a BASIC program. It is used in the direct mode to continue execution of a program ceased due to an error or user intervention. If a program has been edited while stopped, CONT cannot be used. If an error condition has not been corrected, CONT cannot be used. CONT is essentially identical in use on every machine, except that it is spelled CON for Apple Integer BASIC.

COPY

APPLE IIe & II+

Simulate it with the following routine:

```
10 ONERR GOTO 200
20 D$=CHR$(4)
30 PRINT D$;"OPEN file1"
40 PRINT D$;"OPEN file2"
50 PRINT D$;"READ file1"
60 INPUT A$
70 PRINT D$;"WRITE file2"
80 PRINT A$
90 GOTO 50
200 PRINT D$;"CLOSE file1"
210 PRINT D$;"CLOSE file2"
```

Note that this copies only sequential data files, and only one at a time.

IBM PC & PCjr

Simulate it with the following routine with **file1** (the file you wish to copy) and **file2** (the resulting copy):

```
10 OPEN "file1" FOR INPUT AS
   #1
20 OPEN "file2" FOR OUTPUT
   AS #2
30 WHILE NOT EOF(1)
40 LINE INPUT #1,I$
50 PRINT #2,I$
60 WEND
70 CLOSE
```

COMMODORE 64

COPY (usually abbreviated C) this command makes a duplicate copy of a program or sequential file under another name on the same disk when a single disk drive is used. Format is as follows, with **File1** the source file and **File2** the destination file. 8 is the drive number.

```
10 OPEN 15,8,15: PRINT#15,
   "C0:File2=File1": CLOSE
   15
```

TRS-80 Models IV & III

COMMON v1[,v2...] (Model IV) where **v1, v2,...** are variables that will be passed to the chained program. COMMON passes the named variables to a program chained with the CHAIN command. Array variables must have ( ) appended to the variable name. If the ALL option is invoked with the CHAIN command, COMMON is not necessary. It is also not necessary to reDIMension any arrays when using the CHAIN command. You can use any number of COMMON statements, but the same variable cannot appear twice.

To simulate the COMMON instruction on the Model III, protect a block of high memory, POKE the variables you wish to preserve into protected memory, and RUN (or MERGE and RUN) the new program, then retrieve variable values by using PEEK.

TRS-80 Color Computer

Cannot be simulated on COCO. You have to protect a block of high memory with the CLEAR statement. Then POKE the variables you wish to preserve into protected memory, RUN the new program (or merge with the R option) and retrieve the variable values by using PEEK.

COMMENTS

TRS-80 Models IV & III

Simulate it as follows: OPEN the target file as #1 using the "E" option, and OPEN the source file as #2 using the "I" option. Read the data from the source file (1) and write it to the target file (2) until EOF (2) returns true. Then close both files.

TRS-80 Color Computer

COPY "file1" TO "file2" copies **file1** into **file2**. You must specify the drive number at the end of each filename.

COMMENTS

COS

APPLE IIe & II+

COS (x) where x is an angle measured in radians. COS returns the cosine of angle x. The returned value is a floating-point number.

IBM PC & PCjr

Same.

COMMODORE 64

Same.

CSAVE

APPLE IIe & II+

SAVE where no argument is given. Saves on cassette the program currently in memory. Note that the cassette must be ready!

IBM PC & PCjr

SAVE "[CAS1:]filename" [,A][,P] saves the file filename on the cassette. In Cassette BASIC, CAS1: can be omitted. The A option saves it as an ASCII file. The P option saves it in the "protected" mode. If no option is given, the program is saved in binary form.

COMMODORE 64

SAVE"filename" saves the file filename on the cassette.

CSNG

APPLE IIe & II+

Because the Apple does not use double-precision numbers, the CSNG statement cannot be simulated on it. To convert an integer to a floating-point value, just assign it to a variable without the % symbol following it. Thus a=a%. Then use a instead of a%.

IBM PC & PCjr

CSNG(x) converts the numeric expression x to a single-precision expression. A single-precision variable has seven or fewer digits, is an integer in the range −32768-32767, has an exponential form using E, or has a trailing exclamation point (!). If x is an integer, the resulting single-precision expression can be no more accurate than x. If x is a double-precision expression, the single-precision expression is achieved by rounding.

COMMODORE 64

Because Commodore does not use double-precision numbers, the CSNG statement cannot be simulated on it. To convert an integer to a floating-point value, just assign it to a variable without the % symbol following it. Thus a=a%. Then use a instead of a%.

CSRLIN

APPLE IIe & II+

Simulate it with the following routine:

    10 ROW=PEEK(37)+1

where ROW is the variable name denoting the line number, range 1-24.

IBM PC & PCjr

CSRLIN returns the value of the line of the active screen on which the cursor is positioned. Range 1-25.

COMMODORE 64

Simulate it with the following routine:

    10 ROW=PEEK(214)+1

where ROW is the variable name denoting the line number, range 1-25.

TRS-80 Models IV & III	TRS-80 Color Computer	COMMENTS
Same.	Same.	To convert degrees (D) to radians (R), use the following formula: `R=D*3.141593/180`

TRS-80 Models IV & III	TRS-80 Color Computer	COMMENTS
The Model IV cannot access the cassette from BASIC unless it is in the Model III emulation code. **CSAVE "filename"** (Model III) saves the file **filename** on the cassette.	**CSAVE "filename"[,A]** saves the file **filename** on the cassette. If the **A** option is specified, it is saved as an ASCII file. **CSAVEM** writes a machine-language file to the cassette.	

TRS-80 Models IV & III	TRS-80 Color Computer	COMMENTS
CSNG(x) converts the numeric expression **x** to a single-precision expression. A single-precision variable has seven or fewer digits, is an integer in the range −32768-32767, has an exponential form using E, or has a trailing exclamation point (!). If **x** is an integer, the resulting single-precision expression can be no more accurate than **x**. If **x** is a double-precision expression, the single-precision expression is achieved by truncating to seven digits, then rounding with the 4/5 rule to six digits before displaying.	Because the COCO does not use double-precision numbers, the CSNG statement cannot be simulated on it. To convert an integer to a floating-point value, just assign it to a variable without the % symbol following it. Thus **a=a%**. Then use **a** instead of **a%**.	

TRS-80 Models IV & III	TRS-80 Color Computer	COMMENTS

ROW(0) (Model IV) returns the row location of the cursor on the Model IV. Note that the **0** is a dummy argument that should not be changed.
 	
Simulate the command on the Model III by using:
 	
`10 DEF FN ROW(d)=INT((PEEK`
`(16416)+(PEEK(16417)`
	Cannot be easily simulated on the COCO in BASIC.
	
	--- 	
	
	`    AND 3)*256)/64)+1`
	`20 X=FNROW(0)`
	
	FN ROW(0) will return the vertical position of the cursor.	

CVD, CVI, CVS

APPLE IIe & II+

Because of the way it stores data in random files, there is neither a means nor a need to simulate these on Apple.

IBM PC & PCjr

CVI(n) where **n** is a two-byte string, converts a string read from a random access disk file into an integer. It does not change the actual bytes, only the way BASIC interprets them.

CVS(n) where **n** is a four-byte string, converts a string read from a random access disk file into a single-precision number. It does not change the actual bytes, only the way BASIC interprets them.

CVD(n) where **n** is an eight-byte string, converts a string read from a random access disk file into an double-precision number. It does not change the actual bytes, only the way BASIC interprets them.

COMMODORE 64

There is neither a means nor a need to simulate these on Commodore because of the way it stores data in random files.

DATA

APPLE IIe & II+

DATA c[,c]... where **c** is a constant of any form. DATA defines constants to be used by a READ statement. Note that the variable type (numeric or string) defined in the READ statement must agree with the constant type in the DATA statement.

IBM PC & PCjr

Same, except that the use of this command in Cartridge BASIC results in an ILLEGAL FUNCTION CALL if DOS 2.1 is not present.

COMMODORE 64

Same.

DATE$

APPLE IIe & II+

Because the Apple does not have an internal calendar, you must simulate DATE$. Define a string variable, such as D$, as the date string. It will have to be input each time a program is used.

IBM PC & PCjr

DATE$ sets or retrieves the date. Used as a variable, the form is

```
10 v$=DATE$
```

where **v$** is any string variable name. It returns the 10-character string mm-dd-yyyy. The actual date may have been set by DOS prior to entering BASIC, or within BASIC using the DATE$ statement. Used as a statement, the form is

```
DATE$=x$
```

where **x$** has the form mm-dd-yy, mm/dd/yy, mm-dd-yyyy or mm/dd/yyyy. If the first two digits of the year are omitted, it is assumed to be 19yy. The value of yyyy must be in the range 1980-2099.

COMMODORE 64

Because the Commodore 64 does not have an internal calendar, you must simulate DATE$. Define a string variable, such as D$, as the date string. It will have to be input each time the program is used.

TRS-80 Models IV & III

CVI(n) where **n** is a two-byte string, converts a string read from a random access disk file into an integer. It does not change the actual bytes, only the way BASIC interprets them.

CVS(n) where **n** is a four-byte string, converts a string read from a random access disk file into a single-precision number. It does not change the actual bytes, only the way BASIC interprets them.

CVD(n) where **n** is an eight-byte string, converts a string read from a random access disk file into a double-precision number. It does not change the actual bytes, only the way BASIC interprets them.

TRS-80 Color Computer

CVN(n$) where **n$** is a five-byte coded string, this command converts **n$** into a number. This is the complement to MKN$.

COMMENTS

CVI, CVS and CVD are exact opposites of MKI$, MKS$ and MKD$, respectively.

TRS-80 Models IV & III

Same.

TRS-80 Color Computer

Same.

COMMENTS

TRS-80 Models IV & III

DATE$ (Model IV) returns the date. The date can be reset with the following routine:

```
10 D$="DATE " + "mm/dd/yy"
20 SYSTEM D$
```

where **mm** is the month, **dd** is the day and **yy** is the year. Notice that you must enter both digits, for example 01/01/85, as a string argument, and the space **must** be included after the word DATE.

TIME$ (Model III) returns both date and time. When the computer is turned on or reset, these are set to 0. They can be reset with the following routine:

```
10 DEFINT T,I: DIM TM(5)
20 CL=16924
```

TRS-80 Color Computer

Because the COCO does not have an internal calendar, you must simulate DATE$. Define a string variable, such as D$, as the date string. It will have to be input each time a program is used.

```
30 PRINT "INPUT 6 VALUES
   SEPARATED BY COMMAS:
   MONTH, DAY, YEAR, HOUR,
   MINUTES, SECONDS"
40 INPUT TM(0), TM(1),
   TM(2), TM(3), TM(4),
   TM(5)
50 FOR I=0 TO 5
60 POKE CL-I, TM(I)
70 NEXT I
```

COMMENTS

Because AT is a reserved word, do not use DATE or DAT as a variable name. Some BASICs do not allow reserved words to be imbedded in a variable name.

Because the clock is sometimes turned off, such as during cassette operations, clock-dependent programs should allow for occasional resetting of the clock.

DEBUG

is not used within a program.

DEF

APPLE IIe & II+

DEF FNn(a) =e gives a user-defined function. Parameter **n** is a numeric variable and **a** is an argument (a numeric variable name) that will be passed to the function when it is called, and **e** is a numeric expression of less than 239 characters. The function defined must return a numeric value, and no more than one argument may be used. The value of argument **a** is local to the function. That is, it does not matter if you use the same argument name elsewhere in the program.

Be careful not to define two functions whose names have the same first two characters, because only the first two characters of a variable name are significant. Note that all DEFined functions are cleared by the LOMEM command.

IBM PC & PCjr

DEF FNn[(a1[,a2]...)]=e gives a user-defined function where **n** is a string or numeric variable and **a1, a2,...** are variable names that will be replaced with a value when the function is called. If more than one value is provided, they are "plugged in" to the function on a one-to-one basis. The value returned by the function is set by the expression **e**, which shows what operations will be performed on the arguments **a1, a2,...** when the function is called. This must return a value consistent with the variable type named by **n**.

Note that **a1, a2,...** may be the same as variable names found elsewhere in the program, but they do not affect the rest of the program because they are local to the function. If the variable names used in expression **e** are not found within **a1, a2,...** then the function will look for them in the program.

You can define a function that does not require arguments **a1, a2,...** For example,

```
10 DEF FNR=RND8
```

defines a function that returns a random number. If you define a function to require arguments, and then call it without the arguments supplied, you will get a syntax error. Similarly, if you provide too many arguments, you will get a syntax error.

COMMODORE 64

DEF FNn(a) =e gives a user-defined function. Parameter **n** is a numeric variable of one or two characters, and **a** is an argument (a numeric variable name) that will be passed to the function when it is called. Parameter **e** is a numeric expression. The function defined must return a numeric value, and no more than one argument may be used. The value of argument **a** is local to the function. That is, it does not matter if you use the same argument name elsewhere in the program.

On the Commodore 64, **n** may be up to two characters, and **a** is limited to floating-point numeric variables. FNn(a) must be defined by DEFFN(a) before it is called by the program. DEFFNn(a) may be defined in terms of other user-defined functions. Expressions like FNm(FNp(a)) and FNm(X*X) are acceptable.

DEF SEG

APPLE IIe & II+

Not available. Cannot be simulated.

IBM PC & PCjr

DEF SEG [=n] where **n** is a numeric expression in the range 0-65535. Defines the current segment of memory. Note that DEF and SEG **must** be separated by a space, or BASIC will assume you are defining a variable with the name DEFSEG. Any BLOAD, BSAVE, CALL,

COMMODORE 64

Not available. Cannot be simulated.

PEEK, POKE or USR that follows a DEF SEG statement will be relative to that segment. If **n** is omitted, BASIC's data segment is assumed.

TRS-80 Models IV & III

Same as IBM, except that a space is not required between DEF and FN on the Model III.

TRS-80 Color Computer

DEF FNn(a) =e gives a user-defined function. Parameter **n** is a numeric variable, and **a** is an argument (a numeric variable name) that will be passed to the function when it is called. Parameter **e** is a numeric expression. The function defined must return a numeric value, and no more than one argument may be used. The value of argument **a** is local to the function. That is, it does not matter if you use the same argument name elsewhere in the program.

COMMENTS

Many times a short routine that returns only one value may be DEFined as a function rather than used as a GOSUB. This saves disk space, speeds up the program, and allows more program versatility. Variable values remain local to the function, and the program is more readable.

TRS-80 Models IV & III

Not available. Cannot be simulated.

TRS-80 Color Computer

Not available. Cannot be simulated.

COMMENTS

Note that the address you specify should be 1/16th the actual address you want. The address you refer to will be a multiple of 16. DEF SEG

cannot be simulated on other machines, nor is there any reason to do so.

DEFDBL, DEFINT, DEFSNG, DEFSTR

APPLE IIe & II+

Variable types are not explicitly stated in a DEF statement on the Apple. Instead, all variables are implicitly floating-point numeric variables unless they have a trailing % (integer) or $ (string).

IBM PC & PCjr

DEF type letter [-letter] [,letter [-letter]] ... where **type** is INT, SNG, DBL or STR, and **letter** is any letter of the alphabet. This command explicitly DEFines any variable whose name starts with the letter(s) specified as INTegers, SiNGle precision, DouBLe precision or STRings. Default is single precision if DEFtype is not used. A type-declaration character (%, !, # or $) always takes precedence over a DEF statement. The statement should be at the beginning of the program, before any variables it declares are used.

COMMODORE 64

Variable types are not explicitly stated in a DEF statement on Commodore. Instead, all variables are implicitly floating-point numeric variables unless they have a trailing % (integer) or $ (string).

DEF USR

APPLE IIe & II+

Because Apple has only one allowable USR function, DEF USR cannot be simulated in less space than it would take to simply re-POKE the starting address before each USR call.

IBM PC & PCjr

DEF USR[n]=offset where **n** is a digit from 0 to 9 (default=0), specifying which USR routine is being referenced. **Offset** is an integer in the range 0-65535. The offset is added to the segment most recently defined in a DEF SEG to obtain the actual starting address of the USR routine. The USR routine is later called with the command USR[n].

COMMODORE 64

Because Commodore has only one allowable USR function, DEF USR cannot be simulated in less space than it would take to simply re-POKE the starting address before each USR call.

DEL, DELETE

APPLE IIe & II+

DEL a[,b] where **a** and **b** are program line numbers, with **b** the larger line number. DEL is normally used in the command mode, but may be used in programming mode to delete program lines. Program execution will halt after the DELete is completed, and you must type RUN to start it again.

IBM PC & PCjr

DELETE [a][-b] where **a** and **b** are program line numbers, with **b** the larger line number. DELETE is normally used in the command mode, but may be used in the programming mode to delete program lines. Program execution will halt after the DELETE is completed. A period (.) can optionally replace line numbers when referring to the current line.

COMMODORE 64

Although there is no DELETE command on the Commodore 64, the following program lines, which make use of the computer's dynamic keyboard, produce the same effect. This routine will delete all line numbers between **A** and **B**, then terminate the program. If this routine is renumbered, the number 140, which is in quotation marks in line 130, must be changed to reflect the renumbering.

```
100 P=0:GOTO140
110 PRINT CHR$(147)P
120 POKE631,19:POKE
    632,13:POKE633,13:
    POKE198,3
```

TRS-80 Models IV & III

DEF type letter [-letter] [,letter [-letter]] ... where **type** is INT, SNG, DBL or STR, and **letter** is any letter of the alphabet. This command explicitly DEFines any variable whose name starts with the letter(s) specified as INTegers, SiNGle precision, DouBLe precision or STRings. Default is single precision if DEFtype is not used. A type-declaration character (%, !, #, or $) always takes precedence over a DEF statement. The DEF statement should be at the beginning of the program, before any variables it declares are used.

TRS-80 Color Computer

Variable types are not explicitly stated in a DEF statement on the COCO. Instead, all variables are implicitly floating-point numeric variables unless they have a trailing $ (string).

COMMENTS

TRS-80 Models IV & III

DEF USR[n]=address where **n** is a digit from 0 to 9 (default=0), specifying which USR routine is being referenced. **Address** is an integer in the range 0-65535. The address is the actual starting address of the USR routine. The USR routine is later called with the command USR[n]. The space between DEF and USR is significant on the Model IV, but not on the Model III.

TRS-80 Color Computer

DEF USR[n]=address where **n** is a digit from 0 to 9 (default=0), specifying which USR routine is being referenced. **Address** is an integer in the range 0-65535. The address is the actual starting address of the USR routine. The USR routine is later called with the command USR[n].

COMMENTS

TRS-80 Models IV & III

DELETE [a][-b] where **a** and **b** are program line numbers, with **b** the larger line number. DELETE is normally used in the command mode, but may be used in the programming mode to DELETE program lines. Program execution will halt after the DELETE is completed. A period (.) can optionally replace line numbers when referring to the current line.

```
130 PRINT CHR$(19) CHR$(17)
    "P="P+1": GOTO 140": END
140 A=2: B=15: IF P>B THEN
    STOP: REM WILL DELETE ALL
    LINES FROM 2 TO 15
150 IF P<A THEN P=A
160 GOTO 110
```

TRS-80 Color Computer

DEL [a][-b] where **a** and **b** are program line numbers, with **b** the larger line number. DEL is normally used in the command mode, but may be used in the programming mode to DELETE program lines. Program execution will halt after the DELETE is completed.

DEL - without line numbers will delete the entire program.

COMMENTS

DIM

APPLE IIe & II+

DIM arrayname (a [,b...]) [,arrayname (a [,b...])...] where **a** and **b** are values specifying the number of elements in each dimension of **arrayname.** The array name may be either a string or a numeric variable name. Applesoft BASIC allows a maximum of 88 dimensions. The number of elements in each dimension is limited only by the amount of available memory. DIM may specify a list of array names, separated by commas.

Note: DIM is used differently in integer BASIC. Numeric arrays are limited to one dimesion, and string arrays are not allowed. DIM is used with strings to specify maximum string length.

IBM PC & PCjr

DIM arrayname (a [,b...]) [,arrayname (a [,b...])...] where **a** and **b** are values specifying the number of elements in each dimension of **arrayname**. The array name may be either a string or a numeric variable name. The maximum number of dimensions allowed is 255. The maximum number of elements in each dimension is 32767, which may be limited by memory. DIM may specify a list of array names, separated by commas.

Note: The minimum value for subscripts is 0, unless the OPTION BASE statement is used. See **OPTION BASE.**

COMMODORE 64

DIM arrayname (a [,b...]) [,arrayname (a [,b...])...] where **a** and **b** are values specifying the number of elements in each dimension of **arrayname**. The array name may be either a string or a numeric variable name. The maximum number of dimensions allowed is 255. The maximum number of elements in each dimension is 32767, which may be limited by memory. DIM may specify a list of array names, separated by commas.

DIRECTORY

APPLE IIe & II+

CATALOG [,Ss] [,Dd] where **s** specifies slot number 1-7, and **d** specifies drive 1 or 2. CATALOG will display the directory of the specified drive, and may be used in the programming mode when preceded by CHR$(4). If the drive number is omitted, the most recently selected drive will be selected.

IBM PC & PCjr

FILES ["d:"] displays the files on the specified drive, where **d** is the drive name. If the drive is not specified, the currently logged disk drive is used. DIR is used in DOS only.

Use of this command in Cartridge BASIC will result in an ILLEGAL FUNCTION CALL if DOS 2.1 is not present.

COMMODORE 64

Although there is no CATALOG or DIRECTORY command on the Commodore 64, the following program lines produce a similar effect. The program halts after the listing. In fact, the program is no longer in memory. It has been replaced by the directory. If you require a program that reads the directory without destroying the program in memory, see the *1541 Disk Drive User's Manual,* page 47.

```
100 POKE 631,19: POKE
    632,13: POKE 633,13:
    POKE 198,3
110 PRINT CHR$(147) "LIST"
120 LOAD "$",8: END
```

DLOAD

APPLE IIe & II+

Not available.

IBM PC & PCjr

Not available.

COMMODORE 64

Not available.

TRS-80 Models IV & III

DIM **arrayname (a [,b...])[,array-name (a [,b...])...]** where **a** and **b** are values specifying the number of elements in each dimension of **arrayname.** The array name may be either a string or a numeric variable name. The number of dimensions and elements in each dimension is limited only by the amount of available memory. DIM may specify a list of array names, separated by commas.

Note for TRS-80 Model IV: The minimum value for subscripts is 0, unless the OPTION BASE statement is used. See **OPTION BASE.**

TRS-80 Color Computer

DIM **arrayname (a [,b...])[,array-name (a [,b...])...]** where **a** and **b** are values specifying the number of elements in each dimension of **arrayname.** The array name may be either a string or a numeric variable name. The number of dimensions and elements in each dimension is limited only by the amount of available memory. DIM may specify a list of array names, separated by commas.

COMMENTS

An array that is not DIMensioned defaults to 11 elements, numbered 0-10. Thus if A(1) is used, A(0), A(2),...A(10) are automatically available.

TRS-80 Models IV & III

SYSTEM "DIR" (Model IV) will display the directory from BASIC, and may be used in either command or program mode.

CMD "D:d" (Model III) where parameter **d** specifies a currently connected disk-drive number. Displays the directory of the specified drive. Note: Drive specification is not optional. BASIC execution will continue after using CMD "D".

TRS-80 Color Computer

DIR [d] where **d** specifies the drive number to be accessed. DIR will display the directory of the specified drive, and program execution will continue.

COMMENTS

TRS-80 Models IV & III

Not available.

TRS-80 Color Computer

DLOAD "filename","n" downloads a machine-language program from another computer. **Filename** is the name of the file to be transferred. Parameter **n** is either 0 (signifying the transfer at 300 baud) or 1 (signifying 1200 baud). This command is poorly documented by Radio Shack and isn't available on other machines. On most

COMMENTS

computers, external transfer of files is handled by commercially available software.

DOPEN

APPLE IIe & II+

Not available.

IBM PC & PCjr

Not available.

COMMODORE 64

DOPEN#n, "filename",[Lr],Dd,[x]
DOPEN is a reserved word not used on the Commodore 64 unless BASIC 4.0 is being used. In BASIC 4.0, **Lr** indicates the record length of a relative file. If no value is given, then a sequential file is assumed to be in use. Parameter **d** is the number of the disk drive where the file resides. If parameter **x** is R, the file is OPENed for reading. If parameter **x** is W, the file is OPENed for writing. Note that **file-name** may NOT be a string variable.

See **OPEN** for the same command on other computers, as well as normal Commodore 64 operation.

DRAW

APPLE IIe & II+

DRAW n [AT c,r] places a shape on the screen, where **n** specifies a shape in the shape table currently in memory, **c** specifies the column, and **r** specifies the row for DRAWing on the high-resolution screen. If **c** and **r** are omitted, the shape will be drawn at the most recently specified location. Also see **XDRAW**, **ROT=** and **SCALE**.

IBM PC & PCjr

DRAW "[X]n$"
DRAW "X"+VARPTR$(n$) draws the object specified by the graphics language command in **n$**. If **n$** is a constant, it must be enclosed in quotation marks, but X may be omitted. The second method for using DRAW is primarily for those programs that will be compiled, but is legal syntax for interpretive programs too.

COMMODORE 64

Simulating would require extensive machine-language programming. Commercial software is available to give the Commodore 64 similar capabilities.

COMMENTS

GRAPHICS COMMAND LANGUAGE

These are the commands used within the string for the DRAW command on the IBM PC, PCjr and COCO. Commands within a string should be separated by a semicolon, and x and y coordinates should be separated by a comma. Placing a + or − before a coordinate causes motion to be relative to cursor position, rather than absolute.

B Causes the cursor to not DRAW on the next motion command.

N Causes the cursor to return to its previous location following the next motion command.

A n Turns the cursor the relative angle specified by **n**, range 0-3: 0=0°, 1=90°, 2=180°, 3=270°.

C n Changes the drawing color. See **COLOR** for legal values.

P n,m In IBM BASIC 2.0 or Cartridge BASIC only, sets the color. Color for the painting option is specified by **n**. The color for the boundary is set by **m**. See **COLOR** for legal values.

TA n In IBM BASIC 2.0 or Cartridge BASIC only, causes the direction of drawing to be turned by an angle of **n** degrees. Range −360-360.

U n Moves up a distance of **n** times the scaling factor—see option **S** below—from the last point referenced.

D n Moves down a distance of **n** times the scaling factor from the last point referenced.

L n Moves left a distance of **n** times the scaling factor from the last point referenced.

R n Moves right a distance of **n** times the scaling factor from the last point referenced.

E n Moves diagonally up and right a distance of **n** times the scaling factor from the last point referenced.

TRS-80 Models IV & III

Not available.

TRS-80 Color Computer

Not available.

COMMENTS

TRS-80 Models IV & III

Because Models III and IV do not have graphics capabilities, DRAW is not available and cannot be simulated.

TRS-80 Color Computer

DRAW "[X]n$"** draws the object specified by the graphics language commands in **n$. If **n$** is a constant, it must be enclosed in quotation marks, but X may be omitted.

COMMENTS

(See below left.)

F n Moves diagonally down and right a distance of **n** times the scaling factor from the last point referenced.

G n Moves diagonally down and left a distance of **n** times the scaling factor from the last point referenced.

H n Moves diagonally up and left a distance of **n** times the scaling factor from the last point referenced.

M x,y Moves to the coordinate specified by **x** and **y**. Motion is absolute unless **x** is prefixed with either + or −, in which case the move will be relative to the last cursor position.

S n Sets the scaling factor with **n**. The actual scale is n/4. Default for **n** is 4, so the default scaling factor is 1. Range for parameter **n** is 1-255 for IBM; 1-62 for COCO.

Xn$** Calls substring **n$ and continues with the next command.

DRIVE d

APPLE IIe & II+	IBM PC & PCjr	COMMODORE 64
Not available.	Not available.	Not available.

DSKINI

APPLE IIe & II+	IBM PC & PCjr	COMMODORE 64
Disks must be initialized from the command mode.	Disks must be initialized from DOS.	NEW initializes, or formats, a new disk. It is usually abbreviated as **N**. Typical lines to do this follow:

COMMODORE 64 (continued):

```
10 OPEN 15,8,15
20 PRINT#15,
   "N0:diskname,id"
30 CLOSE 15
```

In this code, **id** represents a two-character identifier that you want to assign to the disk. It should be unique for each disk. Diskname is the name you wish to give the disk. The NEW operation takes about two minutes per disk.

DSKI$, DSKO$

APPLE IIe & II+	IBM PC & PCjr	COMMODORE 64
Not available.	Not available.	PRINT#f,"BLOCK-READ:"c,d,t,b

COMMODORE 64 (continued):

PRINT#f,"BLOCK-READ:"c,d,t,b
PRINT#f,"BLOCK-WRITE: "c,d,t,b
PRINT#f,"BLOCK-ALLOCATE: "d,t,b
PRINT#f,"BLOCK-FREE: "d,t,b
PRINT#f,"BUFFER-POINTER: "c,1

These commands allow you to read (BLOCK-READ) and write (BLOCK-WRITE) data directly to disk, allocate space on a disk for data, logically free up space for data (by writing to the RAM, not actually erasing), and change the location of the data pointer.

Here, **f** is the number used to OPEN the file, **c** is the channel number, **d** is the drive number, **t** is the track number and **b** is the block (sector)

TRS-80 Models IV & III

Not available.

TRS-80 Color Computer

DRIVEd changes the logged drive to drive **d**, default=0. The default drive cannot be redefined on other computers covered in this book. You simply include the drive specification in those commands that use non-default values.

COMMENTS

TRS-80 Models IV & III

CMD"I","FORMAT" will allow you to format a disk from BASIC, but you will be returned to DOS afterward, and the program in memory will be lost.

TRS-80 Color Computer

DSKINI d formats the disk in drive number **d**, default=0. Using the command in a program causes the program to be erased from memory.

COMMENTS

TRS-80 Models IV & III

Not available.

number. To use these you must OPEN the command channel (#15) as well as the file buffer. These are often abbreviated with only their first letters (B-R, B-W, B-A, B-F and B-P). These commands may be used from BASIC, but are most useful when used with machine-language programs. They are very hazardous without careful attention to syntax and program structure.

For a full discussion of their proper use, see the *1541 Disk Drive User's Manual.*

TRS-80 Color Computer

DSKI$ d,t,s,s1$,s2$
DSKO$ d,t,s,s1$,s2$
These commands allow you to read (DSKI$) and write (DSKO$) data directly to the disks, where **d** is the number of the disk drive, **t** is the track number, and **s** is the sector number. The strings being input and output are represented by **s1$** and **s2$**. The former represents the first 128 bytes of the sector, the latter the last 128 bytes.

COMMENTS

Direct access to the disk sectors is not available from BASIC on the other computers covered by this book. Data is written onto the disk under the control of the Disk Operating System.

EDIT

Although used in the direct mode to initiate editing a line, EDIT is not used within a program.

ELSE (See IF-THEN-ELSE)

END

APPLE IIe & II+

Terminates program execution and closes all files.

IBM PC & PCjr

Same.

COMMODORE 64

Same.

ENVIRON, ENVIRON$

APPLE IIe & II+

Not available. Do not use it as a variable name because it contains the embedded reserved word ON.

IBM PC & PCjr

These are undocumented reserved words for IBM computers.

COMMODORE 64

Not available. Do not use it as a variable name because it contains the embedded reserved word ON.

EOF

APPLE IIe & II+

Although Apple does not have an EOF function, you can obtain similar results with the following routine. In it, the reading loop reads data from the sequential file **filename**. When the end of the file is reached, an OUT OF DATA error occurs. Line 100 then transfers control to line 500. The POKE resets the error flag, line 510 closes the file and program execution continues.

```
100 ONERR GOTO 500
110 D$=CHR$(4): REM CONTROL
    D
120 PRINT D$; "OPEN filename"
130 PRINT D$; "READ filename"
140 REM
150 REM PLACE A LOOP HERE THAT
160 REM READS THE DESIRED
    DATA
170 REM
500 POKE 216,0
510 PRINT D$; "CLOSE
    filename"
```

IBM PC & PCjr

EOF(n) returns a -1 (True) if the end of file **n** is reached, where **n** is the number of a file that has been OPENed. This is useful for avoiding an END OF FILE error.

COMMODORE 64

The EOF function can be simulated on the Commodore 64 with the following program lines:

```
100 OPEN 8,8,8, "filename,
    S,R"
110 GET#8, A$: A$=A$+CHR$(0)
120 REM
130 REM MANIPULATE A$ HERE
140 REM
150 IF (ST) AND 64=64 THEN
    CLOSE 8: GOTO 170
160 GOTO 110
170 REM PROGRAM EXECUTION
    CONTINUES HERE
```

TRS-80 Models IV & III
Same.

TRS-80 Color Computer
Same.

COMMENTS

TRS-80 Models IV & III
These are undocumented reserved words for the TRS-80 Model IV computer.

TRS-80 Color Computer
Not available.

COMMENTS

TRS-80 Models IV & III
EOF(n) returns a −1 (True) if the end of file **n** is reached, where **n** is the number of a file that has been OPENed. Range for **n** is 1-15. This is useful for avoiding an END OF FILE error.

TRS-80 Color Computer
EOF(n) returns a −1 (True) if the end of file **n** is reached, where **n** is the number of a file that has been opened. For cassette files, **n**=−1. For keyboard files, **n**=0. For disk files, the range for **n** is 1-15. This is useful for avoiding an END OF FILE error.

COMMENTS

EQV

APPLE IIe & II+

xEQVy can be simulated by DEF FNEQV(x,y) = (x OR NOT y) AND (NOT x OR y)

The truth table for this algorithm is:

x	y	(x OR NOT y) AND (NOT x OR y)
T	T	T
T	F	F
F	T	F
F	F	T

Be aware that NOT doesn't perform bitwise operations in the same manner as it does for other computers.

IBM PC & PCjr

xEQVy is a logical operator indicating whether two numeric values x and y are equivalent. The truth table for EQV follows

x	y	xEQVy
T	T	T
T	F	F
F	T	F
F	F	T

COMMODORE 64

xEQVy can be simulated by using the algorithm (x OR NOT y) AND (NOT x OR y)

The truth table for this algorithm (where T = −1 and F = 0) follows:

x	y	(x OR NOT y) AND (NOT x OR y)
T	T	T
T	F	F
F	T	F
F	F	T

ERASE

APPLE IIe & II+

CLEAR is used instead of ERASE. Note that this clears both variables *and* arrays.

IBM PC & PCjr

ERASE name1[,name2]... where name1, name2,... are names of arrays previously used by the program. ERASE selectively eliminates arrays from a program—as opposed to CLEAR, which erases all arrays and variables. This is usually used to free memory space or to allow reDIMensioning of the array.

COMMODORE 64

CLR is used instead of ERASE. Note that it does not allow the reDIMensioning of an array and also CLEARs variables.

ERDEV, ERDEV$

These are undocumented reserved words on IBM.

TRS-80 Models IV & III

xEQVy (Model IV) is a logical operator indicating whether two operators are equivalent. The truth table for EQV follows:

x	y	xEQVy
T	T	T
T	F	F
F	T	F
F	F	T

xEQVy (Model III) can be simulated by **(x OR NOT y) AND (NOT x OR y)**

The truth table for this algorithm follows:

x	y	(x OR NOT y) AND (NOT x OR y)
T	T	T
T	F	F
F	T	F
F	F	T

TRS-80 Color Computer

xEQVy can be simulated by using the algorithm: **(x OR NOT y) AND (NOT x OR y)**

The truth table for this algorithm follows:

x	y	(x OR NOT y) AND (NOT x OR y)
T	T	T
T	F	F
F	T	F
F	F	T

COMMENTS

TRS-80 Models IV & III

ERASE name1[,name2]... (Model IV) where **name1, name2,...** are names of arrays previously used by the program. ERASE selectively eliminates arrays from a program—as opposed to CLEAR, which erases all arrays and variables. This is usually used to free memory space or to allow reDIMensioning of the array.

CLEAR (Model III) is used instead of ERASE. Note that CLEAR also ERASEs all variables.

TRS-80 Color Computer

CLEAR is used instead of ERASE. Note that CLEAR also ERASEs all variables.

COMMENTS

ERL, ERR

APPLE IIe & II+

The line number of the line in which the most recent error occurred can be determined by:

PEEK(218)+PEEK(219)*256

The error number of the most recent error can be determined by:

PEEK(222)

IBM PC & PCjr

ERL is a variable with the value of the line number of the line in which an error occurred. Default=0.

ERR is a variable with the value of the error number that most recently occurred. Default=0.

COMMODORE 64

Cannot be simulated without machine-language programming.

ERROR

APPLE IIe & II+

Not used as a reserved word, but should not be used as a variable name because it contains the embedded reserved word OR. The user-defined, error-code function (as on IBM) cannot be simulated in BASIC.

IBM PC & PCjr

ERRORn simulates the error number **n**. Range=0-255. You should never find this used in a program. It is primarily a debugging tool. However, you may find ERRORn used to define an error code that does not normally exist in BASIC. For example,

```
 10 ON ERROR GOTO 200
 90 INPUT "Select a menu
    choice";A
100 IF A>9 THEN ERROR 220
200 IF ERR=220 THEN PRINT
    "There are only 9
    choices": RESUME 90
```

Thus you can have error routines based on the logic of the program rather than on the limitations of the machine.

COMMODORE 64

Not used as a reserved word, but should not be used as a variable name because it contains the embedded reserved word OR. The user-defined, error-code function (as on IBM) cannot be simulated in BASIC.

EXEC

APPLE IIe & II+

EXEC filename executes the batch-file **filename**. The file may contain DOS commands, and may load and run other BASIC programs. If the batch file calls other BASIC programs, those programs get their input from the batch file. When the batch file is finished, it closes and control returns to the BASIC program that called it.

IBM PC & PCjr

Cannot be simulated without a machine-language routine. But you can work from DOS to BASIC with a batch file. In this way, the batch file calls BASIC programs and/or DOS programs, rather than the other way around, as with EXEC.

COMMODORE 64

Cannot be simulated without a machine-language routine.

TRS-80 Models IV & III	TRS-80 Color Computer	COMMENTS
ERL is a function that returns the value of the line number of the line in which an error occurred. Default=0. If the error occurred in the command mode, then ERL=65535. **ERR** is a function that returns the value of the error number that most recently occurred. Default=0. On the Model III, you must use (ERR/2)+1 to get the actual error code. ERR=(true error code−1)∗2. **ERR** (Model IV) returns the system error number and description of the most recent TRSDOS error. Default=0.	Cannot be simulated without machine-language programming.	

TRS-80 Models IV & III	TRS-80 Color Computer	COMMENTS
ERROR (n) where **n** is a value 0-255, which specifies an error code. Used to simulate errors while debugging error-trapping routines.	Not used as a reserved word. The user-defined, error-code function (as on IBM) cannot be simulated in BASIC.	

TRS-80 Models IV & III	TRS-80 Color Computer	COMMENTS
SYSTEM [command] (Model IV) where **command** is any TRS-DOS library command—except DEBUG or any utility. This does not exactly emulate the EXEC command as used on the Apple, but can simulate it. If you use SYSTEM without the **command**, it returns you to TRS-DOS and the program is lost.	Because DOS and BASIC are transparent to the user, simulating EXEC is not possible. You can CHAIN other programs, and you can initiate DOS commands, such as DSKINI. But the program in memory will be lost.	

EXP

APPLE IIe & II+

EXP(x) returns the mathematical number e raised to the **x** power, where e is the base for natural logarithms. If **x** is greater than 88.0296919, an overflow error will occur.

IBM PC & PCjr

EXP(x) returns the mathematical number e raised to the **x** power, where e is the base for natural logarithms. If **x** is greater than 88.02969, an overflow error will occur.

COMMODORE 64

EXP(x) returns the mathematical number e raised to the **x** power, where e is the base for natural logarithms. If **x** is greater than 88.0296919, an overflow error will occur.

FIELD

APPLE IIe & II+

Apple accesses information in random access files in a different manner from IBM or TRS-80, requiring more information than the FIELD command. In a file having undivided records, you do not define field length. The entire record is one field, which can be read into memory as a string. The various components are then accessed using string functions, such as MID$, LEFT$ and RIGHT$. In a file having divided records, access fields by specifying the first byte of the field with the "B" option. The field is read from the byte specified until it reaches a delimiter. For example,

```
50 PRINT D$;"READ
   FILE1,R22,B25"
60 INPUT A$
```

reads the 22nd record of **FILE1**, from the 25th byte until it reaches a delimiter, and assigns it to string variable **A$**.

IBM PC & PCjr

FIELD[#]n,x AS y[,x AS y]... where **n** is the number of an OPENed file buffer, **x** is the number of characters allocated to the field, and **y** is a string variable that will be used to access the data. FIELD is used to allocate space and position of variables in a random-file buffer. FIELD does not actually insert or retrieve any data into the disk file or buffer. It only designates how that data will be inserted by PUT, and retrieved by GET. The total number of bytes allocated by FIELD is limited to the number specified when the file is opened. Otherwise, you will get a FIELD OVERFLOW ERROR.

When you have assigned a variable name to **y**, do not use that variable name in an INPUT or on the left side of an assignment statement. If you do, you will get some very unexpected results!

COMMODORE 64

FIELD is not supported by the Commodore 64. When manipulating string data, it is the programmer's responsibility to maintain the logistics of specific fields or data areas within a record. When manipulating numeric data, the record length specified in the OPEN command is the maximum length of the field. Maximum record length is 254 characters. See **OPEN**.

Because of this method of accessing random files, FIELD cannot be simulated. Indeed, the whole file-handling routine will need rewriting to bring it into Apple-compatible format.

FILES

APPLE IIe & II+

CATALOG [,Ss][,Dd] where **s** specifies slot number 1-7, and **d** specifies drive 1 or drive 2. CATALOG will display the directory of the specified drive, and may be used in the programming mode when preceded by CHR$(4). If the drive number is omitted, the most recently selected drive will be selected.

IBM PC & PCjr

FILES ["d:"] displays the files on the specified drive, where **d** is the drive name. If the drive is not specified, the currently logged disk drive is used. DIR is used in DOS only.

Use of this command in Cartridge BASIC will result in an ILLEGAL FUNCTION CALL if DOS 2.1 is not present.

COMMODORE 64

Although there is no FILES command on the Commodore 64, the following program lines produce a similar effect. The program halts after the listing. In fact, the program is no longer in memory. It has been replaced by the directory. If you require a program that reads the directory without destroying the program in memory, see the *1541 Disk Drive User's Manual,* page 47.

```
100 POKE 631,19: POKE
    632,13: POKE 633,13:
    POKE 198,3
110 PRINT CHR$(147)"LIST"
120 LOAD "$",8: END
```

TRS-80 Models IV & III	TRS-80 Color Computer	COMMENTS
EXP(x) returns the mathematical number e raised to the **x** power, where e is the base for natural logarithms. If **x** is greater than 87.3365, an overflow error will occur.	**EXP(x)** returns the mathematical number e raised to the **x** power, where e is the base for natural logarithms. If **x** is greater than 87.3365, an overflow error will occur.	

TRS-80 Models IV & III	TRS-80 Color Computer	COMMENTS
FIELD[#]n, x AS y[,x AS y]... where **n** is the number of an OPENed file buffer. Parameter **x** is the number of characters allocated to the field, and **y** is a string variable used to access the data. FIELD is used to allocate space and position of variables in a random-file buffer. FIELD does not actually insert or retrieve any data into the disk file or buffer. It only designates how that data will be inserted by PUT and retrieved by GET. The total number of bytes allocated by FIELD is limited to the number specified when the file is opened. Otherwise, you will get a FIELD OVERFLOW ERROR.	**FIELD#n, x AS y[,x AS y]...** where **n** is the number of an OPENed file buffer: −2 for printer, −1 for cassette, 0 for screen and 1-15 for disk drive buffers. Parameter **x** is the number of characters allocated to the field, and **y** is a string variable that will be used to access data. FIELD is used to allocate space and position of variables in a random-file buffer. FIELD does not actually insert or retrieve any data into the disk file or buffer. It only designates how that data will be inserted in the file buffer by PUT and retrieved by GET.	See **OPEN**.
When you have assigned a variable name to **y**, do not use that variable name in an input or on the left side of an assignment statement. If you do, you will get some very unexpected results!	The total number of bytes allocated by FIELD is limited to the number specified when the file is OPENed. Otherwise you will get a FIELD OVERFLOW ERROR. When you have assigned a variable name to **y**, do not use that variable name in an input or on the left side of an assignment statement. Otherwise, you will get some unexpected results!	

TRS-80 Models IV & III	TRS-80 Color Computer	COMMENTS
SYSTEM "DIR" (Model IV) will display the directory from BASIC, and may be used in either command or program mode.	**DIR [d]** where **d** specifies the drive number to be accessed. DIR will display the directory of the specified drive and program execution will continue.	
CMD "D:d" (Model III) where **d** specifies a currently connected disk drive number. The command will display the directory of the specified drive. Note: The drive specification is not optional. BASIC program execution will continue after the command is used.		

FIX

APPLE IIe & II+

Simulate it with the following routine:

```
20 IF V=INT(V) THEN 40
30 V=INT(V):IF V<0 THEN
   V=V+1
40 RETURN
```

Here **V** is a numeric variable. The decimal portion of **V** will be truncated.

IBM PC & PCjr

FIX (value) where **value** is a numeric expression. FIX will truncate the decimal portion of **value**. FIX is used to obtain the whole-number part of a decimal number.

COMMODORE 64

Simulate it with the following routine:

```
20 IF V=INT(V) THEN 40
30 V=INT(V):IF V<0 THEN
   V=V+1
40 RETURN
```

Here **V** is a numeric variable. The decimal portion of **V** will be truncated.

FLASH

APPLE IIe & II+

FLASH causes subsequent display output to alternately flash between INVERSE and NORMAL.

IBM PC & PCjr

COLOR 16,7 is not precisely the same as FLASH, but it does cause a normal-on-inverse blinking display. You can vary the first digit between 16 and 31 to vary foreground color, and 0 and 7 to vary background color.

COMMODORE 64

Can be simulated with the following routine, where MSG$ is the string to be flashed on line **ROW** at position **COL**. It will flash on and off at the DELAY rate until **KEY$**—in this case the space bar—is pressed.

```
100 MSG$="HELLO":ROW=1:
    COL=2
110 DELAY=100:KEY$=" "
120 POKE 783,0:POKE
    781,ROW:POKE 782,COL
130 SYS 65520:PRINT
    CHR$(18)MSG$
140 FOR I=1 TO DELAY:NEXT
150 POKE 783,0:POKE
    781,ROW:POKE 782,COL
160 SYS 65520:PRINT MSG$
170 GET A$:IF A$=KEY$ THEN
    200
180 FOR I=1 TO DELAY:NEXT
190 GOTO 120
200 REM PROGRAM CONTINUES
    HERE
```

FN

APPLE IIe & II+

FN **N(e)** where **N** is a variable name and **e** is an expression that specifies the value to be evaluated by the function. **FN** is used to call a function

IBM PC & PCjr

Same.

that has been defined by the DEF FN statement.

COMMODORE 64

Same.

TRS-80 Models IV & III

FIX **(value)** where **value** is a numeric expression. FIX will truncate the decimal portion of **value**. FIX is used to obtain the whole-number part of a decimal number.

TRS-80 Color Computer

FIX **(value)** where **value** is a numeric expression. FIX will truncate the decimal portion of **value**. FIX is used to obtain the whole-number part of a decimal number.

COMMENTS

TRS-80 Models IV & III

Can be roughly simulated with the following subroutine. This subroutine will, however, consume a great deal of processor time, and will not operate in a background mode.

```
1000 REM INITIALIZE VARIABLES
1010 REM FLASH = NUMBER OF
     TIMES TO FLASH
1020 REM DLAY=DELAY TIME FOR
     ON/OFF
1030 REM P$=STRING TO BE
     FLASHED
1040 REM LC=SCREEN LOCATION
     (1-1023) FOR FLASHED
     STRING
1050 REM GOSUB 1100 TO CALL
     SUBROUTINE
1100 BL$=STRING$(LEN(P$),
     32)
1110 FOR D1=1 TO FLASH
1120 PRINT@LC,P$;: FOR D2=1
     TO DLAY: NEXT D2
1130 PRINT@LC,BL$;: FOR
     D2=1 TO DLAY: NEXT D2
1140 NEXT D1
1150 PRINT@LC,P$
1160 RETURN
```

Here **FLASH** is a numeric variable containing the number of times to flash **P$**. **DLAY** is a numeric variable affecting the amount of time the string is to remain on and off. **P$** is a string variable containing the string to be flashed. **LC** is the screen location, range 1-1023, at which **P$** is to be flashed.

TRS-80 Color Computer

Can be roughly simulated with the following subroutine:

```
1000 REM INITIALIZE VARIABLES
1010 REM FLASH=NUMBER OF
     TIMES TO FLASH
1020 REM DLAY=DELAY TIME FOR
     ON/OFF
1030 REM P$=STRING TO BE
     FLASHED
1040 REM LC=SCREEN LOCATION
     (0-510) FOR FLASHED
     STRING
1050 REM GOSUB 1100 TO CALL
     SUBROUTINE
1100 BL$=STRING$(LEN(P$),
     32)
1110 FOR D1=1 TO FLASH
1120 PRINT@LC,P$;: FOR D2=1
     TO DLAY: NEXT D2
1130 PRINT@LC,BL$;: FOR
     D2=1 TO DLAY: NEXT D2
1140 NEXT D1
1150 PRINT@LC,P$
1160 RETURN
```

Here **FLASH** is a numeric variable containing the number of times to flash **P$**. **DLAY** is a numeric variable affecting the amount of time the string is to remain on and off. **P$** is a string variable containing the string to be flashed. **LC** is the screen location, range 0-510, at which **P$** is to be flashed.

COMMENTS

TRS-80 Models IV & III

Same.

TRS-80 Color Computer

Same.

COMMENTS

FOR

APPLE IIe & II+

FOR var=v1 TO v2 [STEP i] where **var** is a numeric variable name. This instruction executes a loop, terminated by NEXT, with a beginning value of **v1** and ending value of **v2**, incremented by **STEP i**. **STEP, v1** and **v2** may be negative. **STEP** is optional and is assumed to be +1 if not specified. If you use GOTO or GOSUB to break out of a loop too often, you will encounter OUT OF MEMORY errors. Therefore, plan loops so that they always hit the NEXT statement.

IBM PC & PCjr

FOR var=v1 TO v2 [STEP i] where **var** is a numeric variable name. This instruction executes a loop, terminated by NEXT, with a beginning value of **v1** and ending value of **v2**, incremented by **STEP i**. **STEP, v1** and **v2** may be negative. **STEP** is optional and is assumed to be +1 if not specified.

COMMODORE 64

FOR var=v1 TO v2 [STEP i] where **var** is a numeric variable name. This instruction executes a loop, terminated by NEXT, with a beginning value of **v1** and ending value of **v2**, incremented by **STEP i**. **STEP** is optional and is assumed to be +1 if not specified.

FORMAT

is an undocumented reserved word for TRS-80s. Some computers have a DOS command FORMAT that performs the same function as the TRS-80 COCO command DSKINI.

FRE

APPLE IIe & II+

FRE(e) where **e** is a numeric expression that is not evaluated, but must be present. When used in the form of **PRINT FRE(e)**, FRE will return the amount of available memory. When used in the form of **X=FRE(e)**, FRE will force reorganization of the string storage space. This may take a little time.

IBM PC & PCjr

FRE(e)
FRE(e$) where **e** is any dummy numeric or string value or variable. Returns the amount of free memory available measured in bytes. This doesn't include the space used by the interpreter. Therefore, be very careful not to assume the value given by FRE as the value you could use in a CLEAR statement. If you use FRE immediately after a CLEAR, you will find the free memory is slightly (2K to 4K bytes) smaller than the amount of memory you reserved with the CLEAR. Those 2K to 4K bytes are used by the interpreter.

Use of this command in Cassette BASIC will result in an ILLEGAL FUNCTION CALL if DOS 2.1 is not present.

COMMODORE 64

FRE(e) where **e** is a numeric expression that is not evaluated but must be present. FRE(e) does not always represent the amount of available memory on the Commodore 64. Free memory is calculated by

```
10 M=FRE(0)-(FRE(0)<0)
   *256*256
```

When used in the form PRINT FRE(e) or X=FRE(e), FRE will force reorganization of the string storage space, called *garbage collection*, which could take several minutes.

TRS-80 Models IV & III

FOR var=v1 TO v2 [STEP i] where **var** is a numeric variable name. This instruction executes a loop, terminated by NEXT, with a beginning value of **v1** and ending value of **v2**, incremented by **STEP i**. **STEP**, **v1** and **v2** may be negative. **STEP** is optional and is assumed to be +1 if not specified.

TRS-80 Color Computer

FOR var=v1 TO v2 [STEP i] where **var** is a numeric variable name. This instruction executes a loop, terminated by NEXT, with a beginning value of **v1** and ending value of **v2**, incremented by **STEP i**. **STEP**, **v1** and **v2** may be negative. **STEP** is optional and is assumed to be +1 if not specified.

COMMENTS

TRS-80 Models IV & III

FRE(x$) where **x$** is any dummy string value or variable. Returns the amount of free string space available.

FRE(n) where **n** is any dummy numeric value or variable. Returns the amount of free memory available. Same as **MEM**.

TRS-80 Color Computer

MEM returns the amount of free memory available.

COMMENTS

Also see **MEM**.

FREE

APPLE IIe & II+

Cannot be simulated without machine-language programming.

IBM PC & PCjr

Cannot be simulated without machine-language programming.

COMMODORE 64

Simulate it with the following program lines:

```
2000 OPEN 15,8,15,"I"
2010 PRINT#15,"M-R"
     CHR$(250) CHR$(2)
2020 GET#15,A$:
     A$=A$+CHR$(0)
2030 PRINT#15,"M-R"
     CHR$(252) CHR$(2)
2040 GET#15,B$:
     B$=B$+CHR$(0)
2050 PRINT
     ASC(A$)+256*ASC(B$)"
     BLOCKS FREE"
2060 CLOSE 15
```

GET, GET#

APPLE IIe & II+

GET v\$ [,x\$...] (Keyboard Input) where **v\$** and **x\$** are string variables. GET is used to retrieve a single character from the current input device—usually the keyboard—for each variable listed. GET varies from the INPUT command in that it does not display a prompt. It accepts input without waiting for the RETURN key to be pressed, and continues without displaying the typed character.

GET a\$ (Random File Access)
The format for this command is as follows:

```
10 PRINT CHR$(4);"OPEN
   filename,Vv,Dd,Ss"
20 PRINT CHR$(4);"READ
   filename,Rn"
30 GET a$
```

where **filename** is the file being accessed, **v** is the volume number of the disk, **d** is the disk drive number, **s** is the slot number that contains the disk drive, and **n** is the record number. This code is not as practical as using INPUT in line 30 would be, because GET will get only one character at a time. If you want more than one character, you will have to loop back to line 20 and concatenate a\$ each time you GET it.

IBM PC & PCjr

v\$=INKEY\$ (Keyboard Input) gets the first value at the keyboard buffer and assigns it the value **v\$**. INKEY\$ does not pause for input. If no value is at the buffer, it assigns **v\$** as a null value. If you want it to pause, then you can either loop until INKEY\$ returns a value different from null, or use the INPUT\$(1) function. If you are trying to detect keys with extended codes, use the INKEY\$ function. When a key with extended code is pressed, the INKEY\$ function returns a two-character string. The first character is null, and the second is the extended code.

GET [#]b[,r] (Random File Handling) where **b** is a previously defined buffer number (value 1-15), and **r** specifies a record number. Parameter **r** is optional, and is assumed to be the next available record if it is omitted. GET is used to retrieve a specified record from a random access file. Remember to specify the number of files you will have open when you call BASIC.

GET (x1,y1)-(x2,y2), arrayname (Graphics) where **x** and **y** are used to specify the corner coordinates of a rectangle on the screen and **arrayname** is the name of an array that stores the values of points in the rectangle. This is used for high-speed movement or replication of graphics

COMMODORE 64

GET v[,x...] (Keyboard Input) reads characters from the keyboard buffer. If no character is pending, it returns a null string. To avoid this you can use a loop, as in line 100 below.

```
100 GET V$: IF V$="" THEN
    100: REM LOOP UNTIL A KEY
    IS PRESSED
110 IF V$<"0" OR V$>"9" THEN
    100
120 V=VAL(V$)
```

You could use **V** instead of **V\$** in line 100, but non-numeric input would cause a syntax error. Using **V\$** and adding lines 110 and 120 to this routine allow you to input numeric data, while avoiding syntax errors if a non-numeric key is struck.

Conversely, if you used line 100 alone—with **V\$**—you would get a string variable even if a numeric key were struck. If you wish to get multiple characters, use a string that collects and concatenates them, or use the INPUT instruction.

GET# n, a[\$][,b[\$]]... (Sequential File Access, Screen Access) where **n** is a device or file number, and **a[\$], b[\$],...** are variable names. This instruction reads data from a file or device in the same way GET reads from the keyboard. If device #3 is specified, it reads the characters on the screen sequentially. If no input is received, characters are returned as a null, and numbers are returned as a 0.

TRS-80 Models IV & III

Cannot be simulated without machine-language programming.

TRS-80 Color Computer

FREE (d) reports the number of free granules available on the disk in drive number **d**. This command is used only on the TRS-80 Color Computer.

COMMENTS

TRS-80 Models IV & III

v$=INKEY$ (Keyboard Input) gets the first value at the keyboard buffer and assigns it the value **v$**. INKEY$ does not pause for input. If no value is at the buffer, it assigns **v$** as a null value. If you want it to pause, then you can loop until INKEY$ returns a value different from null.

GET [#]b[,r] (Random File Handling) where **b** is a previously defined buffer number—value 1-15—and **r** specifies a record number. Parameter **r** is optional, and is assumed to be the next available record if it is omitted. GET is used to retrieve a specified record from a random access file.

objects. This command cannot be readily simulated on other computers without using machine language. Therefore, simulation is beyond the scope of this book. You may wish to investigate the use of sprites on the Commodore 64 or the shape table on the Apple.

TRS-80 Color Computer

v$=INKEY$ (Keyboard Input) gets the first value at the keyboard buffer and assigns it the value **v$**. INKEY$ does not pause for input. If no value is at the buffer, it assigns **v$** as a null value. If you want it to pause, then you can either loop until INKEY$ returns a value different from null or use the INPUT function. To retrieve multiple characters, use INPUT.

GET [#]b[,r] (Random File Handling) where **b** is a previously defined buffer number—value 1-15—and **r** specifies a record number. Parameter **r** is optional, and is assumed to be the next available record if it is omitted. GET is used to retrieve a specified record from a random access file.

GET (x1,y1)-(x2,y2), arrayname [,G] (Graphics) where **x** and **y** are used to specify the corner coordinates of a rectangle on the screen, and **arrayname** is the name of an array that will store the values of points in the rectangle. **G** is optional for some uses. When used, **G** tells the computer to store in full graphics detail. This is used for high-speed movement or replication of graphics objects. This command cannot be readily simulated on other computers without using machine language. Therefore, it is beyond the scope of this book. You may wish to investigate using sprites on the Commodore 64 or the shape table on the Apple.

COMMENTS

GET can be a very confusing conversion problem because it is used in many different ways—random file access, keyboard input and graphics. Be careful to identify the results it creates on the source machine before translating it to the target.

GOSUB

APPLE IIe & II+

GOSUB n where **n** is a line number that begins a subroutine terminated by the RETURN statement. GOSUB causes program execution to jump to the specified line, process the instructions found there, and then return to the instruction following the calling GOSUB. Repeatedly breaking out of subroutines with GOTO will cause an OUT OF MEMORY error.

In integer BASIC you can use variables for the line number.

IBM PC & PCjr

GOSUB n where **n** is a line number that begins a subroutine terminated by the RETURN statement. GOSUB causes program execution to jump to the specified line, process the instructions found there, and then return to the instruction following the calling GOSUB. Be sure the subroutines always end in a RETURN statement, rather than branching them with a GOTO.

COMMODORE 64

GOSUB n where **n** is a line number that begins a subroutine terminated by the RETURN statement. GOSUB causes program execution to jump to the specified line, process the instructions found there, and then return to the instruction following the calling GOSUB. Repeatedly breaking out of subroutines with GOTO will cause an OUT OF MEMORY error.

GOTO

APPLE IIe & II+

GOTO n where **n** is a line number in the current program. GOTO causes program execution to jump to the specified line and continue execution from that instruction on. Repeated exits from loops—such as FOR/NEXT or GOSUB—using GOTO will cause an OUT OF MEMORY error.

Apple Integer BASIC allows computed line numbers in a GOTO.

IBM PC & PCjr

GOTO n where **n** is a line number in the current program. GOTO causes program execution to jump to the specified line and continue execution from that instruction on.

COMMODORE 64

GOTO n where **n** is a line number in the current program. GOTO causes program execution to jump to the specified line and continue execution from that instruction on. Repeated exits from loops—such as FOR/NEXT or GOSUB—using GOTO will cause an OUT OF MEMORY error.

GR

APPLE IIe & II+

GR causes the Apple to display the currently specified page of the low-resolution graphic screen. If no page has been specified, page 1 is assumed. This screen will normally be 40 rows by 40 columns with the bottom eight rows open for up to four lines of text. Make a full 48-row-by-40-column screen by following the GR statement with

POKE -16302,0 : CALL -1998

IBM PC & PCjr

SCREEN 1 places the screen into the medium-resolution graphics mode (320x200). Used with the color/graphics adapter only.

SCREEN 2 is the two-color, high-resolution graphics mode (640x200).

SCREEN 3 (Cartridge BASIC Only) places the screen in the low-resolution graphics mode (160x200).

SCREEN 4 (Cartridge BASIC Only) places the screen in the four-color, medium-resolution graphics mode (320x200).

SCREEN 5 (Cartridge BASIC Only) places the screen in the 16-color, medium-resolution graphics mode (320x200). Requires 128K RAM.

COMMODORE 64

POKE 53265,PEEK(53265) OR 32: POKE 53270,PEEK(53270) OR 16 sets the Commodore 64 into the multi-color bit map mode (i.e., medium resolution). This is a very complex mode in BASIC, requiring extensive POKEs to control. A discussion of it is beyond the scope of this book. Instead, see *Commodore 64 Graphics & Sound Programming* by Stan Krute or *How to Program Your Commodore 64* by Carl Shipman.

SCREEN can also take many other arguments. Also see **SCREEN**.

TRS-80 Models IV & III

GOSUB n where **n** is a line number that begins a subroutine terminated by the RETURN statement. GOSUB causes program execution to jump to the specified line, process the instructions found there, and then return to the instruction following the calling GOSUB.

TRS-80 Color Computer

GOSUB n where **n** is a line number that begins a subroutine terminated by the RETURN statement. GOSUB causes program execution to jump to the specified line, process the instructions found there, and then return to the instruction following the calling GOSUB.

COMMENTS

Only Apple Integer BASIC allows computed line numbers in a GOSUB.

TRS-80 Models IV & III

GOTO n where **n** is a line number in the current program. GOTO causes program execution to jump to the specified line and continue execution from that instruction on.

TRS-80 Color Computer

GOTO n where **n** is a line number in the current program. GOTO causes program execution to jump to the specified line and continue execution from that instruction on.

COMMENTS

Only Apple Integer BASIC allows computed line numbers in a GOTO.

TRS-80 Models IV & III

Cannot be simulated because TRS-80 Models III and IV do not have separate graphic screens.

TRS-80 Color Computer

PMODE n where n is 2 or 3. Sets the COCO into medium resolution. PMODE is capable of taking several other arguments not related to medium resolution. Also see **PMODE**.

COMMENTS

HCOLOR

APPLE IIe & II+

HCOLOR=n where **n** is a numeric expression in the range 0-7. Sets the color plotted in the high-resolution graphics mode. Color assignments for **n** are given below. Note that if **n**=3, the dot will be blue if the x coordinate is even, green if the x coordinate is odd, and white only if (x,y) and (x+1,y) are both plotted.

0	Black 1	5	Depends on
1	Green		monitor
2	Blue	6	Depends on
3	White 1		monitor
4	Black 2	7	White 2

IBM PC & PCjr

COLOR [bg] [,[p]] in the SCREEN 1 medium-resolution graphics mode, which requires the color graphics adapter, where **bg** is the background color in the range 0-15 (default=7 or most recently named value) as shown in the chart below. Parameter **p** is the numeric expression in the range 0-255 indicating which palette to use. If **p** is even, palette 0 is selected, which includes red, green and brown. If **p** is odd, palette 1 is chosen, which includes cyan, magenta and white. The color within the palette that will be used is determined when giving a graphics command, such as PSET, PRESET, LINE, CIRCLE, PAINT or DRAW.

Parameter **bg** may be omitted by including a comma before parameter **p**. In this case, the old value of **bg** is considered to still be in effect.

Color-parameter values with the color graphics adapter are:

0	Black	9	Light Blue
1	Blue	10	Light Green
2	Green	11	Light Cyan
3	Cyan	12	Light Red
4	Red	13	Light
5	Magenta		Magenta
6	Brown	14	Yellow
7	White	15	High-
8	Gray		intensity
			White

Using COLOR in the SCREEN 2 high-resolution graphics mode will result in an ILLEGAL FUNCTION CALL error.

COLOR [fg] [,[bg]] (Cartridge BASIC Only) in the SCREEN 6 high-resolution graphics mode selects the foreground attribute and background color. Parameter **fg** is the foreground attribute—range 1-3. Default colors for foreground attributes 1, 2 and 3 are cyan, magenta and white. You can change these defaults with the PALETTE and PALETTE USING commands Parameter **bg** is the background color—range 0-15. The colors associated with the numeric values for the background are the same as in the above table.

COMMODORE 64

To set the color of the screen, border or cursor on the Commodore 64, use one of the following POKEs, with N selected out of the following table:

POKE 53280,N   Colors BORDER
POKE 53281,N   Colors SCREEN
POKE 646,N   Colors CURSOR

The value of **N** must be an integer in the range 0-15, and produces the result indicated in the following table:

0	Black	8	Orange
1	White	9	Brown
2	Red	10	Light Red
3	Cyan	11	Gray 1
4	Purple	12	Gray 2
5	Green	13	Light Green
6	Blue	14	Light Blue
7	Yellow	15	Gray 3

See **HGR** for a further discussion of high-resolution color on the Commodore 64.

TRS-80 Models IV & III

Cannot be simulated on the TRS-80 Models IV or III.

TRS-80 Color Computer

COLOR (f,b) sets the color of the display, where **f** is the color of the foreground, and **b** is the color of the background. Depending on the PMODE selected, the range of **f** and **b** may be 1-2, 1-4 or 1-8, with the actual colors that correspond to the numbers varying.

SET (x,y,c) determines the color of an individual screen point, where **x** and **y** are screen coordinates and **c** is a numeric expression associated with the color. Possible values for c follow:

0	Black	5	Buff
1	Green	6	Cyan
2	Yellow	7	Magenta
3	Blue	8	Orange
4	Red		

COMMENTS

HEX$

APPLE IIe & II+

The following subroutine will return the same value as would be returned by HEX$, stored in the string **R$**. Before calling this subroutine, assign the number you wish to convert to the variable **NUMBER**.

```
1000 DIGIT$="0123456789ABCD
     EF"
1010 R$=""
1015 IF NUMBER<0 THEN
     NUMBER=(65536+NUMBER)
1020 I=NUMBER
1030 Q=INT(I/16)
1040 R=I-Q*16
1050 R$=MID$(DIGIT$,R+1,1)+
     R$
1060 I=Q
1070 IF I>0 GOTO 1030
1080 RETURN
```

IBM PC & PCjr

HEX$(n) where **n** is a numeric expression in the range −32768-65535. This function returns the hexadecimal value of a decimal argument. If **n** is negative, the two's complement form is used. This means that HEX$(−n)=HEX$(65536−n).

COMMODORE 64

The following subroutine will return the same value as would be returned by HEX$, stored in the string **R$**. Before calling this subroutine, assign the number you wish to convert to the variable **NUMBER**.

```
1000 DIGIT$="0123456789ABCD
     EF"
1010 IF NUMBER<0 THEN
     NUMBER=(65536+NUMBER)
1015 R$=""
1020 I=NUMBER
1030 Q=INT(I/16)
1040 R=I-Q*16
1050 R$=MID$(DIGIT$,R+1,1)+
     R$
1060 I=Q
1070 IF I>0 GOTO 1030
1080 RETURN
```

HGR, HGR2

APPLE IIe & II+

HGR[2] causes the computer to display the currently specified page of the high-resolution graphics screen. If no page is specified, page one is assumed. This screen will normally be 280 columns by 160 rows, with a window at the bottom consisting of four rows of text. Following the HGR statement with

```
POKE -16302,0
```

will change the window to graphics, giving a full 280x192 graphics display.

IBM PC & PCjr

SCREEN 2 places the screen in the two-color, high-resolution graphics mode (640x280). Used with the color/graphics adapter only.

SCREEN 6 (Cartridge BASIC Only) places the screen in the four-color, high-resolution graphics mode (640x200). Requires 128K RAM.

SCREEN can take many other arguments. Also see **SCREEN** for more details.

COMMODORE 64

The following program lines set the Commodore 64 into the high-resolution mode, with a 320 column by 200 row, two-color display. The colors are determined by parameters **P** and **B** in line 140. Parameter **P** represents the pixel color, and **B** the background. Parameters **P** and **B** are in the range 0-15. For actual color values, see the list of colors under **COLOR**. In this example, the background is blue and the pixels are black.

```
100 POKE 53272,PEEK(53272)
    OR 8
110 POKE 53265,PEEK(53265)
    OR 32
120 FOR I=8192 TO 16191
130 POKE I,0: NEXT
140 P=0: B=6
150 FOR I=1024 TO 2032
160 POKE I,P*16+B: NEXT
```

Lines 120 and 130 clear the high-resolution screen, which takes about

TRS-80 Models IV & III

HEX$(n) (Model IV) where **n** is a numeric expression in the range −32768-65535. This function returns the hexadecimal value of a decimal argument. If **n** is negative, the two's complement form is used. This means that HEX$(−n)=HEX$(65536−n).

For the Model III, the following subroutine will return the same value as would be returned by HEX$, stored in the string **R$**. Before calling this subroutine, assign the number you wish to convert to the variable **NUMBER**.

```
1000 DIGIT$="0123456789ABCD
     EF"
1010 IF NUMBER< 0 THEN
     NUMBER=(65536+NUMBER)
1015 R$=""
1020 I=NUMBER
1030 Q=INT(I/16)
1040 R=I-Q*16
1050 R$=MID$(DIGIT$,R+1,1)+
     R$
1060 I=Q
1070 IF I> 0 GOTO 1030
1080 RETURN
```

TRS-80 Color Computer

The following subroutine will return the same value as would be returned by HEX$, stored in the string **R$**. Before calling this subroutine, assign the number you wish to convert to the variable **NUMBER**.

```
1000 DIGIT$="0123456789ABCD
     EF"
1010 IF NUMBER< 0 THEN
     NUMBER=(65536+NUMBER)
1015 R$=""
1020 I=NUMBER
1030 Q=INT(I/16)
1040 R=I-Q*16
1050 R$=MID$(DIGIT$,R+1,1)+
     R$
1060 I=Q
1070 IF I> 0 GOTO 1030
1080 RETURN
```

COMMENTS

TRS-80 Models IV & III

Cannot be simulated because TRS-80 Models IV and III do not support high resolution.

45 seconds. If you want, replace them with

```
120 SYS 2024
```

This executes almost immediately. However, prior to calling the line, the following program lines are needed:

```
10 FOR I=2024 TO 2047: READ
   A: POKE I,A: NEXT
20 DATA 169,0,168,132,
   251,162,32,134
30 DATA 252,145,251,200,
   208,251,232,224
40 DATA 64,240,4,134,
   252,208,242,96
```

TRS-80 Color Computer

PMODE n where **n** is 4. Sets the COCO into high-resolution graphics mode with two colors available. PMODE is capable of taking several other arguments not related to high resolution. See **PMODE**.

Other high-resolution screens available on the Commodore 64 are beyond the scope of this book. See *Commodore 64 Graphics & Sound Programming* by Stan Krute.

To return to the low-resolution mode, use the following program lines:

```
200 POKE 53265, PEEK (53265)
    AND 223
210 POKE 53272, 21
```

COMMENTS

HIMEM:

APPLE IIe & II+

HIMEM:m where **m** is to be the upper memory limit for BASIC programs and variable storage. HIMEM: will protect memory above value **m** for reserved use. To find the current value of HIMEM:, use the expression

PEEK(116)*256+PEEK(115)

IBM PC & PCjr

CLEAR [,[n][,m]] where **n** is the total amount of memory for BASIC to use, and **m** is the total stack space to set aside. CLEAR also closes all files and clears all variables. The total amount of memory available to BASIC is found by using the FRE command, and by adding the size of the interpreter workspace—usually 2.5K to 4K. For example, if you have 35K free memory and a 4K interpreter workspace, and you wish to protect 3K memory (35840+4096−3072= 36864), you would use:

CLEAR, 36864

If you have more than 96K memory, there is no need to protect any memory. Everything above 96K is inaccessible to BASIC under normal circumstances. You can use PEEK, POKE and DEF SEG to access this memory, but BASIC will not otherwise know it exists.

COMMODORE 64

Memory locations $C000 to $CFFF are already protected from BASIC on the Commodore 64. If you need more than 4K protected space, you can use the following program lines to protect the top of memory. Because the top of memory is normally at $9FFF, you will be protecting from some address up to $9FFF. The code is

```
10 POKE 51,L: POKE 52,H:
   POKE 55,L: POKE 56,H: CLR
```

where **L** is the decimal value of the right two digits of the address—which is expressed in hexadecimal. **H** is the decimal value of the left two digits. For example, if you wished to protect from $9000 to $9FFF, you would use

```
10 POKE 51,0: POKE 52,144:
   POKE 55,0: POKE 56,144:
   CLR
```

since 90 hexadecimal=144 decimal, and 00 hexadecimal=0 decimal. If the address is in decimal, then **L** and **H** can be calculated by H=INT (address/256) and L=address− H*256.

HLIN

APPLE IIe & II+

HLIN b,e AT r where **b** specifies the beginning column, **e** specifies the ending column, and **r** specifies the row on which to draw the line. Parameters **b** and **e** may have a range of 0-39, while **r** may have a range of 0-47. HLIN is used for drawing horizontal lines on the current low-resolution screen. If HLIN is used in the text mode, it will draw a line of characters. The character used is determined by the current color. If an attempt is made to print in the lower-right corner of the screen, the screen will scroll up.

IBM PC & PCjr

LINE (h1,v1)-(h2,v2) [,[a] [,B[F]] [,style] (Graphics Mode) where **h1** is the beginning horizontal coordinate, **v1** is the beginning vertical coordinate, **h2** is the ending horizontal coordinate, and **v2** is the ending vertical coordinate.

Possible ranges for **h** and **v** are indicated below:

Resolution	h	v
Low (Cart. BASIC only)	0-159	0-199
Medium	0-319	0-199
High	0-639	0-199

The optional value **a** is the color that will be used to draw. See **COLOR** for a list of possible colors.

Specifying **B** will cause a box to be drawn, while BF will draw a filled box. The **style** is used to determine whether to draw a solid line or some sort of

COMMODORE 64

Although there is no HLIN command for the Commodore 64, the following program lines produce a similar effect:

```
100 ROW=1: COL=3: LN=23:
    LI=164
110 POKE 783,0: POKE
    781,ROW: POKE 782,COL
120 SYS 65520
130 FOR I=1 TO LN: PRINT
    CHR$(LI);: NEXT: PRINT
```

This produces a line of length **LN** starting at **ROW, COLumn**. In this case, the line is positioned at the bottom of the cursor. To raise the line, change **LI** from 164 to 114, 102, 96, 99, 100, 101 or 163. If **LI** is 163, the line is at the top of the cursor. Here **ROW** must be in the range 0-24 and **COLumn** in the range 0-39. If an attempt is made to print in the lower-right corner of the screen, the screen will scroll up.

TRS-80 Models IV & III

CLEAR [x][,y] (Model IV) where **x** is the highest memory location you wish to be available to BASIC, and **y** is the number of characters of string storage space to reserve. CLEAR clears all variables, as well as reserving string storage space and protecting high memory.

The Model III does not have a reserved word that protects high memory from within a program. You must do this when BASIC is initiated. The computer will prompt MEMORY SIZE?. You must then enter in the highest memory address—in decimal—you want used.

TRS-80 Color Computer

CLEAR [y][,x] where **y** is the number of characters of string storage space to reserve, and **x** is the highest memory location you want available to BASIC. CLEAR clears all variables, as well as reserving string storage space and protecting high memory. Notice that this syntax is the opposite of the Model IV!

COMMENTS

TRS-80 Models IV & III

May be simulated on Models IV and III with the following subroutine:

```
1000 ROW=ROW-1: PRINT @
     ROW*64+BEGIN,"";
1010 FOR P=BEGIN TO E
1020 PRINT CHR$(176);
1030 NEXT P
1040 RETURN
```

ROW is the row number (1-16) on which to draw the line, **BEGIN** specifies the column for the beginning of the line, and **E** specifies the column for the ending of the line.

TRS-80 Color Computer

LINE (h1,v1)-(h2,v2),a,[b] where **h1** is the beginning horizontal coordinate, **v1** is the beginning vertical coordinate, **h2** is the ending horizontal coordinate, and **v2** is the ending vertical coordinate. **h1** and **h2** may have a range of 0-255, while **v1** and **v2** may have a range of 0-191. Parameter **a** is either PSET or PRESET, one of which is required. PSET sets the line in the foreground color, while PRESET sets the line in the background color. Parameter **b** is either B or BF, both of which are optional. Specifying B will cause a box to be drawn, while BF will draw a filled box.

COMMENTS

dotted line. See the **LINE** statement for further details.

In text mode, you can simulate HLIN with

```
1000 TEMPC=POS(0):
     TEMPR=CSRLIN
1010 IF ROW=25 THEN KEYOFF
1020 LOCATE ROW, BEGIN
1030 PRINT STRING$
     (E-BEGIN+1, PATTERN)
1040 LOCATE TEMPR, TEMPC,1
1050 RETURN
```

ROW is the row on which to draw the line, **BEGIN** is the beginning column, **E** is the ending column, and **PATTERN** is the ASCII value of the character to be used in drawing the line. Some good choices for the value of **PATTERN** are 196, 223, 205 or 178. Any ASCII character may be used except control characters.

HOME

APPLE IIe & II+

HOME clears the current text window and moves the cursor to the upper-left window corner.

IBM PC & PCjr

CLS clears the screen and moves the cursor to the upper-left corner in text mode, or to the center of the screen or active viewport in graphics mode.

COMMODORE 64

Although there is no HOME command on the Commodore 64, the screen can be cleared and the cursor moved to the upper-left corner by using

```
PRINT CHR$(147);
```

HPLOT

APPLE IIe & II+

HPLOT h,v [TO h2,v2]... sets a point on the high-resolution screen, where **h** is the horizontal coordinate, range 0-279, and **v** is the vertical coordinate, range 0-159 (with text window) or 0-191 (without text window). HPLOT h,v is used to set points on the high-resolution screen, while HPLOT h,v TO h2,v2 will draw a line. You can extend the line in any direction by specifying additional TO h3,v3 parameters.

IBM PC & PCjr

Capabilities of the DRAW command exceed those of HPLOT. See **DRAW**.

COMMODORE 64

The following subroutine will set the point **h,v** on the high-resolution screen. For **h** the range is 0-319. For **v** the range is 0-199. Prior to this, the high-resolution screen routine must have been called. See **HGR**. The color of the point set is determined by **P** in that routine.

```
1000 BY=8192+INT(V/8)*320+
     INT(H/8)*8+(V AND 7)
1010 BI=7-(H AND 7)
1020 POKE BY,PEEK(BY) OR
     (2↑BI)
1030 RETURN
```

HTAB

APPLE IIe & II+

HTAB n tabs the cursor horizontally, where **n** is a number between 0 and 255, specifying a horizontal position from the beginning of the current output line. HTAB is similar to TAB, but is used independently from PRINT statements. HTAB can also move the cursor backward to the beginning of the line. TAB cannot.

IBM PC & PCjr

LOCATE [r] [,[c] [,[v] [,[start] [,stop]]]] places the cursor and specifies several options for cursor display. Parameter **r** specifies the row (range 1-25), **c** specifies the column (range 1-40 or 1-80, depending on the current width). If **v**=0, the cursor is invisible. If **v**=1, the cursor is visible. **Start** and **stop** indicate the cursor scan start and stop lines—range 0-31. **Start**, **stop** and **v** do not apply in graphics mode. If **r**=25, then you must use the KEY OFF command prior to the LOCATE command.

COMMODORE 64

Not available on the Commodore 64. The following program lines produce a similar effect:

```
100 ROW=10:COL=4:
    MSG$="HELLO"
110 POKE 783,0:POKE
    781,ROW:POKE 782,COL
120 SYS 65520:PRINT MSG$
```

The above program will print the contents of MSG$ on line **ROW** starting at position **COL**.

TRS-80 Models IV & III

CLS clears the screen and moves the cursor to the upper-left corner.

TRS-80 Color Computer

CLS clears the text screen and moves the cursor to the upper-left corner.

COMMENTS

TRS-80 Models IV & III

Cannot be simulated because TRS-80 Models IV and III do not have high-resolution graphics.

TRS-80 Color Computer

Capabilities of the DRAW command exceed those of HPLOT. See **DRAW**.

COMMENTS

TRS-80 Models IV & III

PRINT @ n (Model IV) or **PRINT @ (r,c)** where **n** is a screen position in the range 0-1919, and **(r,c)** is a pair of coordinates specifying the row— range 0-23—and the column— range 0-79. This command places the cursor at the specified position.

PRINT @ n (Model III) where **n** is a screen position in the range 0-1023. This command places the cursor at the specified position.

TRS-80 Color Computer

PRINT @ n where **n** is a screen position in the range 0-511. This command places the cursor at the specified position.

COMMENTS

IF-THEN-ELSE

APPLE IIe & II+

IF a THEN b

or

IF a [THEN][GOTO] c where a is a logical or arithmetic expression, b is an instruction or line number, and c is a line number. In the second usage, you may use either THEN or GOTO or both, but you must use at least one of them. This instruction set causes the program to perform a conditional branch, based upon whether the test a returns true. If a is true, THEN (or GOTO) is executed. If a returns false, THEN (or GOTO) is ignored. Note that if you have other commands on the same line with the IF-THEN instruction—even if separated by a colon—they will be executed only if a returns true.

If the source program has an ELSE command in it, you can simulate this by adding another IF-THEN that covers the other condition. For example,

```
10 IF A=1 THEN PRINT
   "GOODBYE" ELSE PRINT
   "HELLO"
```

in the source program would become:

```
10 IF A=1 THEN PRINT
   "GOODBYE"
20 IF A<>1 THEN PRINT
   "HELLO"
```

IBM PC & PCjr

IF a [,] THEN b [[,]ELSE d]

or

IF a [,] GOTO c [[,]ELSE d] where a is a logical or arithmetic expression, b is an instruction or line number, c is a line number, and d is an instruction—including, possibly, another IF-THEN-ELSE instruction—or line number. Commas are optional. Use them for increased readability. This instruction set causes the program to perform a conditional branch, based on whether the test a is true. If a is true (not zero), THEN (or GOTO) is executed. If a is false (zero), THEN (or GOTO) is ignored and the optional ELSE is executed. Note that if you have other commands on the same line with the IF-THEN instruction—even if separated by a colon—but before the ELSE, they will be executed only if a is true.

COMMODORE 64

IF a THEN b

or

IF a [THEN] [GOTO] c where a is a logical or arithmetic expression, b is an instruction or line number, and c is a line number. In the second usage, you may use either THEN or GOTO or both, but you must use at least one of them. This instruction set causes the program to perform a conditional branch, based on whether the test a returns true. If a is true, THEN (or GOTO) is executed. If a returns false, THEN (or GOTO) is ignored. Note that if you have other commands on the same line with the IF-THEN instruction—even if separated by a colon—they will be executed only if a returns true.

If the source program has an ELSE command in it, you can simulate this by simply adding another IF-THEN that covers the other condition. For example,

```
10 IF A=1 THEN PRINT
   "GOODBYE" ELSE PRINT
   "HELLO"
```

in the source program would become

```
10 IF A=1 THEN PRINT
   "GOODBYE"
20 IF A<>1 THEN PRINT
   "HELLO"
```

IMP

APPLE IIe & II+

Simulate it by using NOT x OR y. This will work logically, but not bitwise. On the Apple, 1 is True and 0 is False.

x	y	NOT x OR y
T	T	T
T	F	F
F	T	T
F	F	T

IBM PC & PCjr

x IMP y where x and y are numeric expressions. IMP is a logical and bitwise operator that returns the following truth table:

x	y	x IMP y
T	T	T
T	F	F
F	T	T
F	F	T

COMMODORE 64

Simulate it by using NOT x OR y. On the Commodore −1 is True and 0 is False.

x	y	NOT x OR y
T	T	T
T	F	F
F	T	T
F	F	T

TRS-80 Models IV & III

IF a THEN b [ELSE c]

or

IF a [THEN] command [ELSE c]
where **a** is an expression that is either true or false, **b** is executed if **a** is true, and **c** is executed if **a** is false. **Command** may be any BASIC instruction. In the second case, THEN is optional if no ambiguity exists. Parameter **a** may be a logical, arithmetic or Boolean statement. Parameters **b** and **c** may be any instruction or a line number.

TRS-80 Color Computer

IF a THEN b [ELSE c]

or

IF a [THEN] command [ELSE c]
where **a** is an expression that is either true or false, **b** is executed if **a** is true, and **c** is executed if **a** is false. **Command** may be any BASIC instruction. In the second case, THEN is optional if no ambiguity exists. Parameter **a** may be a logical, arithmetic or Boolean statement. Parameters **b** and **c** may be any instruction or a line number.

COMMENTS

TRS-80 Models IV & III

x IMP y (Model IV) where **x** and **y** are numeric expressions. IMP is a logical and bitwise operator that returns the following truth table:

x	y	x IMP y
T	T	T
T	F	F
F	T	T
F	F	T

Simulate it on the Model III by using **NOT x OR y**

x	y	NOT x OR y
T	T	T
T	F	F
F	T	T
F	F	T

TRS-80 Color Computer

Simulate it by using **NOT x OR y**

x	y	NOT x OR y
T	T	T
T	F	F
F	T	T
F	F	T

COMMENTS

IN#

APPLE IIe & II+

IN#**x** where **x** is a numeric expression. IN# redirects input to come from the slot specified by **x**.

IBM PC & PCjr

It is not necessary to redirect input because all input commands specify which buffer the input is to come from.

COMMODORE 64

It is not necessary to redirect input because all input commands specify which buffer the input is to come from.

INKEY$

APPLE IIe & II+

GET **v$** [,**x$**...] is used to retrieve a single character from the current input device—usually the keyboard—for each variable listed, where **v$** and **x$** are string variables. GET varies from the INPUT command in that it does not display a prompt. It accepts input without waiting for the RETURN key to be pressed and continues without displaying the typed character.

IBM PC & PCjr

v$=INKEY$ gets the first value at the keyboard buffer and assigns it the value **v$**. INKEY$ does not pause for input. If no value is at the buffer, it assigns **v$** as a null value. If you want it to pause, then you can either loop until INKEY$ returns a value different from null or use the INPUT$(1) function. If you are trying to detect keys with extended codes, use the INKEY$ function. When a key with extended code is pressed, the INKEY$ function returns a two-character string. The first character is null, and the second is the extended code.

COMMODORE 64

GET **v$[,x...]** (Keyboard Input) reads characters from the keyboard buffer. If no character is pending, it returns a null string. To avoid this you can use a loop, as in line 100 below:

    100 GET V$: IF V$="" THEN 100

If you wish to get multiple characters, use a routine that collects and concatenates them, or use the INPUT instruction.

INP

APPLE IIe & II+

Using ports on the Apple is not accomplished without assembly language routines or extensive PEEKs and POKEs. Therefore, it is beyond the scope of this book. A good reference on the subject is *The Apple Connection* by James W. Coffron.

IBM PC & PCjr

INP(**n**) reads a byte from the port specified by **n**, where **n** is a port address in the range 0-65535. The ports supported by IBM are indicated in the *Technical Reference Manual*. Additional devices that use ports not supported by IBM usually document which port addresses they use.

COMMODORE 64

Using ports is not possible without assembly-language routines or extensive PEEKs and POKEs. Therefore, it is beyond the scope of this book.

TRS-80 Models IV & III	TRS-80 Color Computer	COMMENTS
It is not necessary to redirect input because all input commands specify which buffer the input is to come from.	It is not necessary to redirect input on COCO because all input commands specify which buffer the input is to come from.	

TRS-80 Models IV & III	TRS-80 Color Computer	COMMENTS
v$=INKEY$ gets the first value at the keyboard buffer and assigns it the value **v$**. INKEY$ does not pause for input. If no value is at the buffer, it assigns **v$** as a null value. If you want it to pause, then you can loop until INKEY$ returns a value different from null.	**v$=INKEY$** gets the first value at the keyboard buffer and assigns it the value **v$**. INKEY$ does not pause for input. If no value is at the buffer, it assigns **v$** as a null value. If you want it to pause, then you can either loop until INKEY$ returns a value different from null or use the INPUT instruction. To retrieve multiple characters, use the INPUT instruction.	

TRS-80 Models IV & III	TRS-80 Color Computer	COMMENTS
INP(n) reads a byte from the port specified by **n**, where **n** is a port address in the range 0-255. Ports supported by Tandy are indicated in the *Technical Reference Manual*.	Using a port requires assembly-language routines or extensive PEEKs and POKEs. Therefore, it is beyond the scope of this book.	Also see **OUT** and **WAIT**.

INPUT

APPLE IIe & II+

INPUT ["prompt[] ";] x1[,x2]... pauses program execution to await input from the keyboard, where **prompt** is any string constant that fits on one line, and **x1, x2,...** are string or numeric variable names or array elements to be assigned. The keyboard input must be terminated with a carriage return and must agree in type with the variable name.

If multiple variables are to be assigned, the user may either enter them all on the same line separated by commas, or delimit each with a carriage return. If the **prompt** is omitted, just a question mark is printed as a prompt. If the **prompt** is included, it does not print the question mark. Only one space is permitted at the end of the **prompt**. A null value—just a carriage return—will be accepted if **x1** is to be a string, but not if **x1** is a number.

Quotation marks within the input are allowed only if the first character is also a quotation mark. CTRL-X and CTRL-M are not allowed within a string-input response. If the string begins with a quotation mark, comma and colon are also not allowed.

IBM PC & PCjr

INPUT[;]["prompt ";] x1[,x2]... pauses program execution to await input from the keyboard, where **prompt** is any string constant that will fit on one line, and **x1, x2,...** are string or numeric variable names or array elements to be assigned. The keyboard input must be terminated with a carriage return and must agree in type with the variable name.

If multiple variables are to be assigned, the user must enter them all on the same line, separated by commas. If too many or too few responses are entered, ?REDO FROM START will be displayed, and the INPUT command will be re-executed. If the semicolon after INPUT is included, the user's carriage return is not echoed to the screen. If the **prompt** is omitted, a question mark is printed as a **prompt**. The **prompt** will be followed by a question mark when displayed. If the **prompt** in the command is followed by a comma instead of a semicolon, the question mark is not displayed.

The keyboard input must be terminated with a carriage return and must agree in type with the variable name. If a colon is used as a character, it and the data up to the next carriage return are ignored.

If a string response is to include a comma, it must be completely enclosed in quotation marks.

COMMODORE 64

INPUT ["prompt",] x1[,x2]... causes program execution to await input from the keyboard while printing the optional **prompt** and a question mark. The **prompt** may be any string constant less than 38 characters long. Parameters **x1, x2, ...** are string or numeric variable names or array elements to be assigned.

While the routine is INPUTting, the cursor will continue flashing, and the keyboard input will echo to the screen. The keyboard input must be terminated with a carriage return and must agree in type with the variable name. If multiple variables are to be assigned, the user may enter them all on the same line, separated by commas. If too few responses are entered, the symbol ?? will be displayed while the computer awaits the missing inputs. If too many responses are entered, the message ?EXTRA IGNORED appears and the extra responses are rejected.

Commas and colons are treated as separators by INPUT, so their inadvertent use usually results in too many responses being entered. If the input does not agree in type with the variable name, the message ?REDO FROM START will be displayed, and INPUT awaits the correct type of data.

Leading spaces are ignored, although shifted spaces are not. If a colon is used as a character, it and the data up to the next carriage return are ignored. If a string response is to include a comma, a colon, a leading space or any of the screen-editing characters, then it should be completely enclosed in quotation marks.

If a string response begins with a quotation mark, it cannot contain embedded quotation marks without the ?REDO FROM START message occurring. INPUT accepts the entire line that the cursor is on, including characters after the cursor. The sum of the number of characters in the prompt plus the number of characters in the input string cannot exceed 78 characters. Otherwise, you will get unexpected results. Expressed another way, (number of characters available for **input$**)=78−LEN(**prompt$**).

TRS-80 Models IV & III

INPUT[;] ["prompt";] x1[,x2]...
(Model IV) pauses program execution to await input from the keyboard, where **prompt** is any string constant that will fit on one line, and **x1, x2,...** are string or numeric variable names or array elements to be assigned. The keyboard input must be terminated with a carriage return and must agree in type with the variable name.

If multiple variables are to be assigned, the user must enter them all on the same line, separated by commas. If too many or too few responses are entered, ?REDO FROM START will be displayed, and the INPUT command will be re-executed. If the semicolon after INPUT is included, the user's carriage return is not echoed to the screen. If the prompt is omitted, a question mark is printed as a prompt. The prompt will be followed by a question mark when displayed. If the prompt in the command is followed by a comma instead of a semicolon, the question mark is not displayed. If a string response is to include leading blanks, a comma or a colon, it must be completely enclosed in quotation marks.

INPUT ["prompt";] x1[,x2]...
(Model III) pauses program execution to await input from the keyboard, where **prompt** is any string constant that will fit on one line, and **x1, x2,...** are string or numeric variable names or array elements to be assigned. The keyboard input must be terminated with a carriage return and must agree in type with the variable name.

If multiple variables are to be assigned, the user may enter them all on the same line separated by commas or on separate lines. If too many responses are entered, ?EXTRA IGNORED will be displayed and program execution will continue. If the prompt is omitted, a question mark is printed as a prompt. The prompt will be followed by a question mark when displayed. If a string response is to include leading blanks, a comma or a colon it must be completely enclosed in quotation marks.

TRS-80 Color Computer

INPUT   ["prompt";]   x1[,x2]...
pauses program execution to await input from the keyboard, where **prompt** is any string constant that will fit on one line, and **x1, x2,...** are string or numeric variable names or array elements to be assigned. The keyboard input must be terminated with a carriage return and must agree in type with the variable name.

If multiple variables are to be assigned, the user may enter them all on the same line separated by commas or on separate lines. If too many responses are entered, ?EXTRA IGNORED will be displayed, and program execution will continue. If the prompt is omitted, a question mark is printed as a prompt. The prompt will be followed by a question mark when displayed. If a string response is to include leading blanks, a comma or a colon, it must be completely enclosed in quotation marks.

COMMENTS

Syntax for INPUT varies widely. Be careful to use the right combination of quotation marks and punctuation!

INPUT#

APPLE IIe & II+

INPUT v1[,v2]... will get input from a sequential file if the file was previously specified by using a routine similar to the one below. While the routine is in effect, input comes only from the file, not the keyboard.

```
10 PRINT CHR$(4);"OPEN
   filename"
20 PRINT CHR$(4);"READ
   filename"
```

IBM PC & PCjr

INPUT #n,v1[,v2]... gets a value or a string from sequential filenumber **n** and assigns the value to variable **v1, v2,...** The variables may be string or numeric, but the data must agree with the variable in type. If a string value begins with a quotation mark, it cannot include embedded quotation marks. The value delimiters may be commas, colons, carriage returns or line feeds. Thus, these characters may not be included as part of the data—except that commas and colons may be included inside quoted strings.

The file numbered **n** must have previously been OPENed for input, and may be KYBD:, a COM port, or any other device providing a sequential data stream. If INPUT # is used with a random file, it simply gets the next value after the pointer. GET does not change the position of the pointer in a random file. To use INPUT # with a random file, the file must have delimiters in it. Therefore, INPUT$ may be a better choice.

COMMODORE 64

INPUT# n,v1[,v2...] gets a value or a string from a sequential file number **n** and assigns the value to the variables **v1, v2,...** The variables may be string or numeric, but the data must agree with the variable in terms of type. The value delimiter is usually a carriage return, although a comma can be used to separate multiple entries. If multiple variables are to be assigned, the user may enter them separated by commas or carriage returns. If too few or too many responses are entered, no error message occurs, although in the latter case data will be lost. If a colon is used as a character, it and the data up to the next carriage return are ignored.

Leading spaces are ignored. If a string response is to contain a comma, a colon, or any of the screen-editing characters, then it should be completely enclosed in quotation marks. If a string value begins with a quotation mark, it cannot include embedded quotation marks without the error message ?FILE DATA ERROR appearing. After that, the program halts execution.

The file numbered **n** must have been previously OPENed and may be the keyboard (device 0), the cassette (device 1) or the disk drive (device 8). In the case of the keyboard, no prompt question mark is displayed. If the string exceeds 79 characters, the message ?STRING TOO LONG ERROR appears and execution halts.

TRS-80 Models IV & III

INPUT #n,v1[,v2]... gets a value or a string from a sequential file number **n** and assigns the value to the variables **v1, v2,...** The variables may be string or numeric, but the data must agree with the variable in terms of type.

If a string value begins with a quotation mark, it cannot include embedded quotation marks. The value delimiters may be commas, colons, carriage returns or line feeds. Thus these characters may not be included as part of the data—except that commas and colons may be included inside quoted strings. The file numbered **n** must have previously been OPENed for INPUT.

TRS-80 Color Computer

INPUT #n,v1[,v2]... gets a value or a string from a sequential file number **n** and assigns the value to the variables **v1, v2,...** The variables may be string or numeric, but the data must agree with the variable in terms of type.

If a string value begins with a quotation mark, it cannot include embedded quotation marks. The value delimiters may be commas, colons, carriage returns or line feeds. Thus, these characters may not be included as part of the data—except that commas and colons may be included inside quoted strings. The file numbered **n** must have previously been OPENed for INPUT. If **n** is −1, the variable will be input from the cassette.

COMMENTS

INPUT$

APPLE IIe & II+

To simulate INPUT$ on the Apple, redirect input from the keyboard to the file—unless you want the input to come from the keyboard. Then use GET with a loop to concatenate the number of characters you wish to GET. For example,

```
 10 PRINT CHR$(4);"OPEN
    filename"
 20 PRINT CHR$(4);"READ
    filename"
 30 CC=5: REM THE CHARACTER
    COUNT YOU WISH TO READ
    FROM THE FILE
 40 GOSUB 1000
 50 PRINT "": PRINT IS$
 60 PRINT CHR$(4);"CLOSE
    filename"
 70 END
1000 REM SUBROUTINE TO READ CC
    CHARACTERS INTO
    VARIABLE IS$
1010 IS$=""
1020 FOR I=1 TO CC
1030 GET I$: IS$=IS$+I$
1040 NEXT I
1050 RETURN
```

IBM PC & PCjr

INPUT$(n[,[#] f]) where **n** is the number of characters to read in from file number **f**. File **f** must have been previously OPENed for input or as a random file. If **f** is omitted, the characters will be read from the keyboard, but no prompt will be displayed. INPUT$ allows the inclusion of control characters (except CTRL-BREAK) in the input string, and is therefore preferred for use with COM files.

COMMODORE 64

Can be simulated with the following program lines. Line 40 may generate an unusual screen display if graphics characters are read in.

```
 10 OPEN
    8,8,8,"filename,S,R"
 20 CC=5: REM THE CHARACTER
    COUNT
 30 GOSUB 1000
 40 PRINT IS$
 50 CLOSE 8
 60 REM: PROGRAM CONTINUES
    HERE
1000 IS$=""
1010 FOR I=1 TO CC
1020 GET#8,I$: IS$=IS$+I$
1030 NEXT: RETURN
```

INSTR

APPLE IIe & II+

Can be simulated on the APPLE with the following routine. Here, **big$** is the string to be searched, and **find$** is the string to be found, and **n** specifies the position in **big$** at which to begin searching for **find$**. GOSUB 1000 will return the position of the first occurrence of **find$** within **big$**—returned in variable **R**. If **find$** is not found in **big$**, **R** will be returned equal to 0.

```
1000 BIG=LEN(big$):FIND=LEN
    (find$): N=4
1010 R=0: FOR J=N TO BIG
1020 IF MID$(big$,J,FIND)=
    find$ THEN R=J: J=BIG
1030 NEXT: RETURN
```

IBM PC & PCjr

INSTR([n,] s1$, s2$) where **n** is an integer between 1 and 255 that specifies the position of **s1$** at which to begin searching for **s2$**. Optional parameter **n** is assumed to be 1 if omitted. Parameter **s1$** specifies the string to be searched and **s2$** specifies the string to be found. INSTR will return a value specifying the position of the first occurrence of **s2$** within **s1$**. If **s2$** cannot be found, if **n**>LEN(**s1$**), or if **s1$** is a null, the function returns a 0. If **s2$** is a null, the function returns a 1.

COMMODORE 64

Simulate it with the following routine. Here, **big$** is the string to be searched, **find$** is the string to be found, and **n** specifies the position in **big$** at which to begin searching for **find$**. GOSUB 1000 will return the position of the first occurrence of **find$** within **big$**—returned in variable **R**. If **find$** is not found in **big$**, **R** will be returned equal to 0.

```
1000 BIG=LEN(big$):FIND=LEN
    (find$):N=4
1010 R=0: FOR J=N TO BIG
1020 IF MID$(big$,J,FIND)=
    find$ THEN R=J: J=BIG
1030 NEXT: RETURN
```

TRS-80 Models IV & III

INPUT$(n[,[#] f]) (Model IV) where n is the number of characters to read in from file number f. File f must be a sequential file previously OPENed for input. If f is omitted, the characters will be read from the keyboard, but no prompt will be displayed.

TRS-80 Color Computer

Simulate it with the following subroutine. In this routine, you should replace n with the number of the file to be OPENed, −1 for cassette, range 1-15 for disk.

```
  10 OPEN "I",n,"filename"
  20 GOSUB 1000
  30 REM PROGRAM EXECUTION
     CONTINUES HERE
 100 CLOSE
 110 END
1000 REM SUBROUTINE TO
     SIMULATE
     A$=INPUT$(CC,n) WHERE
     CC IS THE NUMBER OF
     CHARACTERS TO READ
1010 L=LEN(B$):C$=""
1015 IF L<CC AND EOF(n) THEN
     1080
1020 IF L<CC THEN LINE
     INPUT#n,C$ ELSE 1050
1030 B$=B$+C$+CHR$(13):
     L=LEN(B$):REM IF L>255
     YOU WILL GET OVERFLOW
     ERROR
1040 IF L<CC GOTO 1015
1050 A$=LEFT$(B$,CC)
1060 B$=RIGHT$(B$,L-CC)
1070 RETURN
1080 PRINT "NOT ENOUGH DATA IN
     filename"
1090 RETURN
```

COMMENTS

TRS-80 Models IV & III

INSTR([n,] s1$, s2$) where n is an integer between 1 and 255 that specifies the position of s1$ at which to begin searching for s2$. Optional parameter n is assumed to be 1 if omitted. Parameter s1$ specifies the string to be searched and s2$ specifies the string to be found. INSTR will return a value specifying the position of the first occurrence of s2$ within s1$. If s2$ cannot be found, if n>LEN(s1$), or if s1$ is a null, the function returns a 0. If s2$ is a null, the function returns a 1.

TRS-80 Color Computer

INSTR([n,] s1$, s2$) where n is an integer between 1 and 255 that specifies the position of s1$ at which to begin searching for s2$. Optional parameter n is assumed to be 1 if omitted. Parameter s1$ specifies the string to be searched and s2$ specifies the string to be found. INSTR will return a value specifying the position of the first occurrence of s2$ within s1$. If s2$ cannot be found, if n>LEN(s1$), or if s1$ is a null, the function returns a 0. If s2$ is a null, the function returns a 1.

COMMENTS

INT

APPLE IIe & II+

INT(n) where n is a number to be converted into an integer. INT will truncate the fractional part of n and return the next lower integer.

IBM PC & PCjr

INT(n) where n is a number to be converted into an integer. INT will truncate the fractional part of n and return the next lower integer.

COMMODORE 64

INT(n) where n is a number to be converted into an integer. INT will usually truncate the fractional part of n and return the next lower integer. However, INT(.9999999996)=1, while INT(.9999999995)=0.

INTER$

is an undocumented reserved word on IBM.

INVERSE

APPLE IIe & II+

INVERSE causes anything printed to the screen to be reversed in color from normal. INVERSE is cancelled by the NORMAL command.

IBM PC & PCjr

COLOR x,y simulates an inverse image if x and y are valid foreground and background colors other than those previously in use. Preferably, they would be the opposite of those previously in use. For valid colors, see COLOR.

COMMODORE 64

Using the keys RVS ON (CTRL 9) and RVS OFF (CTRL 0) or the codes CHR$(18) and CHR$(146) will toggle output between reverse (inverse) and normal. When you include your PRINT statement, simply insert RVS ON after you type your opening quotation marks and insert RVS OFF before you type your closing quotation marks. The message between the quotation marks will then print in reverse. A carriage return automatically turns off reverse printing, so RVS OFF is sometimes omitted at the end of a message.

IOCTL, IOCTL$

are undocumented reserved words on IBM.

TRS-80 Models IV & III

INT(n) where n is a number to be converted into an integer. INT will truncate the fractional part of n and return the next lower integer.

TRS-80 Color Computer

INT(n) where n is a number to be converted into an integer. INT will truncate the fractional part of n and return the next lower integer.

COMMENTS

TRS-80 Models IV & III

Enabled on the Model IV by PRINTing CHR$(16), and disabled by PRINTing CHR$(17).

Not available on the Model III.

TRS-80 Color Computer

SHIFT-0 will toggle output between normal and inverse on the COCO. When you include your PRINT statement, just toggle to inverse after you type your opening quotation marks and back to normal before typing your closing quotation marks. The message between the quotation marks will print inverse.

COMMENTS

JOYSTK

APPLE IIe & II+

PDL(n) where **n** is an integer in the range 0-225. If values other than 0, 1, 2 or 3 are used, the PDL function will give erratic and unpredictable results! Values of 0-3 return a "resistance variable" for the respective paddle between 0 and 150K ohms. This value must then be interpreted to produce the desired results. Note that this will require extensive programming changes when converting to or from other computers.

Although it can handle four paddles, the Apple can read the status only of three paddle buttons. This is accomplished with PEEK(−16287) for the value of the button on paddle 0, PEEK(−16286) for paddle 1, and PEEK(−16285) for paddle 2. If the value returned is greater than 127, then the button is being pressed.

IBM PC & PCjr

STICK(n) where **n** is an integer in the range 0-3. STICK returns the coordinates of the joysticks. STICK(0) obtains the values of both joysticks, but returns the x coordinate of joystick A.

STICK(1), STICK(2) and STICK(3) do not sample the joystick, but return the coordinates retrieved by the most recent STICK(0). STICK(1) returns the y coordinate of joystick A. STICK(2) returns the x coordinate of joystick B. STICK(3) returns the y coordinate of joystick B.

STRIG ON
v=STRIG(n)
STRIG OFF where **n** is an integer from 0-3 in BASIC, or 0-7 in Advanced BASIC, Cartridge BASIC or Compiler BASIC. STRIG ON causes the program to begin checking the status of the joystick buttons at the beginning of execution of each program line. STRIG OFF ceases checking. Interpret the value returned by STRIG(n) with the table below:

n Value	Button Number	Value If Button Has Been Pressed	Value If Button Is Being Pressed	Default
0	A1	−1		0
1	A1		−1	0
2	B1	−1		0
3	B1		−1	0

The following apply to Advanced, Cartridge and Compiler BASIC only.

4	A2	−1		0
5	A2		−1	0
6	B2	−1		0
7	B2		−1	0

STRIG(n) ON
ON STRIG(n) GOSUB line
STRIG(n) STOP
STRIG(n) OFF
These commands control event trapping for the specified joystick button **n**. The value of **n** is indicated by the chart below. The parameter **line** specifies a line to GOSUB if the specified button has been pressed.

n	Button
0	A1
2	B1
4	A2
6	B2

When STRIG(n) ON has been specified and the ON STRIG(n) GOSUB line command is in effect, BASIC

COMMODORE 64

The Commodore 64 supports two game ports, 1 and 2. The joystick in port 1 is read by PEEKing 56321. Port 2 is read by PEEKing 56320. The number returned by the PEEK is logically ANDed with 15 to indicate the direction according to the chart below:

NW=10	North=14	NE=6
West=11	Home=15	East=7
SW=9	South=13	SE=5

To read the "fire" button, the number returned is logically ANDed with 16. If the value resulting is 16, the button is not pressed. If the value is 0, the button is pressed.

The following program lines demonstrate how to read Port 2:

```
10 FOR I=0 TO 10: READ
   D$(I): NEXT
20 DATA SE,NE,E,,SW,NW,
   W,,S,N,H,
30 F$(0)="FIRE":
   F$(1)="SAFE"
40 PRINT CHR$(147);
50 PRINT CHR$(19)D$((PEEK
   (56320)AND 15)-5)
60 PRINT F$((PEEK(56320)
   AND 16)/16)
70 GOTO 50
```

checks at the beginning of execution of each line to see if the button has been pressed. If it has, the GOSUB is executed. If not, program execution continues uninterrupted. STRIG(n) STOP causes trapping to cease, but the computer remembers whether the button was pressed. If so, when a STRIG(n) ON is executed, the GOSUB is executed immediately. STRIG(n) OFF causes trapping to cease, and even if the button is pressed it will not be remembered.

TRS-80 Models IV & III

Joysticks and paddles are not currently supported on Models IV or III, although some independent manufacturers have devised joysticks that work through the cassette port.

TRS-80 Color Computer

JOYSTK(n) where **n** is an integer from 0-3. This function returns a coordinate of the joystick. If **n**=0, it returns the horizontal coordinate of the right joystick. If **n**=1, it returns the vertical coordinate of the right joystick. If **n**=2, it returns the horizontal coordinate of the left joystick. If **n**=3, it returns the vertical coordinate of the left joystick.

Joystick buttons are accessed by PEEKing memory location 65280. PEEK(65280) will return 127 or 255 if no button is pressed. It will return 126 or 254 if the right button is pressed, or 125 or 253 if the left button is pressed.

COMMENTS

KEY

APPLE IIe & II+

Cannot be simulated.

IBM PC & PCjr

KEY ON causes the current assignments of the function keys to be displayed in abbreviated form on the screen line 25.

KEY OFF removes the function-key display from the screen line 25 and frees it for use by the programmer. This is useful because line 25 does not scroll with the rest of the screen.

KEY LIST displays the current function-key assignments—all 15 characters.

KEY n,x$** assigns the value of x$ to function key number **n. Note: LEN(**x$**) cannot be more than 15 characters.

KEY n, CHR$(x) + CHR$(y) (BASIC 2.0 or Cartridge BASIC Only) defines a key to be trapped, where **n** is a numeric expression (range 15-20), **x** is a numeric value corresponding to the hex value for the "latched" keys (see below), and **y** is a scan code for the key to be trapped (range 1-83). Key-scan codes may be determined by referring to the *BASIC Reference Manual,* Appendix K.

Hex values for the "latched" keys are:

Caps Lock &H40
Num Lock &H20 (Not on PCjr)
Alt &H08
Ctrl &H04
Shift &H01, &H02, &H03

You can add these values together to achieve a combined value. For example, &H0C would require that the Alt and Ctrl keys both be depressed.

ON KEY(n) GOSUB line causes execution of the subroutine at the specified line if a KEY(n) ON has been executed, and function key **n** has been depressed. In BASIC 2.0 and Cartridge BASIC, the extended keys specified by KEY(n) may also be trapped.

COMMODORE 64

Cannot be simulated without extensive machine-language programming.

KEY(n) ON enables the trapping of the specified function key—or extended keys in BASIC 2.0 or Cartridge BASIC. Causes BASIC to check at the beginning of the execution of each line to see if the specified key has been depressed. If it has, the routine specified by ON KEY(n) GOSUB will be executed.

KEY(n) STOP causes BASIC to stop checking for **n** at the beginning of execution of each line. But if **n** has been depressed, it is remembered. When the program encounters a KEY(n) ON, it checks to see if the key has been depressed, and acts accordingly.

KEY(n) OFF causes checking for the specified key **n** to stop. Even if the key is depressed, it will not be remembered and no action will be taken.

KEY$

is an undocumented reserved word on the IBM PC.

TRS-80 Models IV & III

Cannot be simulated.

TRS-80 Color Computer

Cannot be simulated.

COMMENTS

KILL

APPLE IIe & II+

Simulate it with the following program lines

```
10 PRINT CHR$(4);"OPEN
   filename"
20 PRINT CHR$(4);"DELETE
   filename"
```

IBM PC & PCjr

KILL"**filename**" erases **filename** from the disk. The file must have been previously CLOSEd. Filename can include a disk drive specification and must include the extension. For example,

```
KILL"b:file.bas"
```

Use of this command in Cartridge BASIC will result in an ILLEGAL FUNCTION CALL if DOS 2.1 is not present.

COMMODORE 64

Called **SCRATCH** and abbreviated **S** by Commodore, it is simulated with the following program lines:

```
10 OPEN 15,8,15,
   "S0:filename"
20 CLOSE 15
```

LEFT$

APPLE IIe & II+

LEFT$(x$,n) returns a string expression consisting of the left **n** characters of **x$**, where **n** is a numeric expression and **x$** is any string. The range for **n** is 1-255. If **n**>LEN(**x$**), **x$** is returned. If **n**=0, the null string is returned.

IBM PC & PCjr

LEFT$(x$,n) returns a string expression consisting of the left **n** characters of **x$**, where **n** is a numeric expression and **x$** is any string. The range for **n** is 0-255. If **n**>LEN(**x$**), **x$** is returned. If **n**=0, the null string is returned.

COMMODORE 64

LEFT$(x$,n) returns a string expression consisting of the left **n** characters of **x$**, where **n** is a numeric expression and **x$** is any string. The range for **n** is 0-255. If **n**>LEN(**x$**), then **x$** is returned. If **n**=0, the null string is returned.

LEN

APPLE IIe & II+

LEN(x$) returns a value equal to the number of characters—including any blanks or unprintable characters—in **x$**, where **x$** is any string expression.

IBM PC & PCjr

Same.

COMMODORE 64

Same.

LET

APPLE IIe & II+

[LET]n=x assigns the value of **x** to variable **n**. The only restriction is that **x** and **n** must be of the same data type. **LET** is optional. The equals sign alone is sufficient to make this assignment.

IBM PC & PCjr

Same.

COMMODORE 64

Same.

TRS-80 Models IV & III

KILL "**filename**" erases the file **filename** from the disk. The file must have been previously CLOSEd. **Filename** can include a disk drive specification and must include the extension. For example,

```
KILL "file/bas:2"
```

If no disk drive is specified, the file is deleted from the first drive that has it.

TRS-80 Color Computer

KILL "**filename:d** " erases the file **filename** on disk drive number **d**. If **d** is omitted, drive 0 is assumed.

COMMENTS

Files can be KILLed on cassette-based systems simply by recording over them.

TRS-80 Models IV & III

LEFT$(x$,n) returns a string expression consisting of the left **n** characters of **x$**, where **n** is a numeric expression and **x$** is any string. The range for **n** is 0-255. If **n**>LEN(**x$**), then **x$** is returned. If **n**=0, the null string is returned.

TRS-80 Color Computer

LEFT$(x$,n) returns a string expression consisting of the left **n** characters of **x$**, where **n** is a numeric expression and **x$** is any string. The range for **n** is 0-255. If **n**>LEN(**x$**), then **x$** is returned. If **n**=0, the null string is returned.

COMMENTS

The only variation on this function is that the range of **n** is 1-255 for Apple, 0-255 for all others.

TRS-80 Models IV & III

Same.

TRS-80 Color Computer

Same.

COMMENTS

TRS-80 Models IV & III

Same.

TRS-80 Color Computer

Same. Note: Non-extended color BASIC does not recognize LET.

COMMENTS

LINE

APPLE IIe & II+

HPLOT x1,y1 [TO x2,y2]... will draw a line between two points. Parameters **x1** and **x2** are column numbers in the range 0-279, and **y1** and **y2** are row numbers in the range 0-191 if you have full screen graphics, or 0-159 if you have a text window. To use it, you must have first used HGR and HCOLOR=.

To draw a box, use the following routine:

```
10 HPLOT x1,y1 TO x1,y2 TO
   x2,y2 TO x2,y1 TO x1,y1
```

To draw a filled box, use this routine:

```
1000 FOR y=y1 TO y2
1100 FOR x=x1 TO x2
1200 HPLOT x,y
1300 NEXT X
1400 NEXT Y
```

IBM PC & PCjr

LINE [(h1,v1)] - (h2,v2) [,[a] [,B [F]][,style] (Graphics Mode) where **h1** is the beginning horizontal coordinate, **v1** is the beginning vertical coordinate, **h2** is the ending horizontal coordinate, and **v2** is the ending vertical coordinate.

Possible ranges for **h** and **v** are indicated below:

Resolution	h	v
Low (Cart. BASIC only)	0-159	0-199
Medium	0-319	0-199
High	0-639	0-199

The optional value **a** is the color that will be used to draw. See **COLOR** for a list of possible colors.

Specifying **B** will cause a box to be drawn—with its opposite corners at **h1,v1** and **h2,v2**. Specifying BF will draw a filled box.

The **style** is used to determine whether to draw a solid line or some sort of a dotted line. The placement of the dots is determined by the bit pattern of the number used. For example, if &HCCCC is used, it will display a dashed line with the pattern 1100110011001100, where 1 represents a dot and 0 represents a space (&HCCCC = 11001100110 01100 binary).

Simulate it in text mode in its horizontal line-drawing capabilities by:

```
1000 TEMPC=POS(0):
     TEMPR=CSRLIN
1010 IF ROW=25 THEN KEY OFF
1020 LOCATE ROW, BEGIN
1030 PRINT STRING$(E-BEGIN
     +1, PATTERN)
1040 LOCATE TEMPR, TEMPC,1
1050 RETURN
```

where **ROW** is the row on which to draw the line, **BEGIN** is the beginning column, **E** is the ending column, and **PATTERN** is the ASCII value of the character to be used in drawing the line. Some good choices for the value of **PATTERN** are 196, 223, 205 or 178. Any ASCII character may be used except control characters.

Similarly, boxes may be constructed using LOCATE and the graphics characters represented by ASCII 169-223.

COMMODORE 64

Can be simulated by the following routine. You must define these variables before entering the routine:

x1 The x coordinate of the start point in the range 0-319.

y1 The y coordinate of the start point in the range 0-199.

x2 The x coordinate of the end point in the range 0-319.

y2 The y coordinate of the end point in the range 0-199.

You must also insert a high-resolution screen routine, such as the one listed under **HGR**. The subroutine at line 1000 is the set-point subroutine, such as the one listed under **HPLOT**.

```
100 REM HIGH RES SCREEN GOES
    HERE
300 IF x1=x2 THEN 380
310 M=(y1-y2)/(x1-x2): IF
    ABS(M)>1 THEN 350
320 FOR I=0 TO (x2-x1) STEP
    SGN(x2-x1)
330 H=x1+I: V=INT(y1+I*
    M+.5): GOSUB 1000
340 NEXT: GOTO 500
350 FOR I=0 TO (y2-y1) STEP
    SGN(y2-y1)
360 V=y1+I:
    H=INT(x1+I/M+.5)
    :GOSUB 1000
370 NEXT: GOTO 500
380 FOR I=0 TO (y2-y1) STEP
    SGN(y2-y1)
390 H=x1: V=(y1+I): GOSUB
    1000
400 NEXT: GOTO 500
500 REM PROGRAM CONTINUES
    HERE
1000 REM PLOTTING SUBROUTINE
     GOES HERE
```

To draw a box you can put this routine into a loop that repeats four times—with new x and y coordinates each time. You can draw a filled box by using it as a line, but increment either the x coordinates or the y coordinates enough times to produce the desired effect.

TRS-80 Models IV & III

Simulate it in its horizontal line-drawing capabilities on the Model III and Model IV with the following subroutine, where **x1,y1** is the starting point, and **x2,y2** is the ending point. You must declare the x and y coordinates before entering this routine. The range for the x coordinates is 0-47. The range for the y coordinates is 0-127. To draw a box, you can repeat this routine four times—with new x and y coordinates each time.

```
300 IF x1=x2 THEN 380
310 M=(y1-y2)/(x1-x2):IF
    ABS(M)>1 THEN 350
320 FOR I=0 TO (x2-x1) STEP
    SGN(x2-x1)
330 H=x1+I:V=INT(y1+I*
    M+.5):GOSUB 1000
340 NEXT:GOTO 500
350 FOR I=0 TO (y2-y1) STEP
    SGN(y2-y1)
360 V=y1+I:H=INT(x1+I/
    M+.5):GOSUB 1000
370 NEXT:GOTO 500
380 FOR I=0 TO (y2-y1) STEP
    SGN(y2-y1)
390 H=x1:V=(y1+I):GOSUB
    1000
400 NEXT:GOTO 500
500 REM PROGRAM CONTINUES
    HERE
1000 SET(H,V):RETURN
```

A filled box can be drawn with the following routine:

```
 10 X1=0:X2=47:REM RANGE
    X=0 TO 47
 20 Y1=0:Y2=127:REM RANGE
    Y=0 TO 127
 30 GOSUB 1000
 40 END
1000 FOR Y=Y1 TO Y2
1100 FOR X=X1 TO X2
1200 SET(X,Y)
1300 NEXT X
1400 NEXT Y
1500 RETURN
```

TRS-80 Color Computer

LINE [(h1,v1)]-(h2,v2),a,[b] draws a line, where **h1** is the beginning horizontal coordinate, **v1** is the beginning vertical coordinate, **h2** is the ending horizontal coordinate, and **v2** is the ending vertical coordinate. If **(h1,v1)** is omitted, the end point from the previous LINE statement is used. Parameters **h1** and **h2** may have a range of 0-255, while **v1** and **v2** may have a range of 0-191.

Parameter **a** is either PSET or PRESET, one of which is required. PSET sets the line in the foreground color, while PRESET sets the line in the background color. Parameter **b** is either B or BF, both of which are optional. Specifying B will cause a box to be drawn. Specifying BF will draw a filled box.

COMMENTS

LINE INPUT

APPLE IIe & II +

Simulate it with the following routine. IS$ will be the value that would have been returned by LINE INPUT.

```
1000 REM SUBROUTINE TO
     SIMULATE LINE INPUT
1010 IS$=""
1020 GET I$: PRINT I$;
1030 IF I$=CHR$(13) THEN
     RETURN
1035 IF I$=CHR$(20) THEN
     IS$=LEFT$(IS$,LEN(IS$)
     -1): GOTO 1020
1040 IS$=IS$+I$
1050 IF LEN(IS$)=255 THEN
     RETURN
1060 GOTO 1020
```

IBM PC & PCjr

LINE INPUT[;]["prompt ";]x$** allows input of up to 254 characters—including commas and other delimiters—where **x$ is any string variable. **Prompt** is a message that will appear on the screen. Using a semicolon after LINE INPUT will allow you to input on the same line as the prompt. A question mark is not displayed unless it is part of the prompt. Trailing blanks are ignored in the input.

COMMODORE 64

Can be simulated with the following routine. IS$ will be the value which would have been returned by LINE INPUT. It will accept any key except a carriage return.

```
1000 REM SUBROUTINE TO
     SIMULATE LINE INPUT
1010 IS$=""
1020 GET I$: PRINT I$;
1030 IF I$=CHR$(13) THEN
     RETURN
1035 IF I$=CHR$(20) THEN
     IS$=LEFT$(IS$,LEN(IS$)
     -1): GOTO 1020
1040 IS$=IS$+I$
1050 IF LEN(IS$)=255 THEN
     RETURN
1060 GOTO 1020
```

LINE INPUT

APPLE IIe & II +

Simulate it with the following routine. **IS$** will be the value that would have been returned by LINE INPUT #. Note that the file must have been previously OPENed for input, and input must have been activated with

```
PRINT CHR$(4); "READ
filename"
```

```
1000 REM SUBROUTINE TO
     SIMULATE LINE INPUT #
1010 IS$=""
1020 GET I$: PRINT I$;
1030 IF I$=CHR$(13) THEN
     RETURN
1040 IS$=IS$ + I$
1050 IF LEN (IS$)=255 THEN
     RETURN
1060 GOTO 1020
```

IBM PC & PCjr

LINE INPUT #n,x$** allows input of up to 254 characters from a sequential data file—including commas and other delimiters—where **x$ is any string variable and **n** is the number of a sequential data file previously OPENed for input. You can also use LINE INPUT # to read from random files if they have embedded carriage returns.

COMMODORE 64

Simulate it with the following routine. IS$ will be the first string returned from the filename after this routine.

```
10 OPEN
   8,8,8,"filename,S,R"
20 GOSUB 1000
30 PRINT IS$:
   REM-MANIPULATE IS$ HERE
40 CLOSE 8
50 END
1000 REM SUBROUTINE TO
     SIMULATE LINE INPUT#
1010 IS$=""
1020 GET#8,I$: PRINT I$;
1030 IF I$=CHR$(13) THEN
     RETURN
1040 IS$=IS$ + I$
1050 IF LEN(IS$)=255 THEN
     RETURN
1060 GOTO 1020
```

LIST

APPLE IIe & II +

LIST [x][-[y]] lists the program to the screen, where **x** is the beginning—or only—line number and **y** is the ending line number. If **y** is omitted, but the dash included, the program is listed from **x** to the end. If you wish for the program or portion of the program to be listed to a disk file, you must have first opened the file and specified that output be written to it.

IBM PC & PCjr

LIST [x][-[y]][,file] lists the program to the screen or file, where **x** is the first (or only) line number to be listed, **y** is the final line number to be listed, and **file** is the filename to be listed to, in ASCII form. If **y** is omitted, but the dash included, the program is listed from **x** to the end. If the file name is omitted, the program is listed to the screen.

COMMODORE 64

LIST [x][-[y]] lists the program to the screen, where **x** is the beginning—or only—line number and **y** is the ending line number. If **y** is omitted, but the dash included, the program is listed from **x** to the end. LISTing a program during execution will cause the execution to halt.

TRS-80 Models IV & III

LINE INPUT[;][prompt;]x$** allows input of up to 254 characters (240 for the Model III)—including commas and other delimiters—where **x$ is any string variable. **Prompt** is a message that will appear on the screen. Using a semicolon after LINE INPUT on the Model IV will allow you to input on the same line as the prompt, but a semicolon without a prompt is not allowed on the Model III. A question mark is not displayed unless it is part of the prompt. Trailing blanks are ignored in the input.

TRS-80 Color Computer

LINE INPUT["prompt";]x$** allows input of up to 249 characters—including commas and other delimiters—where **x$ is any string variable and **prompt** is a message that will appear on the screen. A semicolon is not allowed without a prompt. A question mark is not displayed unless it is part of the prompt. Trailing blanks are ignored in the input.

COMMENTS

TRS-80 Models IV & III

LINE INPUT #n,x$** allows input of up to 255 characters from a sequential data file—including commas and other delimiters—where **x$ is any string variable and **n** is the number of a sequential data file previously OPENed for input. You can also use LINE INPUT # to read from random files if they have embedded carriage returns.

TRS-80 Color Computer

LINE INPUT #n,x$** allows input of up to 249 characters from a sequential data file—including commas and other delimiters—where **x$ is any string variable and **n** is the number of a sequential data file previously OPENed for INPUT.

COMMENTS

TRS-80 Models IV & III

Causes Models IV and III to return to command mode when used in a program.

TRS-80 Color Computer

Causes COCO to return to command mode when used in a program.

COMMENTS

LLIST

APPLE IIe & II+

To list a program on the printer with Apple, use the following routine, where **x** is the slot number of your printer—normally #1. You can also specify the starting and ending line numbers after the LIST.

```
100 PR#x: LIST: PR#0
```

IBM PC & PCjr

LLIST [x][-[y]] where **x** is the beginning line number and **y** is the ending line number. LLIST will cause the program—or specified lines—to print on the printer, and then return BASIC to the command level. You must then RUN or CONTinue the program.

If you wish to get around this limitation, use the following subroutine. The program will LLIST, then continue. It does so because lines 1010 and 1020 POKE the word RETURN into the keyboard buffer. Afterward the program returns to the command level, the word RETURN is obtained from the keyboard, and the program continues. Thus line 1040 is superfluous. It is included only for clarity.

```
1000 DEF SEG=0
1010 POKE 1050,30: POKE
     1052,44: POKE 1054,82:
     POKE 1056,69: POKE
     1058,84
1020 POKE 1060,85: POKE
     1062,82: POKE 1064,78:
     POKE 1066,13
1030 LLIST
1040 RETURN
```

COMMODORE 64

The following routine will list a program on the printer, where **X** is the device number of your printer—usually 4. You can also specify the starting and ending line numbers after the LIST command. This routine will return you to the command mode.

```
10 PRINT CHR$(147)
   "PRINT#3: CLOSE 3"
20 POKE 198,3: POKE 631,19:
   POKE 632,13: POKE
   633,13: X=4
30 OPEN 3,X: CMD 3: LIST
```

LOAD

APPLE IIe & II+

LOAD filename loads the specified file, where **filename** is the name of the file with any appropriate device designation, such as d1. If no **filename** is specified, the next file on the cassette is assumed. All variables are CLEARed and data files CLOSEd. After LOADing, BASIC returns to the command mode.

IBM PC & PCjr

LOAD "filename"[,R] loads the specified file and optionally runs it, where **filename** is the name of the file with any appropriate device designation, such as CAS1: or A:. Without DOS, device CAS1: is assumed. If the extension is left off the filename, an extension of .BAS is assumed. All variables are CLEARed and data files closed, unless the **R** option is chosen. In this case all data files are left open. If the **R** option is chosen, the program is immediately run. Otherwise BASIC returns to the command mode.

COMMODORE 64

LOAD ["filename"] [,device] [,location] loads a file into memory, where **filename** is the name of the file you wish to load. Default is the next file on cassette. **Device** is the storage device—cassette=1, disk=8, default=1. **Location** is the type of load you wish to achieve. 0 is the default and loads in at the start of BASIC, 1 loads in from where it was saved. **Filename** is not optional for a disk load.

Although LOAD closes all files, when used as a statement within a program it does not clear variables. Nor does it reset the BASIC memory pointers. After the load is complete, it automatically RUNs the BASIC program in memory. LOAD "filename" on the Commodore is equivalent to RUN "filename" on other

TRS-80 Models IV & III

LLIST **[x][-[y]]** where **x** is the beginning line number and **y** is the ending line number. LLIST will cause the program—or specified lines—to be printed on the printer, and then return BASIC to command level. LLIST is identical to LIST but lists the program to the printer. See **LIST**.

TRS-80 Color Computer

LLIST **[x][-[y]]** where **x** is the beginning line number and **y** is the ending line number. LLIST will cause the program—or specified lines—to be printed on the printer, and then return BASIC to the command level. LLIST is identical to LIST but lists the program to the printer.

COMMENTS

TRS-80 Models IV & III

LOAD **"filename"[,R]** loads the specified file and optionally runs it, where **filename** is the name of the file with any appropriate device designation, such as :0 or :1. If no device is specified, BASIC searches all drives, starting with 0. In cassette BASIC the cassette is assumed. All variables are CLEARed and data files closed, unless the **R** option is chosen, in which case all data files are left open. If the **R** option is chosen, the program is immediately run. Otherwise BASIC returns to the command mode.

TRS-80 Color Computer

LOAD **"filename"[,R]** loads the specified file and optionally runs it, where **filename** is the name of the file. In a cassette-based system the cassette is assumed. All variables are CLEARed and data files closed, unless the **R** option is chosen. In this case all data files are left open. If the **R** option is chosen, the program is immediately run. Otherwise, BASIC returns to the command mode.

computers. Be careful when using LOAD to chain BASIC programs together. The first program that has the initial LOAD in it must be longer than any programs subsequently LOADed.

COMMENTS

Also be careful when LOADing machine-language programs to avoid repeatedly reLOADing the same program. See **BLOAD.** If you wish to LOAD and RUN a long BASIC program from a shorter one, you can use the dynamic keyboard with the routine below, but remember that all variables will be cleared.

```
10 PRINT CHR$(147) "LOAD"
   CHR$(34) "filename"
   CHR$(34) ",8"
20 POKE 214,4: PRINT: PRINT
   "RUN"
30 POKE 198,4: POKE 631,19
40 FOR I=2 TO 4: POKE
   630+I,13: NEXT
50 END
```

LOADM (See BLOAD)

LOC

APPLE IIe & II+	**IBM PC & PCjr**	**COMMODORE 64**
Not available. Cannot be simulated.	**LOC(x)** returns the position of the pointer in a file, where **x** is the number of an open file. For random files, it returns the number of the most recently addressed record. For sequential files, it returns the number of records—128 byte blocks—written to or read from the file since it was opened. For a file that is actually a COM buffer, it returns the number of characters in the input buffer, up to a maximum of 255.	Not available. Cannot be simulated.

LOCATE

APPLE IIe & II+	**IBM PC & PCjr**	**COMMODORE 64**

HTAB n where **n** is a number between 0 and 255, specifying a horizontal position from the beginning of the current output line. HTAB is similar to TAB, but is used independently from PRINT statements. HTAB may also move the cursor backward to the beginning of the line. TAB may not.
 	
VTAB n where **n** is a numeric expression between 1 and 24. VTAB moves the cursor to line **n**. Columns remain unchanged and only row position changes.
	LOCATE [r] [,[c] [,[v] [,[start] [,stop]]]] places the cursor and specifies several options for cursor display. Parameter **r** specifies the row—range 1-25. Parameter **c** specifies the column— range 1-40 or 1-80, depending on current width. If **v**=0, the cursor is invisible. If **v**=1, the cursor is visible. **Start** and **stop** indicate the cursor scan start and stop lines—range 0-31. **Start**, **stop** and **v** do not apply in graphics modes. If **r**=25, then you must use the KEY OFF command prior to the LOCATE command.	Simulate it with the following program lines. They will place the cursor on line **ROW** at column **COL**. Of course, you must assign values to **ROW** and **COL** before calling the subroutine.
		
		`1000 POKE 783,0: POKE`
		`     781,ROW: POKE 782,COL`
		`1010 SYS 65520`
		`1020 RETURN`

LOF

APPLE IIe & II+	**IBM PC & PCjr**	**COMMODORE 64**
Not available. It is the programmer's responsibility to keep track of file length by using a counter. Usually the counter is the first item in the file. It is read when the file is opened and incremented each time data is written to the file. Before the file is closed, you must go back and rewrite the new value into the first position.	**LOF(x)** where **x** is the number of an open file. Returns the length of the file in bytes. If the file was created under BASIC 1.1, the number returned will be a multiple of 128. If it was created outside BASIC or under BASIC 2.0 or Cartridge BASIC, the number will be the actual number of bytes. If the file is a COM buffer, LOF will return the amount of free space in the buffer.	Not available. It is the programmer's responsibility to keep track of file length by using a counter. Usually the counter is the first item in the file. It is read when the file is opened and incremented each time data is written to the file. Before the file is closed, you must go back and rewrite the new value into the first position.

TRS-80 Models IV & III

LOC(x) returns the position of the pointer in the file, where **x** is the number of an open file. For random files, it returns the number of the most recently addressed record. For sequential files, it returns the number of records—256 byte blocks—written to or read from the file since it was opened.

TRS-80 Color Computer

LOC(x) returns the position of the pointer in the file, where **x** is the number of an open file.

COMMENTS

TRS-80 Models IV & III

PRINT @ n or **PRINT** @ **(r,c)** (Model IV) places the cursor at the specified position, where **n** is a screen position in the range 0-1919 and **(r,c)** is a pair of coordinates specifying the row (range 0-23) and column (range 0-79).

PRINT @ **n** (Model III) places the cursor at the specified position, where **n** is a screen position in the range 0-1023.

TRS-80 Color Computer

PRINT @ **n** places the cursor at the specified position, where **n** is a screen position in the range 0-511.

COMMENTS

TRS-80 Models IV & III

LOF(x) returns the number of the last record in file **x**, where **x** is the number of an open file.

TRS-80 Color Computer

LOF(x) returns the number of the last record in file **x**, where **x** is the number of an open file.

COMMENTS

LOF cannot be used with a cassette-based system. You can keep track of the length by using a counter variable. Usually the counter is the first item in the file. It is read when the file is opened and incremented each time data is written to the file. Before the file is closed you must go back and rewrite the new value into the first position.

LOG

APPLE IIe & II+
LOG(x) returns the natural logarithm of x, where x is a numeric expression greater than 0.

IBM PC & PCjr
Same.

COMMODORE 64
Same.

LOMEM:

APPLE IIe & II+
LOMEM:x sets the lowest memory location available to the program for variable storage, where x is a numeric expression representing a valid memory location. This is contrasted with HIMEM:, which sets the highest memory location available for variable storage. LOMEM: can only be set higher than its current location, not lower. LOMEM: clears all variable values and erases all functions defined with DEF FN, so it should not normally be used in a program. Or, use it only at the very beginning.

LOMEM: has no equivalent on other machines, and no need to be simulated on them.

IBM PC & PCjr
Not available.

COMMODORE 64
Not available.

LPOS

APPLE IIe & II+
Not available. Cannot be simulated. However, the most common use of LPOS—to insert a carriage return in a string of data being printed—can be achieved with the following routine. You must define the string you wish printed as T$ before entering the subroutine. You can vary W to be whatever width you want up to 255 characters. For output to go to the printer or to a sequential file, you must use the proper output routine before calling this subroutine:

```
1000 W=40:P=1
1010 T2$=MID$(T$,P,W):IF
     LEN(T2$)=0 THEN 1030
1020 PRINT T2$:P=P+W:GOTO
     1010
1030 RETURN
```

IBM PC & PCjr
LPOS(n) returns the logical position of the printer printhead in a buffer specified by n. If n=0 or 1, then the buffer is LPT1:. If n=2, then the buffer is LPT2:. If n=3 then the buffer is LPT3:. The range for n is limited to 0 or 1 in Cartridge BASIC. Note that this is not the physical position of the printhead, but the logical position.

COMMODORE 64
Not available. Cannot be simulated. However, the most common use of LPOS—to insert a carriage return in a string of data being printed—can be achieved with the following routine. You must define the string you wish printed as T$ before entering the subroutine. You can vary W to be whatever width you want up to 255 characters. For output to go to the printer or to a sequential file, you must use the proper output routine before calling this subroutine:

```
1000 W=40:P=1
1010 T2$=MID$(T$,P,W):IF
     LEN(T2$)=0 THEN 1030
1020 PRINT T2$:P=P+W:GOTO
     1010
1030 RETURN
```

TRS-80 Models IV & III	TRS-80 Color Computer	COMMENTS
Same.	Same.	

TRS-80 Models IV & III	TRS-80 Color Computer	COMMENTS
Not available.	Not available.	

TRS-80 Models IV & III

LPOS(n) (Model IV) returns the logical position of the printer printhead. The argument **n** is a dummy numeric expression. Note that this is not the physical position of the printhead, but the logical position.

Not available. Cannot be simulated on the Model III. However, the most common use of LPOS—to insert a carriage return in a string of data being printed—can be achieved with the following routine. You must define the string you wish printed as **T$** before entering the subroutine. You can vary **W** to be whatever width you want up to 255 characters. For output to go to a sequential file, you must use PRINT# in line 1020 instead of LPRINT.

TRS-80 Color Computer

POS(−2) returns the position of the printhead. POS(0) returns the position of the cursor on the screen.

```
1000 W=40: P=1
1010 T2$=MID$(T$,P,W): IF
     LEN(T2$)=0 THEN 1030
1020 LPRINT T2$: P=P+W: GOTO
     1010
1030 RETURN
```

COMMENTS

LPRINT, LPRINT USING

APPLE IIe & II+

To send output to the printer you must redefine the output slot. The printer is usually slot #1. After sending output to the printer, you must then redefine output to go only to the monitor—slot #0. Therefore, you could use the following program lines:

```
50 PRINT CHR$(4);"PR#1"
60 PRINT "MESSAGE TO BE
   PRINTED"
70 PRINT CHR$(4);"PR#0"
```

Apple lacks the extensive formatting capabilities of LPRINT USING. These capabilities are not easily simulated and are beyond the scope of this book. You might consider converting any numeric expressions into string expressions with STR$ and operating on them with LEFT$, RIGHT$ and other string-handling commands. You can then print them out in the format you desire. For formatting dollars and cents, you can use the following subroutine, where **AMT** is the actual figure you wish converted into dollars and cents. This routine will prevent you from getting values returned in fractional cents, will force zeros to be added after the decimal—so you don't get such things as $10.9—and will right-justify the amounts to give you nice-looking columns.

```
1000 AMT=100*(AMT+.005):
     AMT=INT(AMT)
1010 PRINT "$";
     SPC((AMT<100000)+(AMT<
     10000)+(AMT<1000));
     AMT/100;
1020 IF INT(AMT-INT(AMT/100)
     *100)=0 THEN PRINT
     ".00";:GOTO1040
1030 IF
     INT(AMT-INT(AMT/10)*10
     )=0 THEN PRINT "0";
1040 AMT=AMT/100: PRINT:
     RETURN
```

IBM PC & PCjr

LPRINT [n][;]... causes the numeric or string expression **n** to be printed to the printer. If the semicolon is included, the next expression is printed on the same line. LPRINT inserts a carriage return after the 80th character printed on any one line. Thus if you print exactly 80 characters plus a carriage return, you will have a blank line. You can change the value of the line length with the WIDTH command.

LPRINT USING v$;list where **v$** is a string constant or variable that contains special formatting characters. **List** is a list of expressions to be LPRINTed. This command formats the printed output in specific ways depending upon the contents of **v$**. Detailed explanation of the formatting characters is beyond the scope of this book. For BASIC 2.0, refer to the *BASIC Reference Manual,* pages 4-219 through 4-223. For Cartridge BASIC, refer to the *BASIC Reference Manual,* pages 4-286 through 4-291.

COMMODORE 64

PRINT#n,[m][;] causes the numeric or string expression **m** to be printed if file **n** has been opened to the printer. If the semicolon is included, the next expression will be printed on the same line. For example,

```
50 OPEN 4,4
60 PRINT#4, "MESSAGE TO BE
   PRINTED"
70 CLOSE 4
```

Commodore lacks the extensive formatting capabilities of LPRINT USING. These capabilities are not easily simulated and are beyond the scope of this book. As a starter, you might consider converting any numeric expressions into string expressions with STR$ and operating on them with LEFT$, RIGHT$, and other string-handling commands. You can then print them in the format you desire.

TRS-80 Models IV & III

LPRINT [n][;]... causes the numeric or string expression **n** to be printed to the printer. If the semicolon is included, the next expression is printed on the same line.

LPRINT USING v$;list where **v$** is a string constant or variable that contains special formatting characters. **List** is a list of expressions to be LPRINTed. This command formats the printed output in specific ways depending upon the contents of **v$**. Detailed explanation of the formatting characters is beyond the scope of this book. Refer to *Operation and BASIC Language Reference Manual*, pages 136-140 for the Model III and to *Disk System Owner's Manual*, pages 2-150 through 2-153 for the Model IV.

TRS-80 Color Computer

PRINT#-2,[n][;]... causes the numeric or string expression **n** to be printed to the printer. If the semicolon is included, the next expression is printed on the same line.

LPRINT -2, USING v$;list where **v$** is a string constant or variable that contains special formatting characters. **List** is a list of expressions to be LPRINTed. This command formats the printed output in specific ways depending upon the contents of **v$**. Detailed explanation of the formatting characters is beyond the scope of this book. Refer to *Going Ahead With Extended Color BASIC*, pages 129-132.

COMMENTS

LSET, RSET

APPLE IIe & II+

Simulate LSET with the following routine:

```
1000 REM ROUTINE TO SIMULATE
     LSET, WHERE L=LENGTH OF
     FIELD AND S$ IS THE
     STRING BEING MANIPULATED
1100 IF LEN(S$)>L THEN
     S$=LEFT$(S$,L):RETURN
1200 IF LEN(S$)<L THEN
     S$=S$+" ":GOTO 1200
1300 RETURN
```

Simulate RSET with the following routine:

```
1000 REM ROUTINE TO SIMULATE
     RSET, WHERE L=LENGTH OF
     FIELD AND S$ IS THE
     STRING BEING MANIPULATED
1100 IF LEN(S$)>L THEN
     S$=LEFT$(S$,L):RETURN
1200 IF LEN(S$)<L THEN
     S$=S$+" ":GOTO 1200
1300 RETURN
```

IBM PC & PCjr

LSET v$=x$

RSET v$=x$ moves data into a random-file buffer, where **v$** is the name of a string variable defined with a FIELD statement, and **x$** is a string variable to be placed into that field. These commands are used in preparation for PUTting the data into a random file. If **x$** requires fewer bytes than were allocated for **v$**, then **x$** is left-justified in the field by LSET, or right-justified by RSET. The field is padded with blanks. If **x$** requires more bytes than were allocated for **v$**, then either instruction truncates **x$** on the right. Note that these instructions operate only upon strings. Numeric data must be converted into a string with MKI$, MKS$ or MKD$ before they are LSET or RSET.

You can also use these instructions with a variable name that was not defined in a FIELD statement to format output to the printer. For example,

```
100 A$="          ":REM 10 BLANKS
110 LSET A$=X$
```

will cause **x$** to be left-justified in a field of 10 blanks.

COMMODORE 64

Simulate LSET with the following routine:

```
1000 REM ROUTINE TO SIMULATE
     LSET, WHERE L=LENGTH OF
     FIELD AND S$ IS THE
     STRING BEING MANIPULATED
1100 IF LEN(S$)>L THEN
     S$=LEFT$(S$,L):RETURN
1200 IF LEN(S$)<L THEN
     S$=S$+" ":GOTO 1200
1300 RETURN
```

Simulate RSET with the following routine:

```
1000 REM ROUTINE TO SIMULATE
     RSET, WHERE L=LENGTH OF
     FIELD AND S$ IS THE
     STRING BEING MANIPULATED
1100 IF LEN(S$)>L THEN
     S$=LEFT$(S$,L):RETURN
1200 IF LEN(S$)<L THEN
     S$=S$+" ":GOTO 1200
1300 RETURN
```

M-E (See MEMORY-EXECUTE)

M-R (See MEMORY-READ)

M-W (See MEMORY-WRITE)

MEM

APPLE IIe & II+

FRE(0) may be used to simulate MEM. It returns the amount of free memory available to the user when used in the form

```
PRINT FRE(0)
```

When FRE is used as an assignment statement, such as

```
X=FRE(0)
```

FRE causes string space to be reorganized.

IBM PC & PCjr

FRE(x) where **x** is a dummy string or numeric argument. FRE returns the amount of memory available to the program, not including the interpreter work area. It also causes the computer to do "housecleaning," compacting the string storage space as much as possible.

COMMODORE 64

FRE(x) returns a value that may be used to calculate the free memory space, where **x** is a numeric expression that is not evaluated but must be present. The actual amount of free memory is calculated by

```
10 MEM=FRE(0)-(FRE(0)<0)*
   256*256
```

When used in the form PRINT FRE(0) or X=FRE(0), FRE will force reorganization of the string

TRS-80 Models IV & III

LSET v$ = x$
RSET v$ = x$** moves data into a random file buffer, where **v$ is the name of a string variable defined with a FIELD statement, and **x$** is a string variable to be placed into that field. These commands are used in preparation for PUTting the data into a random file. If **x$** requires fewer bytes than were allocated for **v$**, then **x$** is left-justified in the field by LSET, or right-justified by RSET. The field is padded with blanks. If **x$** requires more bytes than were allocated for **v$**, then either instruction truncates **x$** on the right. Note that these instructions operate only upon strings. Numeric data must be converted into a string with MKI$, MKS$ or MKD$ before they are LSET or RSET.

You can also use these instructions with a variable name that was not defined in a FIELD statement to format output to the printer. For example,

```
100 A$=" ":REM 10 BLANKS
110 LSET A$=X$
```

will cause **x$** to be left-justified in a field of 10 blanks.

TRS-80 Color Computer

LSET v$ = x$
RSET v$ = x$** moves data into a random file buffer, where **v$ is the name of a string variable defined with a FIELD statement, and **x$** is a string variable to be placed into that field. These commands are used in preparation for PUTting the data into a random file. If **x$** requires fewer bytes than were allocated for **v$**, then **x$** is left-justified in the field by LSET, or right-justified by RSET. The field is padded with blanks. If **x$** requires more bytes than were allocated for **v$**, then either instruction truncates **x$** on the right. Note that these instructions operate only upon strings. Numeric data must be converted into a string with MKI$, MKS$ or MKD$ before they are LSET or RSET.

You can also use these instructions with a variable name that was not defined in a FIELD statement to format output to the printer. For example,

```
100 A$=" ":REM 10 BLANKS
110 LSET A$=X$
```

will cause **x$** to be left-justified in a field of 10 blanks.

COMMENTS

TRS-80 Models IV & III

MEM returns the amount of free memory available to the user.

TRS-80 Color Computer

MEM returns the amount of free memory available to the user.

COMMENTS

storage space, called *garbage collection*. This could take several minutes under some circumstances.

MEMORY-EXECUTE

APPLE IIe & II+
Not available.

IBM PC & PCjr
Not available.

COMMODORE 64

It's possible to execute machine language that is present in the 1541 Disk Drive's own ROM or RAM. The M-E command is used as follows:

```
10 SA=60064:
   H=INT(SA/256):
   L=SA-H*256
20 OPEN 15,8,15
30 PRINT#15,
   "M-E"CHR$(L)CHR$(H)
40 CLOSE 15
```

In this code, **SA** is the start address in decimal of the machine-language code to be executed. **L** and **H** are the decimal low and high bytes of **SA** when written in hexadecimal. Because memory maps of the 1541's operating system are not widely available, this code is seldom encountered. The command is roughly equivalent to CALL or SYS on other machines. It cannot be simulated on other machines because their disk drives do not have their own memory area.

MEMORY-READ

APPLE IIe & II+
Not available.

IBM PC & PCjr
Not available.

COMMODORE 64

MEMORY-READ
On the Commodore 64 it is possible to PEEK into the 1541 Disk Drive's RAM and ROM areas using the M-R command as follows:

```
10 OPEN 15,8,15
20 PRINT#15,
   "M-R"CHR$(L)CHR$(H)
30 GET#15, A$: IF A$=""
   ""THEN A$=A$+CHR$(0)
40 CLOSE 15
```

L and **H** are the decimal low and high bytes of the address in hexadecimal of the location to be read. Large amounts of data PEEKed this way may take several minutes to complete. This command cannot be simulated on other machines because their disk drives do not have their own memory area.

TRS-80 Models IV & III
Not available.

TRS-80 Color Computer
Not available.

COMMENTS

TRS-80 Models IV & III
Not available.

TRS-80 Color Computer
Not available.

COMMENTS

MEMORY-WRITE

APPLE IIe & II+

Not available.

IBM PC & PCjr

Not available.

COMMODORE 64

MEMORY-WRITE

It is possible to POKE the RAM a~~ of the Commodore 1541 Disk D~ using the M-W command as follow~

```
10 OPEN 15,8,15
20 PRINT#15,
   "M-W"CHR$(L)CHR$(H)
   CHR$(N)X$
30 CLOSE 15
```

L and **H** are the decimal low and ~ bytes of the start address in hexad~ mal of the code, **N** is the length of ~ code—range 1-34—and **X$** is the c~ concatenated as character strings. ~ example, if the 3 bytes $FF $09 ~ were to be placed in the 1541's R~ at $0500, then L=0, H=5, N=3, X$= CHR$(255) + CHR$(9) ~ CHR$(16). This command is equ~ lent to POKE. It cannot be simul~ on other machines because their ~ drives do not have their own men~ area.

MERGE

APPLE IIe & II+

Not available, but you can CHAIN programs in integer BASIC. In Applesoft you can use the CHAIN program on the DOS master disk to get the same effect. Remember that CHAIN does not keep the old program in memory, but does keep variables common.

IBM PC & PCjr

MERGE "file" where **file** is a valid BASIC file that was saved in ASCII format residing on disk (or on cassette if DOS is not present). MERGE merges the file in memory with the file specified. If the line numbers in memory are duplicated on disk, the ones from the disk will replace the ones in memory. If lines in memory or on disk are not duplicated in the other file, they will reside in memory after the merge. MERGE always returns BASIC to the command level. You must then RUN or CONTinue the program.

If you wish to get around this limitation, you can use following subroutine. The program will MERGE, then continue. It does so because lines 1010 and 1020 POKE the word RUN into the keyboard buffer. After the MERGE the program returns to the command level, the word **RUN** is obtained from the keyboard, and the merged program executes. Thus line 1040 is superfluous. It is included only for

COMMODORE 64

Not easily accomplished on Commodore 64 from within BAS~ It is beyond the scope of this book.

clarity. Be sure to include the corr~ file name in line 1030.

Note that MERGE destroys variable values.

```
1000 DEF SEG=0
1010 POKE 1050,30: POKE
     1052,38: POKE 1054,82
1020 POKE 1056,85: POKE
     1058,78: POKE 1060,13
1030 MERGE file
1040 RUN
```

TRS-80 Models IV & III

Not available.

TRS-80 Color Computer   COMMENTS

Not available.

TRS-80 Models IV & III

MERGE **"file"** where **file** is a valid BASIC file on disk. MERGE merges the file in memory with the file specified. The file on disk must have been saved with the A option. If the line numbers in memory are duplicated on disk, those from disk will replace those in memory. If lines in memory or on disk are not duplicated in the other file, they will reside in memory after the merge. MERGE always returns BASIC to the command level. You must then RUN the program.

TRS-80 Color Computer

MERGE **"file"** **[,R]** where **file** is a valid BASIC file residing on disk. MERGE merges the file in memory with the file specified. The file on disk must have been saved with the A option. If the line numbers in memory are duplicated on disk, those from the disk will replace those in memory. If lines in memory or on disk are not duplicated in the other file, they will reside in memory after the merge. MERGE always returns BASIC to the command level. If you include the **R**, the program will immediately RUN. If you do not include the **R**, you will be left in the command mode.

COMMENTS

MID$

APPLE IIe & II+

MID$(S1$,n1[,n2]) (Function) returns the specified portion of string S1$. Parameter n1 specifies the first character of S1$ to be returned, while n2 specifies the total number of characters to be returned. If n2 is omitted, MID$ will return the right portion of S1$, beginning with the character in the n1 position.

IBM PC & PCjr

MID$ (S1$, n1 [,n2]) = S2$ (Command) replaces a portion of string S1$ with S2$. Parameter n1—an integer in the range 1-255—specifies the position of the first character in S1$ to be replaced. Parameter n2—an integer in the range 0-255—specifies the number of characters to be replaced. Parameter n2 is optional, and is assumed to be LEN(S2$) if it is omitted. If n2>LEN(S2$), then n2 will be considered equal to LEN(S2$). If n2> LEN (RIGHT$ (S1$,n1), then n2 will be considered equal to LEN (RIGHT$ (S1$,n1). Thus S1$ will not change in length due to this operation.

MID$(S1$,n1[,n2]) (Function) returns the specified portion of S1$. Parameter n1—an integer in the range 1-255—specifies the first character of S1$ to be returned. Parameter n2—an integer in the range 0-255 —specifies the total number of characters to be returned. If n2 is omitted, MID$ will return the right portion of S1$, beginning with the character in the n1 position. If n2<=0, a null string is returned. If n1>LEN(S1$), a null string is returned.

COMMODORE 64

MID$(S1$,n1[,n2]) (Function) returns the specified portion of S1$. Parameter n1 specifies the first character of S1$ to be returned. Parameter n2 specifies the total number of characters to be returned. If n2 is omitted, MID$ will return the right portion of S1$, beginning with the character in the n1 position.

MKD$

APPLE IIe & II+

There is neither a way nor a need to simulate MKD$ on Apple because of the way it stores data in random files.

IBM PC & PCjr

MKD$(n) converts the double-precision value n into an eight-byte string value so it can later be retrieved from a random file as a numeric value. MKD$ varies from STR$ in that it does not actually cause n to be stored as the ASCII value of the numerals. It stores them as numbers with the data-type specifier indicating it is a string. This must be done prior to LSETing or RSETing, which must also be done prior to PUTing a value to a random-access disk file.

You cannot perform string functions on a string created with MKD$ or print it on the screen. It is just for the purpose of random file storage. MKD$ is the inverse of CVD$, which is used for retrieving a string converted with MKD$.

COMMODORE 64

There is neither a way nor a need to simulate MKD$ because of the way it stores data in random files.

TRS-80 Models IV & III

MID$ (S1$, n1 [,n2]) = **S2$** (Command) replaces a portion of **S1$** with **S2$**. Parameter **n1**—an integer in the range 1-255—specifies the position of the first character in **S1$** to be replaced. Parameter **n2**—an integer in the range 0-255—specifies the number of characters to be replaced. Parameter **n2** is optional, and is assumed to be LEN(**S2$**) if it is omitted. If **n2**>LEN(**S2$**), then **n2** will be considered equal to LEN(**S2$**). If **n2**>LEN(RIGHT$(**S1$,n1**), then **n2** will be considered equal to LEN (RIGHT$(**S1$,n1**). Thus **S1$** will not change in length due to this operation.

MID$(S1$,n1[,n2]) (Function) returns the specified portion of **S1$**. Parameter **n1**—an integer in the range 1-255—specifies the first character of **S1$** to be returned, while **n2**—an integer in the range 0-255 —specifies the total number of characters to be returned. If **n2** is omitted, MID$ will return the right portion of **S1$**, beginning with the character in the **n1** position.

TRS-80 Color Computer

MID$ (S1$, n1 [,n2]) = **S2$** (Command) replaces a portion of **S1$** with **S2$**. Parameter **n1**—an integer in the range 1-255—specifies the position of the first character in **S1$** to be replaced. Parameter **n2**—an integer in the range 0-255—specifies the number of characters to be replaced. Parameter **n2** is optional, and is assumed to be LEN(**S2$**) if it is omitted. If **n2**>LEN(**S2$**), then **n2** will be considered equal to LEN (**S2$**). If **n2**> LEN (RIGHT$ (**S1$, n1**), then **n2** will be considered equal to LEN(RIGHT$ (**S1$,n1**). Thus **S1$** will not change in length due to this operation.

MID$(S1$,n1[,n2]) (Function) returns the specified portion of **S1$**. Parameter **n1**—an integer in the range 1-255—specifies the first character of **S1$** to be returned. Parameter **n2**—an integer in the range 0-255 —specifies the total number of characters to be returned. If **n2** is omitted, MID$ will return the right portion of **S1$**, beginning with the character in the **n1** position.

COMMENTS

Be sure to identify whether your source program is using MID$ as a function or as a command. The syntax is the clue.

TRS-80 Models IV & III

MKD$(n) converts the double-precision value **n** into a eight-byte string value so that it can later be retrieved from a random file as a numeric value. MKD$ varies from STR$ in that it does not actually cause **n** to be stored as the ASCII value of the numerals, but stores them as numbers with the data-type specifier indicating it is a string. This must be done prior to LSETing or RSETing, which must also be done prior to PUTing a value to a random-access disk file. You cannot perform string functions on a string created with MKD$ or print it on the screen. It is just for the purpose of random file storage. MKD$ is the inverse of CVD$, which is used for retrieving a string converted with MKD$.

TRS-80 Color Computer

See MKN$.

COMMENTS

MKDIR

APPLE IIe & II+
Cannot be simulated.

IBM PC & PCjr
MKDIR path causes a new branch directory to be created where **path** is a valid DOS path. This command cannot be simulated on BASIC 1.1 or on any other computer. It is unique to IBM. If you use this command in Cartridge BASIC, DOS 2.1 must be present.

COMMODORE 64
Cannot be simulated.

MKI$

APPLE IIe & II+
There is neither a way nor a need to simulate MKI$ on Apple because of the way it stores data in random files.

IBM PC & PCjr
MKI$(n) converts the integer value **n** into a two-byte string value so that it can later be retrieved from a random file as a numeric value. MKI$ varies from STR$ in that it does not actually cause **n** to be stored as the ASCII value of the numerals, but stores them as numbers with the data-type specifier indicating it is a string. This must be done prior to LSETing or RSETing, which must also be done prior to PUTing a value to a random access disk file. You cannot perform string functions on a string created with MKI$ or print it on the screen. It is just for the purpose of random file storage. MKI$ is the inverse of CVI$, which is used for retrieving a string converted with MKI$.

COMMODORE 64
There is neither a way nor a need to simulate MKI$ on Commodore because of the way it stores data in random files.

MKN$

APPLE IIe & II+
There is neither a way nor a need to simulate MKN$ on Apple because of the way it stores data in random files.

IBM PC & PCjr
See **MKD$, MKI$** and **MKS$**.

COMMODORE 64
There is neither a way nor a need to simulate MKN$ on Commodore because of the way it stores data in random files.

TRS-80 Models IV & III	TRS-80 Color Computer	COMMENTS
Cannot be simulated.	Cannot be simulated.	

TRS-80 Models IV & III	TRS-80 Color Computer	COMMENTS
MKI$(n) converts the integer value **n** into a two-byte string value so that it can later be retrieved from a random file as a numeric value. MKI$ varies from STR$ in that it does not actually cause **n** to be stored as the ASCII value of the numerals, but stores them as numbers with the data-type specifier indicating it is a string. This must be done prior to LSETing or RSETing, which must also be done prior to PUTing a value to a random access disk file. You cannot perform string functions on a string created with MKI$ or print it on the screen. It is just for the purpose of random file storage. MKI$ is the inverse of CVI$, which is used for retrieving a string converted with MKI$.	See **MKN$**.	

TRS-80 Models IV & III	TRS-80 Color Computer	COMMENTS
See **MKD$**, **MKI$** and **MKS$**.	**MKN$(n)** where **n** is a numeric expression. MKN$ converts the specified value into a five-byte string value for the purpose of random file storage. This must be done prior to LSETing or RSETing, which must also be done prior to PUTing a value to a random access disk file.	

137

MKS$

APPLE IIe & II+

There is neither a way nor a need to simulate MKS$ on Apple because of the way it stores data in random files.

IBM PC & PCjr

MKS$(n) converts the single-precision value **n** into a four-byte string value so that it can later be retrieved from a random file as a numeric value. MKS$ varies from STR$ in that it does not actually cause **n** to be stored as the ASCII value of the numerals, but stores them as numbers with the data-type specifier indicating it is a string. This must be done prior to LSETing or RSETing, which must also be done prior to PUTing a value to a random access disk file. You cannot perform string functions on a string created with MKS$ or print it on the screen. It is just for the purpose of random file storage. MKS$ is the inverse of CVS$, which is used for retrieving a string converted with MKS$.

COMMODORE 64

There is neither a way nor a need to simulate MKS$ on Commodore because of the way it stores data in random files.

MOD

APPLE IIe & II+

n MOD m performs modulo arithmetic on integer values in integer BASIC only. The result is an integer value representing the remainder portion of **n** divided by **m**.

Applesoft (floating-point) BASIC does not recognize MOD. You may simulate it by defining the following function:

```
DEF FNMD(n)=INT((n/m-INT
(n/m))*m+.05)*SGN(n/m)
```

where **n** and **m** are integer values. Parameter **m** must be assigned prior to referencing FNMD(n). Subsequent reference to FNMD(n) will return an integer value representing the remainder portion of **n** divided by **m**.

IBM PC & PCjr

n MOD m performs modulo arithmetic on integer values. If **n** or **m** are not integers, they will be arithmetically rounded prior to execution. The result will be an integer value representing the remainder portion of **n** divided by **m**.

COMMODORE 64

Can be simulated by defining the following function:

```
DEF FNMD(n)=INT((n/m-INT
(n/m))*m+.05)*SGN(n/m)
```

where **n** and **m** are integer values. Parameter **m** must be assigned prior to referencing FNMD(n). Subsequent reference to FNMD(n) will return an integer value representing the remainder portion of **n** divided by **m**.

MOTOR

APPLE IIe & II+

You cannot control the motor of the cassette from within BASIC on the Apple, except possibly through some sort of an external control device. There is no built-in command.

IBM PC & PCjr

MOTOR [n] where **n** is an integer value, MOTOR will turn the cassette motor on or off. If **n**=0, the motor is turned off. If **n** is not zero, the motor will be turned on. If **n** is omitted, the motor will be switched from its current state to its opposite state.

COMMODORE 64

LOAD n turns the cassette motor on, where **n** is the name of a file that you are sure is **not** on the cassette. However, program execution halts and there is no way to turn the motor off.

TRS-80 Models IV & III

MKS$(n) converts the single-precision value **n** into a four-byte string value so that it can later be retrieved from a random file as a numeric value. MKS$ varies from STR$ in that it does not actually cause **n** to be stored as the ASCII value of the numerals, but stores them as numbers with the data-type specifier indicating it is a string. This must be done prior to LSETing or RSETing, which must also be done prior to PUTing a value to a random access disk file. You cannot perform string functions on a string created with MKS$ or print it on the screen. It is just for the purpose of random file storage. MKS$ is the inverse of CVS$, which is used for retrieving a string converted with MKS$.

TRS-80 Color Computer

See **MKN$**.

COMMENTS

TRS-80 Models IV & III

n MOD m performs modulo arithmetic on integer values on Model IV. The result will be an integer value representing the remainder portion of **n** divided by **m**.

The Model III does not recognize MOD. You may simulate it by defining the following function:

```
DEF FNMD(n,m)=(INT(n)-INT
(INT(n)/INT(m))*INT(m))
```

where **n** and **m** are integer values. Subsequent reference to FNMD(n,m) will return an integer value representing the remainder portion of **n** divided by **m**.

TRS-80 Color Computer

Can be simulated by defining the following function:

```
DEF FNMD(n)=(INT(n)-INT
(INT(n)/INT(m))*INT(m))
```

where **n** and **m** are integer values. Parameter **m** must be assigned before referencing the function. Subsequent reference to FNMD(n) will return an integer value representing the remainder portion of **n** divided by **m**.

COMMENTS

TRS-80 Models IV & III

TRS-80 Model IV does not use cassettes in the Model IV mode.

You can activate the cassette motor on the Model III with the following program lines. Be sure you have the earplug out if you wish to hear the audio, and don't have the record button pressed. It will continue to operate until a key is pressed and held

TRS-80 Color Computer

MOTOR e where **e** is ON or OFF. Turns the cassette motor on or off as specified.

for a few seconds.

```
1000 PRINT#-1,""
1010 I$=INKEY$: IF I$="" THEN
     1000
1020 RETURN
```

COMMENTS

There's a good reason to turn on the cassette motor. Perhaps you have a tutorial audio tape you wish to work with the program. Or, perhaps you don't have the cassette plugged in at all, but rather some other device that can be activated by the same signals. See **AUDIO**.

NAME

APPLE IIe & II+

PRINT CHR$(4);"RENAME a,b[,s][,d][,v]" causes **a** to be renamed **b**, where **a** and **b** are valid filenames. Parameters **s**, **d** and **v** are optional. Parameter **s** specifies the slot number, **d** specifies the drive number, and **v** specifies the volume number.

You cannot renumber a BASIC program from within itself on the Apple.

IBM PC & PCjr

NAME "a" AS "b" causes **a** to be renamed **b**, where **a** and **b** are valid filenames. Quotation marks are necessary only if **a** and **b** are literal names rather than string variables. If **a** is not on the specified disk, or if **b** is already on the disk, you will get an error. NAME does not change the contents of the file. If you use this command in Cartridge BASIC, DOS 2.1 must be present.

RENUM [newline] [,[startline] [,increment]] renumbers the program, where **newline** will be the first line number of the renumbered sequence; default=10. **Startline** is the current number of the first line to be renumbered—default=first program line. **Increment** is the increment to be used in renumbering; default=10. If you specify **startline**, you must specify **newline**. Renumbering continues from **startline** to the end of the program. RENUM also makes the necessary adjustments to all GOTOs, GOSUBs and other commands with line numbers. Program execution halts when the RENUM has been completed. You must type RUN to begin the program again.

COMMODORE 64

The following routine causes filename **b** to be renamed as filename **a**:

```
10 OPEN 15,8,15, "R0:a=b"
20 CLOSE 15
```

You cannot easily renumber a BASIC program from within itself on the Commodore 64.

TRS-80 Models IV & III

NAME "a" AS "b" (Model IV) where **a** and **b** are valid filenames, NAME causes **a** to be renamed **b**. Quotation marks are necessary only if **a** and **b** are literal names rather than string variables. If **a** is not on the specified disk, or if **b** is already on the disk, you will get an error. New name **b** cannot contain a password or drive specification. NAME does not change the contents of the file.

A file cannot be easily renamed from within a BASIC program on the Model III. You can use:

```
10 CMD "I","RENAME a b"
```

which will rename **a** to **b**, but will return you to the operating system. Another alternative—which won't return the program to the DOS level but will work only on ASCII files—is to read the file into memory, then write it out with a new file name and kill the old file. The routine below will accomplish this. Note that the CLEAR command in line 10 should appear at the beginning of the program, and that lines 1000 and 1010 require operator input. These can be easily modified to suit your needs:

```
10 CLEAR 10000
1000 CLS:LINE INPUT "OLD FILE
     NAME: ";F1$
1010 LINE INPUT "NEW FILE
     NAME: ";F2$
1020 OPEN "I",1,F1$
1030 OPEN "O",2,F2$
1040 IF EOF(1) THEN 1060
1050 LINE INPUT #1,T$: PRINT
     #2,T$: GOTO 1040
1060 CLOSE: KILL F1$
```

RENUM [newline] [,[startline] [,increment]] renumbers the program, where **newline** will be the first line number of the renumbered sequence; default=10. **Startline** is the current number of the first line to be renumbered—default=first program line. **Increment** is the increment to be used in renumbering; default=10. If you specify **startline**, you must specify **newline**. Renumbering continues from **startline** to the end of the program. RENUM also makes the necessary adjustments to all GOTOs, GOSUBs and other commands with line numbers. Program

TRS-80 Color Computer

RENAME "a" TO "b" causes **a** to be renamed **b**, where **a** and **b** are valid filenames. Quotation marks are necessary only if parameters **a** and **b** are literal names rather than string variables. If parameter **a** is not on the specified disk, or if **b** is already on the disk, you will get an error. If a drive specifier is not used on parameter **a**, BASIC will search drive 0 only. RENAME does not change the contents of the file.

RENUM [newline][,[startline] [,increment]] renumbers the program, where **newline** will be the first line number of the renumbered sequence; default=10. **Startline** is the current number of the first line to be renumbered—default=first program line. **Increment** is the increment to be used in renumbering; default=10. If you specify **startline**, you must specify **newline**. Renumbering continues from **startline** to the end of the program. RENUM also makes the necessary adjustments to all GOTOs, GOSUBs and other commands with line numbers. Program execution halts when the RENUM has been completed, and you must type RUN to begin the program again.

execution halts when the RENUM has been completed, and you must type RUN to begin the program again.

NAME [newline] [,[startline] [,increment]] (Model III) renumbers the program, where **newline** will be the first line number of the renumbered sequence; default=10. **Startline** is the current number of the first line to be renumbered; default=first program line. **Increment** is the increment to be used in renumbering—default=10. If you specify **startline**, you must specify **newline**. Renumbering continues from startline to the end of the program. NAME also makes the necessary adjustments to all GOTOs, GOSUBs and other commands with line numbers. Program execution halts when the NAME has been completed, and you must type RUN to begin the program again.

COMMENTS

Notice that NAME is sometimes used for renaming files, but on the TRS-80 Model III it is used for renumbering program lines.

Notice also that the Commodore file-renaming routine is opposite from the other systems in that the direction of assignment is different.

NEW

APPLE IIe & II+

NEW clears the display screen, deletes the program currently in memory, clears all variables and returns control to the command mode.

IBM PC & PCjr

NEW clears the display screen, deletes the program currently in memory, clears all variables and returns control to the command mode.

COMMODORE 64

NEW clears all variables and returns control to the command mode. The program is deleted in the sense that it is no longer accessible. In fact, it is still in memory and could be recovered—sometimes called *UN-NEW* or *OLD*—if you have an extensive knowledge of the inner workings of the Commodore 64. NEW does not affect machine-language programs.

NEW is also used on the Commodore 64 in a completely different way: As a direct command to the disk drive. When used in this way, it formats previously unused disks, and is usually abbreviated by N. For example, the following program lines will format a disk:

```
10 OPEN 15, 8, 15
20 PRINT#15,
    "N0:diskname,id"
30 CLOSE 15
```

Parameter **id** is a two-character identifier that should be unique to this disk. This use of NEW erases the entire disk and formats it for read/write operations. It takes about two minutes to complete.

NEXT

APPLE IIe & II+

NEXT terminates a FOR-NEXT loop. Program execution either returns to the statement following FOR or "falls through" the NEXT statement to the following statement, depending upon the value of the counter specified in the FOR statement.

It is critical that you not use a GOTO to break out of a FOR-NEXT loop. If you do this repeatedly you will soon get an OUT OF MEMORY error.

IBM PC & PCjr

NEXT terminates a FOR-NEXT loop. Program execution either returns to the statement following FOR or "falls through" the NEXT statement to the following statement, depending upon the value of the counter specified in the FOR statement.

COMMODORE 64

NEXT terminates a FOR-NEXT loop. Program execution either returns to the statement following FOR or "falls through" the NEXT statement to the following statement, depending upon the value of the counter specified in the FOR statement.

It is critical that you not use a GOTO to break out of a FOR-NEXT loop. If you do this repeatedly you will soon get an OUT OF MEMORY error.

TRS-80 Models IV & III

NEW clears the display screen, deletes the program currently in memory, clears all variables and returns control to the command mode.

TRS-80 Color Computer

NEW clears the display screen, deletes the program currently in memory, clears all variables and returns control to the command mode.

COMMENTS

TRS-80 Models IV & III

NEXT terminates a FOR-NEXT loop. Program execution either returns to the statement following FOR or "falls through" the NEXT statement to the following statement, depending upon the value of the counter specified in the FOR statement.

TRS-80 Color Computer

NEXT terminates a FOR-NEXT loop. Program execution either returns to the statement following FOR or "falls through" the NEXT statement to the following statement, depending upon the value of the counter specified in the FOR statement.

COMMENTS

Unstructured use of FOR-NEXT loops—or any other branching—can cause problems. You should always be sure your loops have "one way in and one way out."

NOISE

APPLE IIe & II+

Cannot be simulated without machine-language programming.

IBM PC & PCjr

NOISE s,v,d (Cartridge BASIC Only) causes a noise to be generated through the external speaker, where **s** specifies the noise source—range 0-7. You can change the sound generated for **s**=3 or **s**=7 by changing voice 3 with the PLAY command. See **PLAY**. Parameter **v** controls volume and is an integer in the range 0-15. Parameter **d** is the duration of the noise measured in clock ticks. There are 18.2 ticks per second. You must execute a SOUND command before the NOISE command. Otherwise, you will cause an error condition.

COMMODORE 64

Simulating NOISE on the Commodore 64 requires extensive POKEing, and is beyond the scope of this book. For a good discussion of generating sound from BASIC programs, see *Your Commodore 64,* by Heilborn and Talbot or *How to Program Your Commodore 64* by Carl Shipman.

NORMAL

APPLE IIe & II+

NORMAL restores INVERSE or FLASH to the normal text mode—light characters on a dark background.

IBM PC & PCjr

COLOR x,y gives a normal image on the PC, where **x** and **y** are valid foreground and background colors. See **COLOR** for valid colors.

COMMODORE 64

Not available. If FLASH is being simulated, normal operation will be resumed when you cease simulation.

NOT

APPLE IIe & II+

NOT e where **e** is an expression that may be tested true or false. NOT will return 1 (True) if the expression is false, and 0 (False) if the expression is true.

IBM PC & PCjr

NOT e where **e** is an expression that may be tested true or false. NOT will return 1 (True) if the expression is false, and 0 (False) if the expression is true.

COMMODORE 64

NOT e where **e** is an expression that may be tested true or false. NOT will return -1 (True) if the expression is false, and 0 (false) if the expression is true.

NOTRACE

APPLE IIe & II+

NOTRACE cancels the effects of TRACE.

IBM PC & PCjr

TROFF cancels the effects of TRON.

COMMODORE 64

Not available on the Commodore because TRACE is not used. Simulation is possible but would require extensive machine-language routines beyond the scope of this book.

TRS-80 Models IV & III	TRS-80 Color Computer	COMMENTS
Cannot be simulated without machine language.	Cannot be simulated without machine language, but you can create some similar effects with the SOUND command.	

TRS-80 Models IV & III	TRS-80 Color Computer	COMMENTS
Not available. If FLASH is being simulated, normal operation will be resumed when you cease simulation. If inverse printing is enabled on the Model IV, normal printing may be resumed by PRINT CHR$(17). Inverse is not available on the Model III.	Not available. If FLASH is being simulated, normal operation will be resumed when you cease simulation. If inverse printing is enabled, it can be disabled by SHIFT-0.	

TRS-80 Models IV & III	TRS-80 Color Computer	COMMENTS
NOT e where **e** is an expression that may be tested true or false. NOT will return 1 (True) if the expression is false, and 0 (False) if the expression is true.	**NOT e** where **e** is an expression that may be tested true or false. NOT will return 1 (True) if the expression is false, and 0 (False) if the expression is true.	

TRS-80 Models IV & III	TRS-80 Color Computer	COMMENTS
TROFF cancels the effects of TRON.	**TROFF** cancels the effects of TRON.	

OCT$

APPLE IIe & II+

The following subroutine will return the same value as would be returned by OCT$, stored in the string **R$**. Assign the number you wish to convert to the variable **NUMBER** before calling this subroutine.

```
1000 DIGIT$="012345678"
1010 R$=""
1015 IF NUMBER<0 THEN
     NUMBER=(65536+NUMBER)
1020 I=NUMBER
1030 Q=INT(I/8)
1040 R=I-Q*8
1050 R$=MID$(DIGIT$,R+1,1)+
     R$
1060 I=Q
1070 IF I>0 GOTO 1030
1080 RETURN
```

IBM PC & PCjr

OCT$(n) returns the octal value of a decimal argument, where **n** is a numeric expression in the range −32768-65535. If **n** is negative, the two's complement form is used. This means that OCT$(−n)=OCT$ (65536 −n).

COMMODORE 64

The following subroutine will return the same value as would be returned by OCT$. The result will be stored in the string **R$**. Assign the number you wish to be converted to the variable **NUMBER** before calling this subroutine.

```
1000 DIGIT$="012345678"
1010 IF NUMBER<0 THEN
     NUMBER=(65536+NUMBER)
1015 R$=""
1020 I=NUMBER
1030 Q=INT(I/8)
1040 R=I-Q*8
1050 R$=MID$(DIGIT$,R+1,1)+
     R$
1060 I=Q
1070 IF I>0 GOTO 1030
1080 RETURN
```

ON COM (See COM)

ON ERR GOTO, ON ERROR GOTO, ONERR

APPLE IIe & II+

ONERR GOTO n
When an error is encountered after this statement, program execution will jump to the routine beginning at line **n**, and continue until the word RESUME is encountered.

IBM PC & PCjr

ON ERROR GOTO n
When an error is encountered after this statement, program execution will jump to the routine beginning at line **n**, and continue until the word RESUME is encountered.

COMMODORE 64

Not available. Cannot be easily simulated.

TRS-80 Models IV & III

OCT$(n) (Model IV) returns the octal value of a decimal argument, where n is a numeric expression in the range −32768-65535. This function returns the octal value of a decimal argument. If **n** is negative, the two's complement form is used. This means that OCT$(−n)=OCT$(65536− n).

For the Model III, the following subroutine will return the same value as would be returned by OCT$. The result will be stored in the string **R$**. Assign the number you wish to convert to the variable NUMBER before calling this subroutine.

```
1000 DIGIT$="012345678"
1010 IF NUMBER<0 THEN
     NUMBER=(65536+NUMBER)
1015 R$=""
1020 I=NUMBER
1030 Q=INT(I/8)
1040 R=I-Q*8
1050 R$=MID$(DIGIT$,R+1,1)+
     R$
1060 I=Q
1070 IF I>0 GOTO 1030
1080 RETURN
```

TRS-80 Color Computer

The following subroutine will return the same value as would be returned by OCT$. The result will be stored in the string **R$**. Assign the number you wish to convert to the variable **NUMBER** before calling this subroutine.

```
1000 DIGIT$="012345678"
1010 IF NUMBER<0 THEN
     NUMBER=(65536+NUMBER)
1015 R$=""
1020 I=NUMBER
1030 Q=INT(I/8)
1040 R=I-Q*8
1050 R$=MID$(DIGIT$,R+1,1)+
     R$
1060 I=Q
1070 IF I>0 GOTO 1030
1080 RETURN
```

COMMENTS

TRS-80 Models IV & III

ON ERROR GOTO n
When an error is encountered after this statement, program execution will jump to the routine beginning at line **n**, and continue until the word RESUME is encountered.

TRS-80 Color Computer

Not available and cannot be easily simulated.

COMMENTS

ON-GOSUB

APPLE IIe & II+

ON v GOSUB n1[,n2...] causes conditional program branching, where v is a numeric expression and n1, n2... are the beginning line numbers of subroutines. The value of v determines the line number executed by the GOSUB. If v=1, then GOSUB will reference the first line number. If v=2 then GOSUB will reference the second line number, etc. If v is 0 or greater than the number of lines listed, program execution will "fall through" to the next line. If v is less than zero, an error condition will result.

IBM PC & PCjr

ON v GOSUB n1[,n2...] causes conditional program branching, where v is a numeric expression and n1, n2... are the beginning line numbers of subroutines. The value of v determines the line number executed by the GOSUB. If v=1, then GOSUB will reference the first line number. If v=2, then GOSUB will reference the second line number, etc. If v is 0 or greater than the number of lines listed, program execution will continue with the next line—the GOSUB will not be executed. If v is less than zero, an error condition will result.

COMMODORE 64

ON v GOSUB n1[,n2...] causes conditional program branching, where v is a numeric expression and n1, n2... are the beginning line numbers of subroutines. The value of v determines the line number executed by the GOSUB. If v=1, then GOSUB will reference the first line number. If v=2, then GOSUB will reference the second line number, etc. If v is 0 or greater than the number of lines listed, program execution will continue with the next line—the GOSUB will not be executed. If v is less than zero, an error condition will result.

The following program lines are commonly used on the Commodore as a branching method dependent upon YES and NO responses.

```
10 ON-(A$="Y")-2*(A$=
   "N") GOSUB 100,200
20 REM PROGRAM CONTINUES
   HERE
99 END
100 REM THIS IS REACHED IF
    A$="Y"
110 RETURN
200 REM THIS IS REACHED IF
    A$="N"
210 RETURN
```

If A$="Y", then the first expression in parentheses is true and returns the value −1, while the second expression in parentheses is false and is evaluated as 0. Line 100 will therefore be executed from line 10. If A$="N", then in a similar way the entire statement is evaluated as 2 and line 200 is executed. If A$ is neither "Y" nor "N", then line 20 is executed. If v is less than zero, an error condition will result.

TRS-80 Models IV & III

ON v GOSUB n1[,n2...] causes conditional program branching, where **v** is a numeric expression and **n1, n2...** are the beginning line numbers of subroutines. The value of **v** determines the line number executed by the GOSUB. If **v**=1, then GOSUB will reference the first line number. If **v**=2, then GOSUB will reference the second line number, etc. If **v** is 0 or greater than the number of lines listed, program execution will continue with the next line—the GOSUB will not be executed. If **v** is less than zero, an error condition will result.

TRS-80 Color Computer

ON v GOSUB n1[,n2...] causes conditional program branching, where **v** is a numeric expression and **n1, n2...** are the beginning line numbers of subroutines. The value of **v** determines the line number executed by the GOSUB. If **v**=1, then GOSUB will reference the first line number. If **v**=2, then GOSUB will reference the second line number, etc. If **v** is 0 or greater than the number of lines listed, program execution will continue with the next line—the GOSUB will not be executed. If **v** is less than zero, an error condition will result.

COMMENTS

ON-GOTO

APPLE IIe & II+

ON v GOTO n1[,n2...] causes conditional branching, where v is a numeric expression and **n1, n2...** are the beginning line numbers of routines. The value of v determines the line number executed by the GOTO. If **v**=1, then GOTO will reference the first line number. If **v**=2, then GOTO will reference the second line number, etc. If v is 0 or greater than the number of lines listed, program execution will continue with the next line—the GOTO will not be executed. If v is less than zero, an error condition will result.

IBM PC & PCjr

ON v GOTO n1[,n2...] causes conditional branching, where v is a numeric expression and **n1, n2...** are the beginning line numbers of routines. The value of v determines the line number executed by the GOTO. If **v**=1, then GOTO will reference the first line number. If **v**=2, then GOTO will reference the second line number, etc. If v is 0 or greater than the number of lines listed, program execution will continue with the next line—the GOTO will not be executed. If v is less than zero, an error condition will result.

COMMODORE 64

ON v GOTO n1[,n2...] causes conditional program branching, where **v** is a numeric expression and **n1, n2...** are the beginning line numbers of routines. The value of v determines the line number executed by the GOTO. If **v**=1, then GOTO will reference the first line number. If **v**=2, then GOTO will reference the second line number, etc. If v is 0 or greater than the number of lines listed, program execution will continue with the next line—the GOTO will not be executed. If v is less than zero, an error condition will result.

ON KEY (See KEY)

ON PEN (See PEN)

ON PLAY (See PLAY)

ON STRIG (See STRIG)

ON TIMER (See TIMER)

TRS-80 Models IV & III

ON v GOTO n1[,n2...] causes conditional branching, where **v** is a numeric expression and **n1, n2...** are the beginning line numbers of routines. The value of v determines the line number executed by the GOTO. If **v**=1, then GOTO will reference the first line number. If **v**=2, then GOTO will reference the second line number, etc. If **v** is 0 or greater than the number of lines listed, program execution will continue with the next line—the GOTO will not be executed. If **v** is less than zero, an error condition will result.

TRS-80 Color Computer

ON v GOTO n1[,n2...] causes conditional branching, where **v** is a numeric expression and **n1, n2...** are the beginning line numbers of routines. The value of v determines the line number executed by the GOTO. If **v**=1, then GOTO will reference the first line number. If **v**=2 then GOTO will reference the second line number, etc. If **v** is 0 or greater than the number of lines listed, program execution will continue with the next line—the GOTO will not be executed. If **v** is less than zero, an error condition will result.

COMMENTS

EVENT TRAPPING ON THE IBM PC, XT & PCjr

Event trapping causes the program to test for the occurrence of some event before the execution of each program line. IBM allows event trapping for several actions. If the event has occurred, program control is transferred to the line specified in the GOSUB portion of the command. This powerful feature slows program execution slightly, but the trade-off in power is worth the slight delay. In some cases you may want to use event trapping to slow overall execution of a program.

The commands that allow event trapping are as follows:

ON COM GOSUB
ON KEY(n) GOSUB
ON PEN GOSUB
ON PLAY(n) GOSUB
ON STRIG GOSUB
ON TIMER GOSUB

Notice that ON ERROR, ON ... GOTO and ON ... GOSUB are not event trapping in the sense of checking for an action at the beginning of each program line. Also, KEY ON is not the same as KEY(n) ON.

These commands are active only if a COMMAND ON, such as KEY (n) ON, is executed before them. They are deactivated by a COMMAND OFF, such as KEY(n) OFF. If a COMMAND STOP is executed, such as KEY(n) STOP, event trapping at the beginning of each line ceases. However, if the event occurs after the COMMAND OFF, the computer remembers it, and if a subsequent COMMAND ON is encountered, program control will immediately be transferred to the line specified in the GOSUB portion of the ON COMMAND GOSUB.

For a detailed description of these commands, see COM, KEY(n), PEN, PLAY, STRIG and TIMER.

OPEN

APPLE IIe & II+

PRINT CHR$(4) ; "OPEN filename, Ln [,Ss] [,Dd] [,Vv]" OPENs the file specified, where **filename** is the name of the file, **n** is the length of the records, **s** is the slot of the disk drive controller (default=6), **d** is the drive number (default=currently logged drive), and **v** is the volume number of the disk. If you are opening a sequential file, **Ln** is not used. It is required only for random access files.

IBM PC & PCjr

OPEN "filename" [FOR mode] AS [#]num [LEN=n] or OPEN mode2, [#]num, "filename" [,n] OPENs the specified file, where **filename** is the name and/or path for the file. It can also be a device, such as CAS1: or LPT1:. **Mode** is either OUTPUT if the file is to be written to, INPUT if the file is to be read from, or APPEND if the file is to be appended to. If **mode** is omitted, random access is assumed. **Mode2** is either O if the file is to be written to, I if the file is to be read from, or R if the file is to be accessed randomly. **Num** is the file number—range 1-15. If **num>3**, you must have set the number of files with the /F switch when entering BASIC. Parameter **n** is the record length—range 1-32767, default=128—for random files or for sequential files in BASIC 2.0 or Cartridge BASIC.

For a detailed discussion on all the ramifications of the OPEN statement, refer to the *BASIC Reference Manual,* pages 4-189 through 4-199b or the Cartridge *BASIC Reference Manual,* page 4-233 through 4-239.

If you OPEN a COM adapter with the OPEN statement, there are many other parameters available for setting baud rate, handshaking, etc. This capability does not exist for other computers and cannot be easily simulated. A detailed discussion is beyond the scope of this book. Refer to the *BASIC Reference Manual,* pages 4-194 through 4-199b for a detailed discussion, or the Cartridge *BASIC Reference Manual,* page 4-240 through 4-246.

COMMODORE 64

OPEN n[,d[,sa[,"filename"[,type, mode]]]] To communicate with any device, you must OPEN a file to that device. Parameters that the OPEN command can take are as follows:

Parameter **n** is the logical file number—range 1-255. If **n** is greater than 127, a linefeed will be generated after PRINT#. The number **n** used in GET#n, PRINT#n, CLOSEn, CMDn and INPUT#n causes the command to relate to the file OPENed with the number **n**.

Parameter **d** is the device number of the peripheral—range 0-15. Some commonly encountered device numbers are 0=keyboard, 1=cassette tape, 2=modem, 3=video screen, 4=printer, 8=disk drive.

Parameter **sa** is the secondary address or command channel number. The significance of this depends upon the device. A value of 0-2 may relate to the cassette, 0-10 may relate to the printer, and 2-15 may relate to the disk drives.

Type is the type of file. The default is a program file. If **type**=S, it is a sequential file, and if **type**=R, it is a relative file.

Mode is the mode of access. If **mode**=R, it is for reading. If **mode**=W, it is for writing. And if **mode**=A, it is for appending.

The actual usage of OPEN varies from device to device, so a few examples help clarify its use.

Cassette: Device 1

A secondary address of 0 indicates the file is to be read. A 1 indicates data will be written to it.

```
10 OPEN 2,1,0,"file"
20 INPUT#2, A$: REM GET#2,
   A$ COULD BE USED
30 CLOSE 2
```

The above lines will read one byte of data, **A$**, from a cassette sequential file named **"file"**.

```
10 OPEN 2,1,1,"file"
20 PRINT#2, A$
30 CLOSE 2
```

TRS-80 Models IV & III

OPEN, "mode", num, "filename" [,n] OPENs a file, where **mode** specifies how the file will be used. **Num** is the buffer number—range 1-15. **Filename** is the name of the file, and **n** is the record length for random access files. Parameter **n** is not specified for sequential access files—default=256. The **mode** may be one of the following: O for sequential output, I for sequential input, E for extended mode (appending to sequential files), D or R for random input/output.

The above lines will write one byte of data, **A$**, to a cassette sequential file named "**file**".

Printer: Device 4
Here, you should use nothing after the device number, so OPEN 1,4 will OPEN the printer. There are two different ways of printing to the printer, depending on whether or not CMDn is used.

```
10 OPEN 1,4
20 PRINT#1, A$
30 CLOSE 1
```

will print the string **A$** on the printer. Using CMD diverts all output to file **n**, until a PRINT# statement is encountered, which disables CMD.

```
10 OPEN 1,4
20 CMD 1
30 PRINT A$
40 PRINT# 1
50 PRINT B$
60 CLOSE 1
```

will print A$ to the printer, and B$ to the screen. A secondary address of 7 on the Commodore 1525 printer selects a different character set.

Disk Drive: Device 8
On the disk drive, secondary addresses of 2-14 have no particular significance. But 15 is reserved for the command channel.

```
10 OPEN 1,8,2, "file,S,R"
20 INPUT#1, A$ : REM
   GET#1,A$ COULD ALSO BE
   USED
30 CLOSE 1
```

TRS-80 Color Computer

OPEN "mode", #num,"filename" [,n] OPENs a file, where **mode** specifies how the file will be used, **num** is the buffer number, **filename** is the name of the file, and **n** is the record length for random access files. Parameter **n** is not specified for sequential access files—default=256. The **mode** may be one of the following: O for sequential output, I for sequential input, D for random input/output. Parameter **num** may be 0 for display and keyboard, −1 for cassette, −2 for printer, or 1-15 for disk drives.

will read one byte of data, **A$**, from the disk sequential file named **file**.

Using 15 as a secondary address is illustrated as follows:

```
10 OPEN 1,8,15
20 INPUT#1, E, E$, T, S
30 IF E$ <> "OK" THEN PRINT
   E;E$;T;S: CLOSE 1: END
40 REM REST OF PROGRAM GOES
   HERE
```

This routine identifies any disk drive errors, for example, FILE NOT FOUND. If E$="OK", no error exists. If an error exists, then the error number, error message, track and sector are displayed. This routine resets the error channel to normal. Secondary address 15 is also used to send commands to the disk operating system. For example:

```
10 OPEN 1,8,15
20 PRINT#1, "S0:filename"
30 CLOSE 1
```

will delete (SCRATCH, KILL) the file named **filename** from the disk in the drive. Secondary addresses of 0 and 1 are associated with loading and saving and are undocumented and seldom used.

COMMENTS

OPTION BASE

APPLE IIe & II+

The option base for Apple is always 0. Thus, an array will automatically have 11 elements (0-10) if it is not DIMensioned.

IBM PC & PCjr

OPTION BASE 1 sets the minimum array subscript value to 1. Thus, if an array is not DIMensioned, it will automatically have 10 elements (1-10). If you try to use OPTION BASE after any arrays are DIMensioned or used, an error will occur. In BASIC 1.1 or earlier, a program that is being chained cannot have an OPTION BASE command.

If OPTION BASE is not declared, the option base is 0. In that case an array will automatically have 11 elements (0-10) if it is not DIMensioned.

COMMODORE 64

The option base for the Commodore 64 is always 0. Thus, an array will automatically have 11 elements (0-10) if it is not DIMensioned.

OR

APPLE IIe & II+

OR is a logical and bitwise operator. It allows an evaluation of two items, returning True (1) if either of the values is true or non-zero. The logic table for OR follows:

x	y	x OR y
T	T	T
T	F	T
F	T	T
F	F	F

IBM PC & PCjr

OR is a logical and bitwise operator. It allows an evaluation of two items, returning True (1) if either of the values is true or non-zero. The logic table for OR follows:

x	y	x OR y
T	T	T
T	F	T
F	T	T
F	F	F

COMMODORE 64

OR is a logical and bitwise operator. It allows an evaluation of two items, returning True (-1) if either of the values is true or non-zero. The logic table for OR follows:

x	y	x OR y
T	T	T
T	F	T
F	T	T
F	F	F

OUT

APPLE IIe & II+

Use of ports on the Apple is not possible without assembly-language routines or extensive PEEKs and POKEs, and is thus beyond the scope of this book. A good reference on the subject is *The Apple Connection* by James W. Coffron.

IBM PC & PCjr

OUT n,m sends a byte to a machine output port, where **n** is the port number—range 0-65535—and **m** is a numeric expression representing the data—range 0-255. OUT is the opposite of INP, which reads a byte at a machine port.

COMMODORE 64

Use of ports on the Commodore 64 is not possible without the use of assembly-language routines or extensive PEEKs and POKEs, and is thus beyond the scope of this book.

TRS-80 Models IV & III

OPTION BASE 1 (Model IV) sets the minimum array subscript value to 1. Thus, if an array is not DIMensioned, it will automatically have 10 elements (1-10). If you try to use OPTION BASE after any arrays are DIMensioned or used, an error will occur.

If OPTION BASE is not declared, the option base is 0. In that case an array will automatically have 11 elements (0-10) if it is not DIMensioned.

The option base for the Model III is always 0. Thus, an array will automatically have 11 elements (0-10) if it is not DIMensioned.

TRS-80 Color Computer

The option base for the COCO is always 0. Thus, an array will automatically have 11 elements (0-10) if it is not DIMensioned.

COMMENTS

TRS-80 Models IV & III

OR is a logical and bitwise operator. It allows an evaluation of two items, returning True (1) if either of the values is true or non-zero. The logic table for OR follows:

x	y	x OR y
T	T	T
T	F	T
F	T	T
F	F	F

TRS-80 Color Computer

OR is a logical and bitwise operator. It allows an evaluation of two items, returning True (1) if either of the values is true or non-zero. The logic table for OR follows:

x	y	x OR y
T	T	T
T	F	T
F	T	T
F	F	F

COMMENTS

TRS-80 Models IV & III

OUT n,m sends a byte to a machine output port, where **n** is the port number—range 0-255—and **m** is a numeric expression representing the data—range 0-255. OUT is the opposite of INP, which reads a byte at a machine port.

TRS-80 Color Computer

Use of ports on COCO is not possible without the use of assembly-language routines or extensive PEEKs and POKEs, and is thus beyond the scope of this book.

COMMENTS

PAINT

APPLE IIe & II+

Fill routines, such as accomplished by PAINT, are not easily simulated on the Apple in BASIC. Machine-language graphics utilities are commercially available for this function. If the figure to be PAINTed is a regular figure or has easily defined boundaries, you can use PLOT, HPLOT, LINE or HLINE to define and fill them. For example:

```
10 FOR y=y1 TO y2: FOR x=x1
   to x2
20 HPLOT x,y: NEXT x: NEXT y
```

will draw a solid, filled box at x1,y1 with the diagonally opposite corner at x2,y2. Note: x1 must be less than x2, and y1 must be less than y2.

Similar algorithms may be defined for other regular shapes. These algorithms may be stored in subroutines and recalled as needed. This is not exactly the same as PAINT, but may fulfill the same need in some cases without resorting to machine language.

IBM PC & PCjr

PAINT (x,y) [,color] [,boundary] [,background] fills in an area on a graphics screen with a specified color or pattern, where **x** and **y** are coordinates within the outline to be filled. If parameter **color** is numeric, it specifies the color to use for filling. See **COLOR** for valid numeric values to use for **color**.

If parameter **color** is a string expression—BASIC 2.0 or Cartridge BASIC only—then "tiling" occurs. Tiling allows you to set individual pixels in a specified pattern. A detailed explanation of tiling is beyond the purpose of this book. Refer to the *BASIC Reference Manual,* pages 4-204a through 4-204f for a complete discussion, or Cartridge *BASIC Reference Manual* pages 4-252 through 4-256.

Parameter **boundary** specifies the color of the edges or boundaries of the figure to be filled. Parameter **background** is a one-byte string expression that is used when tiling.

COMMODORE 64

Fill routines, such as accomplished by PAINT, are not easily simulated on the Commodore 64 in BASIC. Machine-language graphics utilities are commercially available for this function. If the figure to be PAINTed is a regular figure or has easily defined boundaries, you can fill it by repeatedly simulating HPLOT. For example:

```
100 REM HIGH RES SCREEN
    ROUTINE GOES HERE
300 FOR V=Y1 TO Y2 STEP
    SGN(Y2-Y1)
310 FOR H=X1 TO X2 STEP
    SGN(X2-X1)
320 GOSUB 1000
330 NEXT: NEXT
999 END
1000 REM PLOT SUBROUTINE GOES
     HERE
```

will draw a solid, filled rectangle at **X1,Y1** with the diagonally opposite corner at **X2,Y2**. Before calling this routine the high-resolution screen routine must be called. See **HGR**. Subroutine 1000 is the set-point subroutine. See **HPLOT**. Similar algorithms may be defined for other regular shapes. Note that this is not exactly the same as PAINT, but may fulfill the same need in some cases without resorting to machine language.

PALETTE, PALETTE USING

APPLE IIe & II+

Not available. Cannot be simulated.

IBM PC & PCjr

PALETTE [attribute] [,color] (Cartridge BASIC Only) assigns the number **color** to the attribute number **attribute**. The range for each is 0-1, 0-3 or 0-15, depending on which SCREEN is in use. See **COLOR** or **SCREEN** for a list of valid color numbers. If **attribute** is omitted, it defaults to the maximum attribute for that SCREEN. If **color** is omitted, the attribute will be reset to its default. If both **attribute** and **color** are omitted, all attributes are reset to their default values. PALETTE does not affect background, only the objects or text in the foreground color.

COMMODORE 64

Not available. Cannot be simulated.

PALETTE USING [arrayname (start)] (Cartridge BASIC Only) assigns the colors for attributes using the values from the array **arrayname**, starting at position **start** within the array. The array must have at least 16 elements past position **start**. The range for the elements is 0-15, based on the number of attributes available for that SCREEN. See **SCREEN**. If you do not wish to change a color, use −1 in the appropriate position in the array. Also see **COLOR**.

TRS-80 Models IV & III

Because TRS-80 Models IV and III do not have color capabilities, PAINT cannot be simulated. See **PRINT@** on the Model IV and **SET** on the Model III to create solid, regular figures.

TRS-80 Color Computer

PAINT (x,y),color,boundary fills a figure with the appropriate color, where **x** and **y** are the coordinates at which to begin filling. Parameter color—range 0-8—specifies the color with which to fill. Parameter boundary—range 0-8—specifies the color of the edges or boundaries of the figure to be filled.

Possible values for color and boundary follow:

0	Black	5	Buff
1	Green	6	Cyan
2	Yellow	7	Magenta
3	Blue	8	Orange
4	Red		

COMMENTS

TRS-80 Models IV & III

Not available. Cannot be simulated.

TRS-80 Color Computer

Not available. Cannot be simulated.

COMMENTS

PCLEAR

APPLE IIe & II+

Apple BASIC has no specific way to reserve memory for graphics. This can be a problem because the program can write over the graphics screens. You can, however, protect an extra page of low-resolution graphics with the following program lines, which must be executed before the program is loaded. This program calls the program **"filename"**, which would be your main program.

```
10 POKE 103,0: POKE 104,12
20 POKE 2048,0
30 RUN "filename"
```

To protect your high-resolution pages, use HIMEM:8192 if your program is small. Or you can use the following program lines. They force some low-memory loss, but not as much as becomes unavailable by using HIMEM:.

```
10 POKE 103,1: POKE 104,96
20 POKE 24576,0
30 RUN "filename"
```

IBM PC & PCjr

The amount of memory available for graphics is static on the PC. It cannot be written over by the program. Therefore, there is no need to simulate PCLEAR.

CLEAR [,[n] [,m] [,v]] (Cartridge BASIC Only) clears memory, where **n** is the optional number of bytes you want for BASIC workspace. Parameter **m** is the optional stack space you desire. Parameter **v** specifies the total number of bytes to set aside for video memory. Used alone, CLEAR frees all memory, erases all DIMs, DEFs and variable values, and sets any SOUND, PLAY, PEN and STRIG values to OFF.

COMMODORE 64

The Commodore 64 has no specific way to reserve memory for graphics. This can be a problem because the program can write over the graphics screens. The high-resolution screen used under HGR could be protected by using the counterpart of HIMEM:

```
10 POKE 51,0: POKE 52,32:
   POKE 55,0: POKE 56,32:
   CLR
```

Protecting other graphics pages could be achieved in a similar way, but a discussion of that is beyond the scope of this book because of the complex nature of other graphics screens.

PCLS

APPLE IIe & II+

HOME clears the screen and places the cursor in the upper-left corner in the text mode.

To clear the high-resolution screen to black, use the following call:

CALL -3086

To clear the high-resolution screen to the most recent HCOLOR, use the following call:

CALL -3082

IBM PC & PCjr

CLS clears the screen or the active viewport to the current background color and places the cursor in the upper-left corner if the computer is in text mode, or center of screen if the computer is in a graphics mode.

COMMODORE 64

PRINT CHR$(147); will clear the screen and move the cursor to the upper-left corner of the screen.

TRS-80 Color Computer

Because TRS-80 Models III and IV do not have graphics, there is no way and no need to simulate PCLEAR.

TRS-80 Color Computer

PCLEAR **n** protects graphics memory, where **n** is a numeric expression in the range 1-8. This specifies the number of memory pages to be reserved, protecting that memory space from being used by the program for other purposes.

COMMENTS

TRS-80 Models IV & III

CLS clears the screen, but always to black.

TRS-80 Color Computer

PCLS [n] clears the current graphics screen, where **n** is an optional parameter specifying the color with which to clear the screen. If **n** is omitted, the current background color is used.

COMMENTS

PCOPY

APPLE IIe & II+

You can quickly move from displaying one graphics screen to another with the following program lines. If you already have the screens DRAWn or BLOADed, you need not use lines 50 and 60. This code assumes that your pictures were BSAVEd in the files **picture1** and **picture2**. If you are switching to page 1, use line 80. If you are switching to page 2, use line 90. Using the code as it is will switch from page 1 to page 2 so fast you probably won't see page 1. You could put a counting loop in line 85 if you want to see them both.

```
50 PRINT CHR$(4);BLOAD
   picture1,A$2000:REM
   LOAD HI-RES PAGE 1
60 PRINT CHR$(4);BLOAD
   picture2,A$4000:REM
   LOAD HI-RES PAGE 2
70 POKE -16304,0: POKE
   -16302,0: POKE -16297,0
80 POKE -16300,0: REM CALLS
   PAGE 1
90 POKE -16299,0: REM CALLS
   PAGE 2
```

IBM PC & PCjr

In the text mode IBM allows only eight pages—numbered 0-7—when the value of WIDTH=40. It allows only four pages—numbered 0-3—when the value of WIDTH=80. You can switch between the page displayed on the screen with the following program lines, where **v** is the page number of the page to be viewed. The three commas are mandatory. See **SCREEN** for an explanation of its other features.

```
10 SCREEN ,,,v
```

BASIC 2.0 and earlier versions allow only one graphics screen. The quickest way to load a complete graphics screen is to BLOAD it with the following program lines:

```
10 DEF SEG=&HB8000: BLOAD
   filename,0
```

where **filename** is the name under which you BSAVEd the screen.

PCOPY [source], [destination] (Cartridge BASIC Only) where **source** and **destination** are the numbers of valid graphics pages. This command copies the contents of **source** onto **destination**. The range for **source** and **destination** are determined by the amount of memory required for each (see **SCREEN**) and by the on-board memory available as determined by the CLEAR command.

COMMODORE 64

Simulating PCOPY on the Commodore would require a machine-language program, or extensive PEEKS and POKES. Such discussion is beyond the scope of this book.

TRS-80 Models IV & III

TRS-80 Models IV and III have only one screen available, so it is not possible to simulate PCOPY on them.

TRS-80 Color Computer

PCOPY source TO destination will copy the contents of graphics page **source** onto graphics page **destination**. Parameters **source** and **destination** may be in the range 1-8, depending on the PMODE.

COMMENTS

PDL

APPLE IIe & II+

PDL(n) returns a value related to the position of the joystick, where **n** is an integer in the range 0-225. If values other than 0, 1, 2 or 3 are used, PDL will give erratic and unpredictable results! Values of 0-3 will return a "resistance variable" for the respective paddle between 0 and 150K ohms. This value must then be interpreted to produce the desired results. This will require extensive programming changes when converting to or from other computers.

Although it can handle four paddles, the Apple can read the status of only three paddle buttons. This is accomplished with PEEK(−16287) for the value of the button on paddle 0, PEEK(−16286) for paddle 1, and PEEK(−16285) for paddle 2. If the value returned is greater than 127, then the button is being pressed.

IBM PC & PCjr

STICK(n) where **n** is an integer in the range 0-3, STICK returns the coordinates of the joysticks. STICK(0) obtains the values of both joysticks, but returns the x coordinate of joystick A. STICK(1), STICK(2) and STICK(3) do not sample the joystick, but return the coordinates retrieved by the most recent STICK(0). STICK(1) returns the y coordinate of joystick A. STICK(2) returns the x coordinate of joystick B. STICK(3) returns the y coordinate of joystick B.

STRIG ON
STRIG(n)

STRIG OFF where **n** is an integer from 0-3 in BASIC—or 0-7 in Cartridge, Advanced or Compiler BASIC—STRIG ON causes the program to begin checking the status of the joystick buttons at the beginning of execution of each program line.

n Value	Button Number	Value If Button Has Been Pressed	Value If Button Is Being Pressed	Default
0	A1	−1		0
1	A1		−1	0
2	B1	−1		0
3	B1		−1	0

The following apply to Advanced, Cartridge and Compiler BASIC only.

4	A2	−1		0
5	A2		−1	0
6	B2	−1		0
7	B2		−1	0

STRIG(n) ON
ON STRIG(n) GOSUB line
STRIG(n) STOP
STRIG(n) OFF

These commands control event trapping for the specified joystick button **n**. The value of **n** is determined by the chart below. The parameter **line**—range 1-65535—specifies a line to GOSUB to if the specified button has been pressed.

n	Button
0	A1
2	B1
4	A2
6	B2

When STRIG(n) ON has been specified and the ON STRIG(n) GOSUB **line** command is in effect, BASIC checks at the beginning of execution of each line to see if the button has been pressed. If it has, the GOSUB is executed. If not, program execution

COMMODORE 64

The Commodore 64 supports two game ports, 1 and 2. The joystick in port 1 is read by PEEKing 56321, while port 2 is read by PEEKing 56320. The number returned by the PEEK is logically ANDed with 15 to indicate the direction according to the chart below.

NW=10	North=14	NE=6
West=11	Home=15	East=7
SW=9	South=13	SE=5

To read the "fire" button, the number returned is logically ANDed with 16. If the value resulting is 16, the button is not pressed. If the value is 0, the button is pressed.

The following program lines demonstrate how to read Port 2:

```
10 FOR I=0 TO 10: READ
   D$(I): NEXT
20 DATA SE,NE,E,,SW,NW,
   W,,S,N,H,
30 F$(0)="FIRE":
   F$(1)="SAFE"
40 PRINT CHR$(147);
50 PRINT CHR$(19)D$((PEEK
   (56320)AND15)-5)
60 PRINT F$((PEEK(56320)
   AND16)/16)
70 GOTO 50
```

continues uninterrupted. STRIG(n) STOP causes trapping to cease, but the computer remembers whether the button was pressed. If so, when a STRIG(n) ON is executed, the GOSUB is executed immediately. STRIG(n) OFF causes trapping to cease, and even if the button is pressed it will not be remembered.

TRS-80 Models IV & III

Joysticks and paddles are not currently supported on TRS-80 Models IV or III, although some independent organizations have devised joysticks that work through the cassette port.

TRS-80 Color Computer

JOYSTK(n) returns a coordinate of the joystick, where **n** is an integer from 0-3. If **n**=0, it returns the horizontal coordinate of the right joystick. If **n**=1, it returns the vertical coordinate of the right joystick. If **n**=2, it returns the horizontal coordinate of the left joystick. If **n**=3, it returns the vertical coordinate of the left joystick.

The buttons of the joystick are accessed by PEEKing memory location 65280. PEEK(65280) will return 127 or 255 if no button is pressed. It will return 126 or 254 if the right button is pressed, or 125 or 253 if the left button is pressed.

COMMENTS

PEEK

APPLE IIe & II+

PEEK(m) where **m** is a valid memory location. The command will return the value of the contents of memory location **m**.

IBM PC & PCjr

PEEK(m) where **m** is a valid memory location offset from the currently DEFined SEGment. The command will return the value of the contents of memory location **m**.

COMMODORE 64

PEEK(m) where **m** is a valid memory location. The command will return the value of the contents of memory location **m**.

MEMORY-READ
It is possible to PEEK into the 1541's RAM and ROM areas by using the M-R command as follows:

```
10 OPEN 15, 8, 15
20 PRINT#15,
   "M-R"CHR$(L)CHR$(H)
30 GET#15, A$: IF A$="" THEN
   A$=A$+CHR$(0)
40 CLOSE 15
```

Here, parameters **L** and **H** are the decimal low and high bytes of the address—in hexadecimal—of the location to be read. Large amounts of data PEEKed in this way take a long time to complete.

PEN

APPLE IIe & II+

The method of interfacing with a light pen on the Apple depends on the specific supplier of the light pen. The necessary documentation and software should accompany the light pen.

IBM PC & PCjr

PEN ON
ON PEN GOSUB line
PEN STOP (Advanced, Cartridge and Compiler BASIC Only)
PEN OFF
These commands enable or disable trapping for the use of the light pen. The parameter **line**—range 1-65535—specifies a line to GOSUB if the pen has been used.

When PEN ON has been specified and the ON PEN GOSUB **line** command is in effect, BASIC checks at the beginning of execution of each line to see if the pen has been used. If it has, the GOSUB is executed. If not, then program execution continues uninterrupted. PEN STOP causes trapping to cease, but the computer remembers whether the pen was used. If so, when a PEN ON is executed, then the GOSUB is executed immediately. PEN OFF causes trapping to cease, and even if the pen is used, it will not be remembered.

Do not use cassette I/O with the pen in use.

COMMODORE 64

Though the Commodore 64 supports a light pen, there is no PEN command. Its simulation is beyond the scope of this book. Refer to the *Commodore 64 Programmer's Reference Manual,* page 348. Any commercially available light pen should come with the appropriate software to read it.

PEN(n) reads the light pen coordinates, where **n** is an integer in the range 0-9. The pen is read according to the following:

n=0 If the pen was used since the last time checked, it returns −1. Otherwise it returns 0.

n=1 Returns the most recent x coordinate where the pen was activated—range 0-319 in medium resolution, 0-639 in high resolution.

n=2 Returns the most recent y coordinate where the pen was activated—range 0-199.

TRS-80 Models IV & III

PEEK(m) where **m** is a valid memory location. The command will return the value of the contents of memory location **m**.

TRS-80 Color Computer

PEEK(m) where **m** is a valid memory location. The command will return the value of the contents of memory location **m**.

COMMENTS

TRS-80 Models IV & III

Light pens are not currently supported by Radio Shack.

TRS-80 Color Computer

Light pens are not currently supported by Radio Shack.

COMMENTS

---

n=3 Returns −1 if the pen is currently down, 0 if the pen is currently up.

n=4 Returns the most recent x coordinate of the pen—range 0-319 in medium resolution, 0-639 in high resolution.

n=5 Returns the most recent y coordinate of the pen—range 0-199.

n=6 Returns the number of the line where the pen was last activated in text mode—range 1-24.

n=7 Returns the number of the column where the pen was last activated in text mode—range 1-40 or 1-80, depending on screen WIDTH.

n=8 Returns the number of the line where the pen was last activated in text mode—range 1-24.

n=9 Returns the number of the column where the pen was last activated in text mode—range 1-40 or 1-80, depending on screen WIDTH.

PLAY

APPLE IIe & II+

Not available. Cannot be simulated without using machine-language subroutines.

IBM PC & PCjr

PLAY s1$

PLAY s1$[,[s2$][,s3$]] (Cartridge BASIC Only) plays notes, where **s1$** is a string expression specifying the note, octave, note length, tempo, volume and pause-length. Parameters **s2$** and **s3$** are similar but control voices 2 and 3 in Cartridge BASIC. Notes are specified with the letters **A** to **G**, with an optional # (sharp), + (sharp), or − (flat). Notes may also be specified with integers in the range 0-84, with 0 representing a rest. The note must actually exist on the piano keyboard.

Octaves are specified by the letter **O**, followed by a numeral from 1-7. If octave is omitted, O4 is used. You can also change octaves by using < to lower the octave and > to raise the octave.

Note lengths are specified by the letter **L**, followed by a numeral from 1-64. If note length is omitted, current note length is used. Actual note length is 1/n, where n is the length specified. Dotted notes are achieved by use of a period after the note.

Tempo is specified by the letter **T**, followed by a numeral from 32-255. If tempo is omitted, T120 is used. **MF** causes program execution to await completion of play of each note (foreground mode).

MB causes the note to be played while program execution continues (background mode). Up to 32 notes may be buffered this way. **MN** causes normal play of the notes. That is, each note plays for 7/8 of the time specified by **L**. **ML** (legato) causes each note to play the full length specified by **L**. **MS** (staccato) causes each note to play 3/4 the length specified by **L**. Pause-length is specified by the letter **P**, followed by a numeral from 1-64.

Volume (Cartridge BASIC only) is controlled by the letter **V**, followed by an integer in the range 0-15 (default=8). Volume is invalid only when a SOUND ON has been executed.

COMMODORE 64

Though the Commodore 64 supports extensive sound capabilities, there is no PLAY command. Its simulation is beyond the scope of this book. For a good discussion of generating sound from BASIC programs, see *Your Commodore 64* by Heilbron and Talbot or *How to Program Your Commodore 64* by Carl Shipman. Also, machine-language sound utilities are commercially available for this function.

You can set up a string variable with music commands and cause them to be executed with the command Xn;, where n is the name of the string. The numbers used in music commands can also be variables, if you use the form C=n;, where C is the command and n is the variable. Note that the semicolon is required, except when using MF, MB, MN, ML, or MS—in which cases it is not allowed.

Variables may also be used in the forms

```
PLAY "C"+VARPTR$(n$)
PLAY "C="+VARPTR$(n)
```

where **C** is the command and **n** is the variable specifying the string to be played or the numeric argument for the command.

PLAY(n) (BASIC 2.0 or Cartridge BASIC Only) returns the number of notes in the music background buffer, where **n** is a dummy numeric argument. This command has meaning only when the music is in the background mode—otherwise it always returns 0. The maximum number of notes that may be buffered is 32.

TRS-80 Models IV & III

Not available on the Models IV or III and cannot be simulated without machine-language subroutines and hardware modification.

TRS-80 Color Computer

PLAY s\$ plays notes, where **s\$** is a string expression specifying the note, octave, note length, tempo, volume and pause-length. Notes are specified with the letters **A** to **G**, or a numeral from 1-12. Octaves are specified by the letter **O**, followed by a numeral from 1-5. If octave is omitted, O2 is used. Note lengths are specified by the letter **L**, followed by a numeral from 1-255. If note length is omitted, the current note length is used. Tempo is specified by the letter **T**, followed by a numeral from 1-255. If tempo is omitted, T2 is used. Volume is specified by the letter **V**, followed by a numeral from 1-31. If volume is omitted, V15 is used. Pause-length is specified by the letter **P**, followed by a numeral from 1-255.

COMMENTS

Differs from SOUND in that SOUND is oriented toward absolute pitch in cycles per second (decimal). PLAY is oriented toward a piano-style note system (octal).

PLAY ON
PLAY OFF
PLAY STOP
ON PLAY (n) GOSUB (line)

These commands enable or disable trapping for the status of the music buffer. The parameter **line**—range 1-65535—specifies a line to GOSUB to if the music buffer has fewer than **n**—range 1-32—notes in it. These commands are used only when music is in the background mode.

When PLAY ON has been specified and the ON PLAY GOSUB **line** command is in effect, BASIC checks at the beginning of execution of each line to see if the music buffer has fewer notes in it than specified by the PLAY(n) statement. If it has, the GOSUB is executed. If not, then program execution continues uninterrupted. PLAY STOP causes trapping to cease, but the computer remembers whether the buffer contains fewer than **n** notes. If so, when a PLAY ON is executed, the GOSUB is executed immediately. PLAY OFF causes trapping to cease, and even if the buffer has fewer notes than **n**, it will not be remembered.

PLOT

APPLE IIe & II+

PLOT h,v places a block at the specified coordinates on the low-resolution screen, using the current low-resolution display color. Parameter **h** specifies the horizontal coordinate—range 0-39—and **v** specifies the vertical coordinate—range 0-39 with text window, 0-47 with full screen graphics.

IBM PC & PCjr

PSET (x,y)[,color] sets a point to the specified color, where **x** and **y** are valid coordinates on a graphics screen. The values available for **color** are determined by the current SCREEN. See **SCREEN**. If **color** is not specified, the point will be set to the foreground color.

DRAW "[X]n$"
DRAW "X" + VARPTR$(n$) draws the object specified by the graphics language commands in **n$**. If **n$** is a constant it must be enclosed in quotation marks, but the **X** may be omitted. The second method of using DRAW is primarily for those programs that will be compiled, but is legal syntax for interpretive programs too. For a discussion of the graphics language commands, see **DRAW**.

COMMODORE 64

Simulate it with the following routine. It will print the letter **A** at row 20, column 30. Of course, any character could be printed in place of **A**, including any graphics character.

```
10 R=20:C=30
20 POKE 783,0: POKE 781,R:
   POKE 782,C
30 SYS 65520: PRINT "A";
```

Here, parameter **R** must be in the range 0-24. Parameter **C** must be in the range 0-39. If you attempt to print in the lower-right screen corner, the screen will scroll up.

PMAP

APPLE IIe & II+

Not available. Cannot be simulated.

IBM PC & PCjr

PMAP (BASIC 2.0 and Cartridge BASIC Only) is used to translate between the world coordinate system and the physical coordinate system as defined by the VIEW and WINDOW commands. These commands cannot be simulated on other machines. See the IBM *BASIC Reference Manual*, page 4-212b or 4-275 through 4-276 in the Cartridge *BASIC Reference Manual* for complete reference to this powerful command.

COMMODORE 64

Not available. Cannot be simulated.

TRS-80 Models IV & III

PRINT @ (v,h) ,CHR$ (191); (Model IV) may be used to simulate PLOT, where **v** specifies the vertical coordinate and **h** the horizontal coordinate. This statement will place a graphics block (CHR$(191)) at the specified screen location. Parameter **v** may be in the range 0-23, and parameter **h** may be in the range 0-79. There is no way to simulate the color function of PLOT on the TRS-80.

SET (h,v) (Model III) may be used to simulate PLOT, where **h** specifies the horizontal coordinate and **v** specifies the vertical coordinate. This statement will place a graphics block at the specified screen location. Parameter **h** may be in the range 0-127, and parameter **v** may be in the range 0-47. There is no way to simulate the color function of PLOT on the TRS-80.

TRS-80 Color Computer

SET(h,v,c) may be used to simulate PLOT, where **h** specifies the horizontal coordinate, **v** specifies the vertical coordinate, and **c** specifies the color to be SET. This statement will place a graphics block at the specified screen location. Parameter **h** may be in the range 0-63. Parameter **v** may be in the range 0-31. Parameter **c** may be in the range 0-8.

COMMENTS

TRS-80 Models IV & III

Not available. Cannot be simulated.

TRS-80 Color Computer

Not available. Cannot be simulated.

COMMENTS

PMODE

APPLE IIe & II+

GR causes the Apple to display the currently specified page of the low-resolution graphic screens. If no page has been specified, page 1 is assumed. This screen will normally be 40 rows by 40 columns with the bottom 8 rows open for up to 4 lines of text. A full 48 row by 40 column screen can be obtained by following the GR statement with POKE −16302,0: CALL−1998.

HGR[2] causes the Apple to display the currently specified page of the high-resolution graphics screen. If 2 is not specified, page 1 is assumed. This screen will normally be 280 columns by 160 rows, with a window at the bottom consisting of 4 rows of text. Following the HGR statement with POKE −16302,0 will change the window to graphics, giving a full 280x192 graphics display.

IBM PC & PCjr

SCREEN [m][,[c][,a][,v]]] sets the screen attributes to be used, and may be used to simulate PMODE. Parameter m represents the SCREEN mode to be used. Default=current SCREEN mode. Possible screens follow:

SCREEN 0 is the text mode at current WIDTH (40 or 80). In Cartridge BASIC, WIDTH 80 is available only if you have 128K RAM.

SCREEN 1 is the four-color, medium-resolution graphics mode (320x200).

SCREEN 2 is the two-color, high-resolution graphics mode (640x200).

SCREEN 3 (Cartridge BASIC Only) is the 16-color, low-resolution graphics mode (160x200).

SCREEN 4 (Cartridge BASIC Only) is the four-color, medium-resolution graphics mode (320x200).

SCREEN 5 (Cartridge BASIC Only) is the 16-color, medium-resolution graphics mode (320x200). Requires 128K RAM.

SCREEN 6 (Cartridge BASIC Only) is the four-color, high-resolution graphics mode (640x200). Requires 128K RAM.

Parameter c enables or disables color. If m=0 and c=0, color is disabled. Otherwise, it is enabled. If m=1, the opposite is true. Color is enabled by c=0, but otherwise disabled. If m=2, c will have no effect. Parameters a and v may be specified only in the text mode (m=0) and have a range of 0-7 if WIDTH=40, or 0-3 if WIDTH=80. Parameter a specifies the active page, that is, the page to be affected by output statements to the screen. Default=current page. Parameter v specifies the visual page, that is, the page displayed. Default=a.

COMMODORE 64

The following program lines set the Commodore 64 into high-resolution mode with a 320 column by 200 row display screen, having two colors available. The colors are determined by parameters P and B in line 140. Parameter P represents the pixel color and B the background. Parameters P and B are in the range 0-15. For actual color values, see COLOR. In this example, the background is blue and the pixels are black.

```
100 POKE 53272,PEEK(53272)
    OR 8
110 POKE 53265,PEEK(53265)
    OR 32
120 FOR I=8192 TO 16191
130 POKE I,0: NEXT
140 P=0: B=6
150 FOR I=1024 TO 2032
160 POKE I,P * 16 + B: NEXT
```

Lines 120-130, which clear the high-resolution screen, take about 45 seconds to execute. If desired, they could be replaced by the single line:

```
120 SYS 2024
```

This line executes almost immediately. However, prior to calling this line, the following program lines are necessary:

```
10 FOR I=2024 TO 2047: READ
   A: POKE I,A: NEXT
20 DATA 169, 0, 168, 132,
   251, 162, 32, 134
30 DATA 252, 145, 251, 200,
   208, 251, 232, 224
40 DATA 64, 240, 4, 134,
   252, 208, 242, 96
```

Other high-resolution screens are available on the Commodore 64, but a discussion of them is beyond the scope of this book.

To return to low-resolution mode, use the following program lines:

```
200 POKE 53265,PEEK(53265)
    AND 223
210 POKE 53272,21
```

For more information on graphics, a good reference is *Commodore 64 Graphics & Sound Programming* by Stan Krute or *How to Program Your Commodore 64* by Carl Shipman.

TRS-80 Models IV & III

Because TRS-80 Models IV and III do not have separate graphics screens, there is no method and no need to simulate PMODE.

TRS-80 Color Computer

PMODE [m][,p] defines the graphics mode, where **m** specifies the mode—range 0-4—and **p** specifies the memory graphics page you wish to start on. Possible modes follow:

PMODE	Grid Size	Color Mode	Pages Required
0	128x96	Two color	1
1	128x96	Four color	2
2	128x192	Two color	2
3	128x192	Four color	4
4	256x192	Two color	4

If **m** is omitted, the most recently assigned value is used. If PMODE has not been previously used, parameter **m** defaults to 2. If **p** is omitted, the most recent value is used. If PMODE has not been previously used, parameter **p** defaults to 1.

COMMENTS

The ranges available for **a** and **v** are in the table below:

m Value	WIDTH Value	Range For a And v
0	40	0-7
0	80	0-3
1*		Not available
2*		Not available
1-6**		Depends on RAM

* Other than Cartridge BASIC
**Cartridge BASIC

If all parameters are valid, the screen is erased, the new mode takes effect, the background and border are set to black, and the foreground is set to white. Don't forget to reset the COLOR after using SCREEN.

POINT

APPLE IIe & II+

SCRN (**h,v**) where **h** specifies a horizontal coordinate and **v** specifies a vertical coordinate. SCRN returns a code for the color currently displayed at the specified coordinates on the low-resolution screen. If the specified coordinate is black—unlit—then a zero is returned. This allows SCRN to effectively simulate POINT.

IBM PC & PCjr

POINT(h,v) returns the color number of the specified point on the screen, where parameters **h** and **v** specify legal absolute horizontal and vertical coordinates. This command will return a value of −1 if the specified coordinates are out of range. The range of color numbers returned depends on the current SCREEN. See **COLOR** for a list of valid color numbers that may be used.

POINT(n) (BASIC 2.0 and Cartridge BASIC Only) returns the value of the current x and y coordinates on the graphics screen. Parameter **n** may have a value of 0-3, where **n**=0 returns the current physical x coordinate and **n**=1 returns the current physical y coordinate. If WINDOW is active, **n**=2 will return the current world x coordinate and **n**=3 will return the current world y coordinate. If WINDOW is not active and parameter **n** has a value of 2 or 3, the value returned will be the same as values returned for **n**=0 and **n**=1.

COMMODORE 64

Different models of the Commodore 64 deal with the color screen in various ways due to different graphics chips that Commodore has installed in their machines from time to time. Therefore, no attempt will be made here to simulate POINT on the Commodore.

POKE

APPLE IIe & II+

POKE (m,n) where **m** specifies a legal memory location, and **n** specifies a value—range 0-255. POKE will store the specified value into the specified memory location.

IBM PC & PCjr

POKE m,n where **m** specifies a legal memory location offset from the currently DEFined SEGment, and **n** specifies a value—range 0-255. POKE will store the specified value into the specified memory location.

COMMODORE 64

POKE m,n where **m** specifies a legal memory location, and **n** specifies a value—range 0-255. POKE will store the specified value into the specified memory location.

MEMORY-WRITE

It's possible to POKE to the 1541 disk drive's RAM area using the M-W command as follows:

```
10 OPEN 15, 8, 15
20 PRINT#15, "M-W"CHR$(L)
   CHR$(H)CHR$(N)X$
30 CLOSE 15
```

Variables **L** and **H** are the decimal low and high bytes of the start address—in hex—of the code. **N** is the length of the code—range 1-34, and **X$** is the code concatenated as CHR$ strings. For example, if the three bytes $FF, $09, and $10 were to be placed in the 1541 Disk Drive's RAM at $0500, then **L**=0, **H**=5, **N**=3 and **X$**=CHR$(255)+CHR$(9)+CHR$(16).

TRS-80 Models IV & III

POINT (h,v) where **h** specifies a horizontal coordinate and **v** specifies a vertical coordinate. POINT returns a True (−1) if the specified coordinate is "lit," or a False (0) if the specified coordinate is not lit. Parameter **h** may have a range of 0-127, and parameter **v** may have a range of 0-47.

TRS-80 Color Computer

POINT (h,v) where **h** specifies a horizontal coordinate and **v** specifies a vertical coordinate. POINT returns a −1 if the specified coordinate is a text character, 0 if the coordinate is not "lit," or the color code (1-8) if the coordinate is "lit." Parameter **h** may have a range of 0-63. Parameter **v** may have a range of 0-31.

COMMENTS

TRS-80 Models IV & III

POKE m,n where **m** specifies a legal memory location, and **n** specifies a value—range 0-255. POKE will store the specified value into the specified memory location.

TRS-80 Color Computer

POKE m,n where **m** specifies a legal memory location, and **n** specifies a value—range 0-255. POKE will store the specified value into the specified memory location.

COMMENTS

POP

APPLE IIe & II+

POP causes the most recent return address to be deleted from the top of the return-address stack. Therefore, the previous return address will be used when a RETURN is encountered. POP is used as a way of modifying program branching. Some experts consider this poor programming practice.

IBM PC & PCjr

Because POP is considered poor programming practice, you should try to modify the program so that this instruction is not necessary. However, if you wish to simulate POP, you can use a variable flag to control the branching, as follows:

```
 10 GOSUB 100
 20 REM THE PROGRAM
    EVENTUALLY RETURNS HERE
100 REM THIS LINE BEGINS
    FIRST SUBROUTINE
110 GOSUB 200
120 IF X=1 THEN 140
130 REM MORE PROGRAM LINES GO
    HERE . . .
140 RETURN
200 REM THIS LINE BEGINS
    SECOND SUBROUTINE
210 X=1 : RETURN
```

Variable flag **X** in line 120 causes the code in line 130 to be ignored. Therefore, the **X**=1 in line 210 takes the place of POP.

COMMODORE 64

Because POP is considered poor programming practice, you should try to modify the program so that this instruction is not necessary. However, if you wish to simulate POP, you can use a variable flag to control the branching, as follows:

```
 10 GOSUB 100
 20 REM THE PROGRAM
    EVENTUALLY RETURNS HERE
100 REM THIS LINE BEGINS
    FIRST SUBROUTINE
110 GOSUB 200
120 IF X=1 THEN 140
130 REM MORE PROGRAM LINES GO
    HERE . . .
140 RETURN
200 REM THIS LINE BEGINS
    SECOND SUBROUTINE
210 X=1 : RETURN
```

Variable flag **X** in line 120 causes the code in line 130 to be ignored. Therefore, the **X**=1 in line 210 takes the place of POP.

POS

APPLE IIe & II+

POS(n) where **n** is a dummy value. POS(n) returns the current horizontal cursor position. Range is 0-39 if in 40-column mode, 0-79 if in 80-column mode.

IBM PC & PCjr

POS(n) where **n** is a dummy value. POS(n) returns the current horizontal cursor position. Range is 1-40 if in 40-column mode, 1-80 if in 80-column mode.

COMMODORE 64

POS(n) where **n** is a dummy value. POS(n) returns the current horizontal cursor position. Range is 0-39.

POSN

is an undocumented reserved word on TRS-80 Model III.

PPOINT

APPLE IIe & II+

SCRN (x,y) returns the color code for the cell at **(x,y)**, where **x** is a column number and **y** is a row number in the medium-resolution mode. SCRN is not meant for use in high-resolution mode.

IBM PC & PCjr

POINT(x,y) returns the color number of the specified point on the screen, where parameters **x** and **y** specify legal absolute horizontal and vertical coordinates. This command will return a value of −1 if the specified coordinates are out of range. The range of color numbers returned depends on the current SCREEN. See **COLOR** for a list of valid color numbers that may be used.

POINT(n) (DOS 2.0 and Cartridge

COMMODORE 64

Different models of the Commodore deal with the color screen in various ways because of the different chips installed in various production series. Therefore, no attempt will be made here to simulate POINT on the Commodore.

BASIC Only) returns the value of the current x and y coordinates on the graphics screen. Parameter **n** may have a value of 0-3, where **n**=0 re-

TRS-80 Models IV & III

Because POP is considered poor programming practice, you should try to modify the program so that this instruction is not necessary. However, if you wish to simulate POP, you can use a variable flag to control the branching, as follows:

```
 10 GOSUB 100
 20 REM THE PROGRAM
    EVENTUALLY RETURNS HERE
100 REM THIS LINE BEGINS
    FIRST SUBROUTINE
110 GOSUB 200
120 IF X=1 THEN 140
130 REM MORE PROGRAM LINES GO
    HERE...
140 RETURN
200 REM THIS LINE BEGINS
    SECOND SUBROUTINE
210 X=1: RETURN
```

Variable flag **X** in line 120 causes the code in line 130 to be ignored. Therefore, the **X**=1 in line 210 takes the place of POP.

TRS-80 Color Computer

Because POP is considered poor programming practice, you should try to modify the program so that this instruction is not necessary. However, if you wish to simulate POP, you can use a variable flag to control the branching, as follows:

```
 10 GOSUB 100
 20 REM THE PROGRAM
    EVENTUALLY RETURNS HERE
100 REM THIS LINE BEGINS
    FIRST SUBROUTINE
110 GOSUB 200
120 IF X=1 THEN 140
130 REM MORE PROGRAM LINES GO
    HERE...
140 RETURN
200 REM THIS LINE BEGINS
    SECOND SUBROUTINE
210 X=1: RETURN
```

Variable flag **X** in line 120 causes the code in line 130 to be ignored. Therefore, the **X**=1 in line 210 takes the place of POP.

COMMENTS

TRS-80 Models IV & III

POS(n) where **n** is a dummy value. POS(n) returns the current horizontal cursor position. Range is 1-80.

TRS-80 Color Computer

POS(−2) returns the current horizontal print head position on the printer.

POS(0) returns the current horizontal cursor position on the display.

COMMENTS

TRS-80 Models IV & III

POINT (x,y) tests whether a cell is on or off, where **x** and **y** are legal screen coordinates. It returns True (−1) if the cell is on, False (0) if the cell is off.

turns the current physical x coordinate and **n**=1 returns the current physical y coordinate. If WINDOW is active, **n**=2 will return the current world x coordinate and **n**=3 will return the

TRS-80 Color Computer

PPOINT (x,y) tests whether or not a screen cell is on or off, where **x** and **y** are screen coordinates. PPOINT returns the color of the specified cell if it is on. See **COLOR** for a list of the numeric values for colors.

current world y coordinate. If WINDOW is not active and parameter **n** has a value of 2 or 3, the value returned will be the same as values returned for **n**=0 and **n**=1.

COMMENTS

PR#

APPLE IIe & II +

PR# n where **n** specifies a slot number—range 1-7. PR# directs subsequent output to the specified slot. When used in a BASIC program, PR# must follow a PRINT statement and must be preceded by CONTROL-D. Common usage of PR# includes sending output to the printer (normally PR#1), "booting" the disk (normally PR#6) and returning output to the screen (PR#0).

IBM PC & PCjr

Because all output statements include a device or file buffer number, PR# is not used on the PC. For example, PRINT# can be used to direct output to any device that has been OPENed with a buffer number. You can also send output to the printer with LPRINT.

COMMODORE 64

CMDn redirects output to file number **n**—range 1-255. File number **n** and the device must have been previously OPENed. CMDn is deactivated by PRINT#n and is normally used to redirect output to the printer—device 4.

PRESET

APPLE IIe & II +

Simulate it by using COLOR or HCOLOR—depending on the resolution mode you are using—to set the current foreground color to the background color. Then use PLOT(x,y) or HPLOT(x,y) to set the point to that color. Don't forget to change the foreground color back to its previous value!

IBM PC & PCjr

PRESET (x,y)[,color] sets a point to the specified color, where **x** and **y** are valid coordinates on a graphics screen. See **COLOR** for a list of valid **color** numbers for each SCREEN mode. If **color** is not specified, the point will be set to the background color. In Cartridge BASIC, **color** will be the attribute—not necessarily the specific color. See **PALETTE**.

COMMODORE 64

Simulate it with the routines under COLOR, PLOT and HPLOT.

TRS-80 Models IV & III

Because all output statements include a device or file buffer number, PR# is not used on the Model IV. For example, PRINT# can be used to direct output to any device that has been OPENed with a buffer number. You can also send output to the printer with LPRINT.

Because the Model III does not use slots, you cannot specify slot numbers. The same functions are usually accomplished with reserved words, such as LPRINT or LLIST (output to the printer), PRINT or LIST (output to the screen).

TRS-80 Color Computer

Because all output statements include a device or file buffer number, PR# is not used on the COCO. For example, PRINT# can be used to direct output to any device that has been OPENed with a buffer number. You can also send output to the printer with LPRINT.

COMMENTS

TRS-80 Models IV & III

RESET (x,y) will turn off, or **reset**, a graphics block specified by coordinates **x** and **y**. Range for parameter **x** is 0-127. Range for parameter **y** is 0-57.

TRS-80 Color Computer

PRESET (x,y) will turn off a graphics point, where **x** and **y** specify valid coordinates of a graphics point to be reset to the background color.

COMMENTS

PRINT, PRINT USING

APPLE IIe & II+

PRINT list will print the specified list, where **list** is a list of expressions to be written to the current output device. Items in **list** are separated by semicolons or commas. String-literal items must be enclosed within double quotation marks.

Apple lacks the extensive formatting capabilities of PRINT USING. These capabilities are not easily simulated and are beyond the scope of this book. As a starter, you might consider converting any numeric expressions into string expressions with STR$ and operating on them with LEFT$, RIGHT$ and the other string-handling commands. You can then PRINT them in the format you desire.

For formatting dollars and cents, you can use the following subroutine. **AMT** is the actual figure you wish converted into dollars and cents. This routine will prevent you from getting values returned in fractional cents, will force zeros to be added after the decimal so you don't get such things as $10.9, and will right-justify the amounts to give you neat columns.

```
1000 AMT=100*(AMT+.005):
     AMT=INT(AMT)
1010 PRINT "$";
     SPC((AMT<100000)
     +(AMT<10000)+(AMT<
     1000));AMT/100;
1020 IF INT(AMT-INT(AMT/100)
     *100)=0 THEN PRINT
     ".00";:GOTO 1040
1030 IF INT(AMT-INT(AMT/10)
     *10)=0 THEN PRINT "0";
1040 AMT=AMT/100:PRINT:
     RETURN
```

IBM PC & PCjr

PRINT list will print the specified list, where **list** is a list of expressions to be written to the current output device. Items in **list** are separated by blank spaces, semicolons or commas. String-literal items must be enclosed within double quotation marks.

PRINT USING v$; list will print the specified list, where **v$** is a string constant or variable that contains special formatting characters. **List** is a list of expressions to be PRINTed. This command formats the printed output in specific ways, depending upon the contents of v$. Detailed explanation of the formatting characters is beyond the scope of this book. Refer to the *BASIC Reference Manual*, pages 4-219 through 4-223 or to the Cartridge *BASIC Reference Manual*, pages 4-286 through 4-291.

COMMODORE 64

PRINT list will print the specified list, where **list** is a list of expressions to be written to the current output device. Items in **list** are separated by semicolons or commas. String-literal items must be enclosed within double quotation marks.

The Commodore 64 lacks the extensive formatting capabilities of PRINT USING. These capabilities are not easily simulated and are beyond the scope of this book. As a starter, you might consider converting any numeric expressions into string expressions with STR$ and operating on them with LEFT$ RIGHT$, and the other string-handling commands. You can then print them out in the format desired.

PRINT@

APPLE IIe & II+

To simulate PRINT@, use

```
10 HTAB x: VTAB y: PRINT list
```

where **x** is the horizontal coordinate—range 1-40—and **y** is the vertical coordinate—range 1-24—of the position to start PRINTing. **List** is the list of items to PRINT.

IBM PC & PCjr

To simulate PRINT@, use

```
10 LOCATE (x,y):PRINT list
```

where **x** and **y** are valid screen coordinates. **List** is the list of items to be printed starting at **(x,y)**.

COMMODORE 64

Although there is no PRINT@ command on the Commodore 64, the following program lines produce a similar effect:

```
100 RO=10: COL=4:
    MSG$="HELLO"
110 POKE 783,0: POKE 781,RO:
    POKE 782,COL
120 SYS 65520: PRINT MSG$
```

This will print the contents of **MSG$** on line **RO** starting at position **COL**.

TRS-80 Models IV & III

PRINT list will print the specified list, where **list** is a list of expressions to be written to the current output device. Items in **list** are separated by semicolons or commas. String-literal items must be enclosed within double quotation marks.

PRINT USING v$; list will print the specified list using the specified format, where **v$** is a string constant or variable containing special formatting characters. **List** is a list of expressions. This command formats the printed output in specific ways depending upon the contents of **v$**. Detailed explanation of the formatting characters is beyond the scope of this book. Refer to the *Operation and BASIC Language Reference Manual,* pages 136 through 140 for the Model III, and to *Disk System Owners Manual,* pages 2-150 through 2-153 for the Model IV.

TRS-80 Color Computer

PRINT list will print the specified list, where **list** is a list of expressions to be written to the current output device. Items in **list** are separated by semicolons or commas. String-literal items must be enclosed within double quotation marks.

PRINT USING v$; list will print the specified list using the specified format, where **v$** is a string constant or variable that contains special formatting characters. **List** is a list of expressions to be PRINTed. This command formats the printed output in specific ways, depending on the contents of **v$**. Detailed explanation of the formatting characters is beyond the scope of this book. Refer to *Going Ahead With Extended Color BASIC,* pages 129 through 132.

COMMENTS

TRS-80 Models IV & III

PRINT @ n, list will print the specified list at the specified screen location, where **n** specifies a location, range 0-1919 (Model IV), or range 0-1023 (Model III). **List** is a list of expressions to be PRINTed.

PRINT @ (r,c), list (Model IV) will print the specified list at the specified location, where **r** specifies the row—range 0-23—and **c** specifies the

TRS-80 Color Computer

PRINT @ n, list will print the specified list at the specified location, where **n** specifies a location in the range 0-511. **List** is a list of expressions to be PRINTed.

column—range 0-79. **List** is a list of expressions to be PRINTed.

COMMENTS

PRINT#, PRINT# USING

APPLE IIe & II+

Because of the way it handles files, Apple does not use PRINT#. When you have used a line such as

```
10 PRINT CHR$(4);"WRITE
   filename"
```

all subsequent PRINT statements will PRINT to the file **filename**. Of course, **filename** must have been previously OPENed for output.

For a method of formatting output similar to PRINT# USING, see **PRINT USING**.

IBM PC & PCjr

PRINT# n, list outputs data to a sequential file, where **n** is the number used to OPEN the file. **List** is a list of expressions to be written to the file. The expressions may be constants or variables, string or numeric. The expressions must be delimited by semicolons or commas. This causes embedded spaces to be printed to the file, just as it would on the screen with a PRINT command. If the items are to be delimited by quotation marks, you must specifically PRINT CHR$(34) to the file. If the items contain embedded spaces, commas, colons or semicolons, you must also delimit them by PRINTing CHR$(34) on each side of the string. You can avoid some of the problems associated with delimiters by using WRITE# instead of PRINT# if your application will allow it.

PRINT# n USING v$; list where **n** is the number used when the file was OPENed, **v$** is a string constant or variable containing special formatting characters, and **list** is a list of expressions to be PRINTed to a sequential file. This command formats the output in specific ways, depending on the contents of **v$**. Detailed explanation of the formatting characters is beyond the scope of this book. Refer to the *BASIC Reference Manual,* pages 4-219 through 4-223, or Cartridge *BASIC Reference Manual,* 4-292 through 4-294.

COMMODORE 64

PRINT#n,list outputs data to a sequential file or device, where **n** is the file number used to OPEN the device. **List** is a list of expressions to be written to it. The expressions may be constants or variables, string or numeric. The expressions must be delimited by semicolons or commas. This will cause embedded spaces to be printed to the file, just as it would be on the screen with a PRINT command. If the items contain embedded spaces, commas, colons, semicolons or screen editing characters, you must enclose each of them in quotation marks. If quotation marks themselves are to be sent, they should be represented by CHR$(34). Devices that can be written to in this way include any storage device, the printer, screen or modem. Also see **OPEN**.

PRINT# works exactly like PRINT. The only difference is that the information in the list gets printed to the sequential file or device specified in the OPEN command, rather than to the monitor. No spaces are permitted between PRINT and #. For example, to write the variable **NUM$** to the file named **PRACTICE**:

```
100 OPEN 1,8,2,
    "0:PRACTICE, S,W"
110 PRINT#1, NUM$;CHR$(13);
```

The **;CHR$(13);** is absolutely necessary to make sure that only a carriage return is placed at the end of the line. Without this coding, a return and a linefeed are written at the end of the line. This can cause problems on the subsequent input of this data from the disk file.

To send a command to the disk, you must access the command channel #15, like this:

```
100 OPEN 15,8,15
110 PRINT#15,"disk command"
```

For a description of possible **disk commands** see **INITIALIZE, VALIDATE, SCRATCH, COPY, RENAME** and **NEW**.

To create a relative file that will contain **NR** records of **LN** length, you would use the following program lines. Parameter **n** is the file number.

TRS-80 Models IV & III

PRINT# n, list outputs data to a sequential file, where **n** is the number used to OPEN the file. **List** is a list of expressions to be written to the file. The expressions may be constants or variables, string or numeric. The expressions must be delimited by semicolons or commas. This will cause embedded spaces to be printed to the file, just as it would on the screen with a PRINT command. If the items are to be delimited by quotation marks, you must specifically PRINT CHR$(34) to the file. If the items contain embedded spaces, commas, colons or semicolons, you must also delimit them by PRINTing CHR$(34) on each side of the string. On the Model IV, you can avoid some of the problems associated with delimiters by using WRITE# instead of PRINT# if your application will allow it.

PRINT# n USING v$; list where **n** is the number used when the file was OPENed, **v$** is a string constant or variable containing special formatting characters, and **list** is a list of expressions to be PRINTed to a sequential file. This command formats the output in specific ways, depending on the contents of **v$**.

Detailed explanation of the formatting characters is beyond the scope of this book. Refer to the *Operation and BASIC Language Reference Manual,* pages 136 through 140 for the Model III, and to *Disk System Owners Manual,* pages 2-150 through 2-153 for the Model IV.

CH is the channel (secondary address) you wish to use. See **OPEN**.

```
100 OPEN 15,8,15
110 OPEN n,8,CH,
    "0:filename,L,"+
    CHR$(LN)
120 PRINT#15,"P"CHR$(CH)CH
    R$(NR)CHR$(0)
130 PRINT#n,CHR$(255);
    CHR$(13);
140 CLOSEn
```

TRS-80 Color Computer

PRINT# n, list outputs data to a sequential file, where **n** is the number that was used to OPEN the file, and **list** is a list of expressions to be written to the file. The expressions may be constants or variables, string or numeric. The expressions must be delimited by semicolons or commas. This will cause embedded spaces to be printed to the file, just as it would on the screen with a PRINT command. If the items are to be delimited by quotation marks, you must specifically PRINT CHR$(34) to the file. If the items contain embedded spaces, commas, colons or semicolons, you must also delimit them by PRINTing CHR$(34) on each side of the string.

PRINT# n USING v$; list where **n** is the number used when the file was OPENed, **v$** is a string constant or variable containing special formatting characters, and **list** is a list of expressions to be PRINTed to a sequential file. This command formats the output in specific ways, depending on the contents of **v$**.

Detailed explanation of the formatting characters is beyond the scope of this book. Refer to *Going Ahead With Extended Color BASIC,* pages 129 through 132.

To access a relative file, use the following:

```
100 OPEN 15,8,15
110 OPEN n,8,CH,"relative
    file"
120 R1=NR: R2=0: IF R1>255
    THEN R2=INT(R1/256):
    R1=R1-256*R1
130 PRINT#15,
    "P"CHR$(CH)CHR$
    (R1)CHR$(R2)CHR$(P)
```

COMMENTS

"P" indicates that you wish to position the pointer. The **CH** must be the same as in the OPEN command. **R1** and **R2** are the high- and low-byte addresses for the record number you are using (**RN**). And parameter **P** is the exact position within the record you are interested in accessing.

After accessing a record within a relative file in the manner shown, you can either input data from the file—see **INPUT#**—or write data to the record of interest by using PRINT#. Within the record you are writing, all data is lost to the right of where you are writing new data. To write to the middle of a record and preserve all data to the right of your position, you must first input and save each field in the record starting with the one you wish to change. Then rewrite these fields back to the record, including any changes you wish to make.

PRINT#n is also used as the opposite of CMDn, before closing the previously OPENed file **n**. See **CMD**. For further details on Commodore file I/O, see **OPEN**.

PSET

APPLE IIe & II+

Simulate it by using COLOR or HCOLOR to set the desired foreground color. Then use PLOT(x,y) or HPLOT(x,y) to set the point.

IBM PC & PCjr

PSET (x,y)[,color] sets a point to the specified color, where **x** and **y** are valid coordinates on a graphics screen. See **COLOR** for a list of valid **color** numbers for each **SCREEN** mode. In Cartridge BASIC, **color** will be the attribute—not necessarily the specific color. See **PALETTE**. If **color** is not specified, the point will be set to the foreground color.

COMMODORE 64

Simulate it by using the subroutine at HGR to set the desired background and pixel colors, and the subroutine listed under HPLOT to set the desired point.

PUT

APPLE IIe & II+

Applesoft BASIC does not recognize a PUT command because it writes directly to the disk file instead of to a buffer. For random access file handling, records are PRINTed under the auspices of OPEN and WRITE. See **OPEN** and **WRITE**.

IBM PC & PCjr

PUT [#] n [,r] (File Handling) writes a record from a random buffer to a file, where **n** is the number used when the file was OPENed, and **r** is the record number to be written to. If parameter **r** is omitted, the record goes into the next available record. If **n** refers to a COM file, **r** is the number of bytes to write. The record must have been previously placed into the buffer with PRINT#, PRINT# USING, WRITE#, LSET or RSET. Use of this command in Cartridge BASIC requires the presence of DOS 2.1.

PUT (x,y), array [,action] (Graphics) is the opposite of the graphics usage of GET, in that it converts information from array into screen display with **(x,y)** being the upper-left corner of the resulting display. The action taken with the data from the array can take five forms. These operators are actually operating on the binary representation of the value of the colors on the screen versus the colors in the array.

XOR, the default action, is used for animation. It causes screen points to be inverted where a point exists in the array image. If an array is PUT to the same location a second time, the previous background is restored unchanged.

PSET takes the data from the array and puts it directly onto the screen—the exact opposite of GET. PRESET causes a negative image of

COMMODORE 64

The Commodore 64 does not recognize a PUT command because it writes directly to the disk file instead of to a buffer. For random access file handling, records are PRINTed under the auspices of OPEN and PRINT#. See **OPEN** and **PRINT#**.

To simulate the graphics usage of PUT, you can use sprites. A discussion of sprites is beyond the scope of this book. Refer to the *Commodore 64 Programmer's Reference Guide,* pages 139 to 182, or *How to Program Your Commodore 64* by Carl Shipman.

the data in the array to be PUT on the screen. AND is used to set a point only if the point is already set on the screen. OR superimposes the image onto the existing image.

TRS-80 Models IV & III

SET (x,y) turns on a screen point, where **x** and **y** specify the coordinates of a graphics block to be set, or turned on. Range for parameter **x** is 0-127, and range for parameter **y** is 0-57.

TRS-80 Color Computer

PSET (x,y) turns on a screen point, where **x** and **y** specify valid coordinates of a graphics point to be set to the foreground color.

COMMENTS

TRS-80 Models IV & III

PUT n [,r] (File Handling) moves data from a buffer to a file, where **n** specifies a buffer number that has been OPENed. See **OPEN**. Parameter **r** specifies the record number to be added to an OPEN random file—range 1-65535. Parameter **r** is optional. Default is the next record. If **r** is greater than the end of file, then the new end of file will be equal to parameter **r**.

The graphics usage of PUT cannot be simulated on the Model IV or Model III.

TRS-80 Color Computer

PUT#n [,r] (File Handling) moves data from a buffer to a file, where **n** specifies a buffer number that has been OPENed. See **OPEN**. Parameter **r** specifies the record number to be added to an OPEN random file. Parameter **r** is optional. Default is the next record. If **r** is greater than the end of file, then the new end of file will be equal to parameter **r**.

PUT (x1,y1)-(x2,y2),source,action is the opposite of the graphics usage of GET, in that it converts information from array into screen display with **(x1,y1)** being the upper-left corner of the resulting display. Parameter **(x1,y1)** specifies the starting point and **(x2,y2)** specifies the ending point. **Source** specifies an array containing the graphics data to be displayed. Parameter **action** specifies how the array will be displayed. **Action** may take five forms: PSET sets the points contained in the array. PRESET resets the points contained in the array. AND performs a bitwise comparison of the points in the array and the points on the screen. Any point set in both will be set on the final screen. OR performs a bitwise comparison (like AND) and sets any points on the final screen that exist in either the array or the original screen. NOT reverses the state of each point in the original screen, regardless of the array contents.

COMMENTS

RANDOM, RANDOMIZE

APPLE IIe & II+

RND(n) reseeds the random number generator, where **n** is any negative integer. The new random sequence will be different from that generated by power-up, but the same seeds will generate the same sequences each time the program runs.

IBM PC & PCjr

RANDOMIZE reseeds the random number generator. When this command is used, the program will prompt for a random number seed. If you do not wish the program to stop and prompt for a number, you can include the TIMER command. It will then get its seed from the current value of the timer. To use TIMER with Cartridge BASIC, have DOS 2.1 present. Example:

```
10 RANDOMIZE TIMER
```

COMMODORE 64

RND(n) reseeds the random number generator, where **n** is any negative number. The new random sequence will be different from that generated by power-up, but the same seeds will generate the same sequences. To reseed the random number generator in a random manner, use RND(-TI). It uses the current timer value as the seed.

READ

APPLE IIe & II+

READ n1[,n2...] reads data from DATA statements in the program and assigns the values to the variables **n1, n2,...** READ is always used in conjunction with a DATA statement. The variables may be string or numeric, but the data read must agree in type with the variable name. Subsequent READ statements read the next data item following the one most recently read. Trying to READ more data than is contained in the DATA statements will produce an error condition.

IBM PC & PCjr

Same.

COMMODORE 64

Same.

RECALL

APPLE IIe & II+

RECALL n reads values from the cassette into array **n**.

IBM PC & PCjr

INPUT#b,n(1)[,n(2)...] may be used to simulate RECALL, where **b** is the buffer number used to OPEN the data file, and **n(1), n(2)...** specify the array elements to be input.

COMMODORE 64

INPUT# b, n(1)[,n(2)]... inputs data **n1, n2...** from a sequential file, where **b** is the number used to open the file. For more details on its use and limitations, see **INPUT#**.

TRS-80 Models IV & III

RANDOM will reseed the random number generator, so that each run will produce a different series of random numbers.

TRS-80 Color Computer

RND(n) reseeds the random number generator, where **n** is any negative integer. The new random sequence will be different from that generated by power-up, but the same seeds will generate the same sequences each time the program runs.

COMMENTS

TRS-80 Models IV & III

Same.

TRS-80 Color Computer

Same.

COMMENTS

TRS-80 Models IV & III

Model IV does not support cassette tapes, so RECALL cannot be simulated for cassette input. To input data from disk, use

```
INPUT#b,n(1)[,n(2)...]
```

Parameter **b** is the buffer number used to OPEN the data file, and **n(1), n(2)...** specify the array elements to be input.

INPUT #−1,n(1)[,n(2)...] causes the Model III to turn on the tape player and input the variables specified into the array. Notice the minus sign between # and 1. This specifies cassette tape. The command **INPUT #1 ,n(1)[,n(2)...]** (without the minus sign) specifies disk input from the file OPENed as #1.

TRS-80 Color Computer

INPUT #−1,n(1)[,n(2)...] causes the COCO to turn on the tape player and input the variables specified into the array. Notice the minus sign between # and 1. This specifies cassette tape. The command **INPUT #1 ,n(1)[,n(2)...]** (without the minus sign) specifies disk input from the file OPENed as #1.

COMMENTS

RECORD#n, RN, P is a reserved word not available on the Commodore 64 unless it is using BASIC 4.0. It is very unlikely that you will encounter it. In BASIC 4.0, this command looks at position **P** in record **RN** in the previously opened file **n**. Using a file # different from that used in the OPEN command causes a FILE NOT OPEN ERROR. If position **P** is not specified, then position 1 is assumed. If parameter **n**, **RN** or **P** is determined by a loop, then that variable must be enclosed within parentheses.

REM

APPLE IIe & II+

REM specifies that the data following the REM is not executable code.

IBM PC & PCjr

REM specifies that the data following the REM is not executable code. REM may be abbreviated with a single quotation mark (').

COMMODORE 64

REM specifies that the data following the REM is not executable code.

RENAME

APPLE IIe & II+

PRINT CHR$(4);" RENAME a, b[,s] [,d] [,v]" where **a** and **b** are valid filenames. RENAME causes file **a** to be renamed **b**. Parameters **s**, **d** and **v** are optional, where parameter **s** specifies the slot number, **d** specifies the drive number, and **v** specifies the volume number.

IBM PC & PCjr

NAME "a" AS "b" where **a** and **b** are valid filenames. NAME causes file **a** to be renamed **b**. Quotation marks are necessary only if **a** and **b** are literal names rather than string variables. If **a** is not on the specified disk, or if **b** is already on the disk, you will get an error. NAME does not change the contents of the file. Use of this command in Cartridge BASIC will result in an ILLEGAL FUNCTION CALL if DOS 2.1 is not present.

COMMODORE 64

10 OPEN 15,8,15, "R0:a=b" where **a** and **b** are valid filenames. This routine causes file **b** to be renamed **a**. Notice that this syntax is the opposite of other computers!

TRS-80 Models IV & III

REM specifies that the data following the REM is not executable code. REM may be abbreviated with a single quotation mark (').

TRS-80 Color Computer

REM specifies that the data following the REM is not executable code. REM may be abbreviated with a single quotation mark (').

COMMENTS

TRS-80 Models IV & III

NAME "a" AS "b" (Model IV) where **a** and **b** are valid filenames. NAME causes file **a** to be renamed **b**. Quotation marks are necessary only if **a** and **b** are literal names rather than string variables. If **a** is not on the specified disk, or if **b** is already on the disk, you will get an error. The new name **b** cannot contain a password or drive specification. NAME does not change the contents of the file.

A file cannot be easily renamed from within a BASIC program on the Model III. You can use

    10 CMD "I", "RENAME a b"

It will rename file **a** to **b**, but will return you to the operating system. Another alternative will not return the program to the DOS level, but will work only on ASCII files: Read the file into memory, write it out with a new file name, then kill the old file. The following routine will accomplish this. Note that the CLEAR command in line 10 should appear at the beginning of the program. Lines 1000 and 1010 require operator input. You can modify them to suit your needs.

```
  10 CLEAR 10000
1000 CLS:LINE INPUT "OLD FILE
     NAME: ";F1$
1010 LINE INPUT "NEW FILE
     NAME: ";F2$
1020 OPEN "I",1,F1$
1030 OPEN "O",2,F2$
1040 IF EOF(1) THEN 1060
1050 LINE INPUT #1,T$: PRINT
     #2,T$: GOTO 1040
1060 CLOSE: KILL F1$
```

TRS-80 Color Computer

RENAME "a" TO "b" where **a** and **b** are valid filenames. RENAME causes file **a** to be renamed **b**. Quotation marks are necessary only if **a** and **b** are literal names rather than string variables. If file **a** is not on the specified disk, or if **b** is already on the disk, you will get an error. If a drive specifier is not used for file **a**, BASIC will search drive 0 only. RENAME does not change the contents of the file.

COMMENTS

Notice that NAME is sometimes used for renaming files, but on the TRS-80 Model III it is used for renumbering program lines.

RENUM

APPLE IIe & II+

You cannot renumber a BASIC program from within itself on the Apple.

IBM PC & PCjr

RENUM [newline] [,[startline] [,increment]] renumbers the program, where **newline** will be the first line number of the renumbered sequence; default=10. **Startline** is the current number of the first line to be renumbered—default=first program line. **Increment** is the increment to be used in renumbering; default=10. If you specify **startline**, you must specify **newline**. Renumbering continues from **startline** to the end of the program. RENUM also adjusts all GOTOs, GOSUBs and other commands that include line references. Program execution halts when RENUM has been completed. You must type RUN to start the program again.

COMMODORE 64

You cannot renumber a BASIC program from within itself on the Commodore 64.

TRS-80 Models IV & III

RENUM [newline] [,[startline] [,increment]] (Model IV) renumbers the program, where **newline** will be the first line number of the renumbered sequence; default=10. **Startline** is the current number of the first line to be renumbered—default=first program line. **Increment** is the increment to be used in renumbering; default=10. If you specify **startline**, you must specify **newline**. Renumbering continues from **startline** to the end of the program. RENUM also adjusts all GOTOs, GOSUBs and other commands that include line references. Program execution halts when RENUM has been completed. You must type RUN to start the program again.

NAME [newline] [,[startline] [,increment]] (Model III) renumbers the program, where **newline** will be the first line number of the renumbered sequence—default=10. **Startline** is the current number of the first line to be renumbered—default=first program line. **Increment** is the increment to be used in renumbering; default=10. If you specify **startline**, you must specify **newline**. Renumbering continues from **startline** to the end of the program. NAME also corrects all GOTOs, GOSUBs and other commands that include line references. Program execution halts when the operation has been completed. You must type RUN to start the program again.

TRS-80 Color Computer

RENUM [newline] [,[startline] [,increment]] renumbers the program, where **newline** will be the first line number of the renumbered sequence; default=10. **Startline** is the current number of the first line to be renumbered—default=first program line. **Increment** is the increment to be used in renumbering; default=10. If you specify **startline**, you must specify **newline**. Renumbering continues from **startline** to the end of the program. RENUM also adjusts all GOTOs, GOSUBs and other commands that include line references. Program execution halts when RENUM has been completed. You must type RUN to start the program again.

COMMENTS

Notice that some computers use NAME for renaming files, but on the TRS-80 Model III it is used for renumbering program lines.

RESET

APPLE IIe & II+

CLOSE (File Handling) can be used to simulate the IBM command RESET. Used without any parameters, it will close all open files.

PLOT h,v (Graphics) may be used to simulate the TRS-80 command RESET, where **h** specifies the horizontal coordinate—range 0-39—and **v** specifies the vertical coordinate—range 0-39 with text window, 0-47 with full screen graphics. PLOT will place a block at the specified coordinates on the low-resolution screen, using the current low-resolution display color. Therefore, if you set the current color to the background color, the point will be "reset."

IBM PC & PCjr

RESET (File Handling) closes all files and clears the system buffer. DOS 2.1 must be present before using RESET in Cartridge BASIC.

PRESET (x,y) [,color] resets a point, where **x** and **y** are valid screen coordinates, and **color** is a valid color number or attribute number for the SCREEN in use. If **color** is omitted, the background color (0) is used. For a discussion of valid color numbers, see **COLOR**.

COMMODORE 64

Simulate it in its file-handling sense by executing

SYS 65511

to close all files.

Simulate it as a graphics command by using the subroutine under PLOT and printing a blank space in the background color. The number of the background color can be determined with

(PEEK(53281) AND 15)

RESTORE

APPLE IIe & II+

RESTORE resets the DATA pointer to the first DATA statement, allowing DATA lines to be accessed more than one time.

IBM PC & PCjr

RESTORE [n] where **n** specifies a program line containing a DATA statement. RESTORE n resets the DATA pointer to that line, allowing DATA lines to be accessed more than one time. If parameter **n** is omitted, the next READ will access the first DATA line in the program.

COMMODORE 64

RESTORE resets the DATA pointer to the first DATA statement, allowing DATA lines to be accessed more than one time.

RESUME

APPLE IIe & II+

RESUME returns control from an error-handling routine to the statement that caused the error.

IBM PC & PCjr

RESUME [n]
RESUME NEXT returns from an error-handling routine. Parameter **n** specifies a line number where execution is to RESUME. If **n** is zero, or omitted, program execution will RESUME at the statement that caused the error. If RESUME NEXT is used, program execution will RESUME at the statement following the statement that caused the error.

COMMODORE 64

Because Commodore does not support ON ERROR type statements, there is no way and no need to simulate RESUME.

TRS-80 Models IV & III

PRINT @ (v,h),CHR$(32) (Model IV Graphics) may be used to simulate RESET, where **v** specifies the vertical coordinate and **h** specifies the horizontal coordinate. Used in this way, PRINT @ will place a blank space—CHR$(32)—at the specified screen location. Parameter **v** may be in the range 0-23, and parameter **h** may be in the range 0-79.

RESET (h,v) (Model III Graphics) where **h** specifies the horizontal coordinate and **v** specifies the vertical coordinate, RESET will place a blank space at the specified screen location. Parameter **h** may be in the range 0-127. Parameter **v** may be in the range 0-47.

CLOSE (File Handling) simulates IBM's RESET. The difference is that CLOSE will close the cassette files. RESET will not.

TRS-80 Color Computer

RESET(h,v) (Graphics) where **h** specifies the horizontal coordinate, and **v** specifies the vertical coordinate. RESET will turn off a graphics block at the specified screen location. Parameter **h** may be in the range 0-63. Parameter **v** may be in the range 0-31

CLOSE (File Handling) simulates IBM's RESET. The difference is that CLOSE will close the cassette files. RESET will not.

COMMENTS

TRS-80 Models IV & III

RESTORE resets the DATA pointer to the first DATA statement, allowing DATA lines to be accessed more than one time.

TRS-80 Color Computer

RESTORE resets the DATA pointer to the first DATA statement, allowing DATA lines to be accessed more than one time.

COMMENTS

TRS-80 Models IV & III

RESUME [n]
RESUME NEXT returns from an error-handling routine. Parameter **n** specifies a line number where execution is to RESUME. If **n** is zero, or omitted, program execution will RESUME at the statement that caused the error. If RESUME NEXT is used, program execution will RESUME at the statement following the statement that caused the error.

TRS-80 Color Computer

Because COCO does not support ON ERROR type statements, there is no way and no need to simulate RESUME.

COMMENTS

RETURN

APPLE IIe & II+

RETURN causes program execution to return from a subroutine to the statement immediately following the calling GOSUB.

IBM PC & PCjr

RETURN [n] causes program execution to return from a subroutine to the statement immediately following the calling GOSUB. If parameter **n** is included, program execution will return from the subroutine to the line number specified by **n**.

COMMODORE 64

RETURN causes program execution to return from a subroutine to the statement immediately following the calling GOSUB.

RIGHT$

APPLE IIe & II+

RIGHT$(x$,n) where **n** is a numeric expression and **x$** is any string. This function returns a string expression consisting of the right **n** characters of **x$**. The range for **n** is 1-255. If **n**>LEN(x$), then **x$** is returned. If **n**=0 then an ILLEGAL QUANTITY ERROR will result.

IBM PC & PCjr

RIGHT$(x$,n) where **n** is a numeric expression and **x$** is any string. This function returns a string expression consisting of the right **n** characters of **x$**. The range for **n** is 0-255. If **n**>LEN(x$), then **x$** is returned. If **n**=0 then the null string is returned.

COMMODORE 64

RIGHT$(x$,n) where **n** is a numeric expression and **x$** is any string. This function returns a string expression consisting of the right **n** characters of **x$**. The range for **n** is 0-255. If **n**>LEN(x$), then **x$** is returned. If **n**=0 then the null string is returned.

RMDIR

APPLE IIe & II+

Cannot be simulated.

IBM PC & PCjr

RMDIR **path** where **path** is a string expression that specifies the subdirectory to be removed from the existing disk directory. Because none of the other computers covered by this book has a multiple directory, there is no method of simulating RMDIR. To use this command in Cartridge BASIC, you must have DOS 2.1 present.

COMMODORE 64

Cannot be simulated.

TRS-80 Models IV & III

RETURN causes program execution to return from a subroutine to the statement immediately following the calling GOSUB.

TRS-80 Color Computer

RETURN causes program execution to return from a subroutine to the statement immediately following the calling GOSUB.

COMMENTS

TRS-80 Models IV & III

RIGHT$(x$,n) where n is a numeric expression and x$ is any string. This function returns a string expression consisting of the right n characters of x$. The range for n is 0-255. If n>LEN(x$), then x$ is returned. If n=0 then the null string is returned.

TRS-80 Color Computer

RIGHT$(x$,n) where n is a numeric expression and x$ is any string. This function returns a string expression consisting of the right n characters of x$. The range for n is 0-255. If n>LEN(x$), then x$ is returned. If n=0 then the null string is returned.

COMMENTS

The only variation on this function is that the range of n is 1-255 for Apple and 0-255 for all others.

TRS-80 Models IV & III

Cannot be simulated.

TRS-80 Color Computer

Cannot be simulated.

COMMENTS

RND (Also See RANDOM, RANDOMIZE)

APPLE IIe & II+

RND(n) returns a pseudo-random number, where **n** is any numeric argument. If the sign of **n** is positive, RND will return a random number between 0 and 1. If **n** has a value of zero, RND will return the same number produced by the previous RND call. If the sign of **n** is negative, the value of **n** will act as the seed for a new random number sequence. The same seed number always produces the same number sequence.

To obtain a number in a range other than 0-1, multiply the returned RND value times a constant—such as 10.

IBM PC & PCjr

RND(n) returns a pseudo-random number, where **n** is any numeric argument. If the sign of **n** is positive, RND will return a random number between 0 and 1. If **n** has a value of zero, RND will return the same number produced by the previous RND call. If the sign of **n** is negative, the value of **n** will act as the seed for a new random number sequence. The same seed number always produces the same number sequence.

To obtain a number in a range other than 0-1, substitute the value of the upper limit for **n** in the following formula:

```
R=INT(RND*(n+1))
```

COMMODORE 64

RND(n) generates a floating point pseudo-random number between 0 and 1—excluding 0 and 1. The numeric argument **n** dictates the sequence of numbers generated. If parameter **n** is positive, then the same sequence of numbers is generated from power-up, independent of the magnitude of **n**. If the sign of **n** is negative, then the value of **n** will act as the seed for a new number sequence. Different seeds generate different sequences of random numbers. The same seed generates the same sequence of numbers. For example, the program

```
10 R=RND(-1):PRINT RND(1)
```

always generates the same results, no matter how often it is run. If **n**=0, then a random number is generated by the computer's clock. The usual way to generate a random seed is to use RND(-TI), which uses the current value in the timer as the seed.

To generate a random integer between the integers **a** and **b**, including **a** and **b**, use the following formula:

```
10 R=INT(RND(1)*(b-a+1)
   +a)
```

ROT=

APPLE IIe & II+

ROT=n specifies the amount of rotation to be applied to a high-resolution graphics shape prior to DRAWing or XDRAWing it on the screen. Parameter **n** is a numeric argument representing 1/64 of a circle. For example, ROT=32 specifies 180 degrees of rotation.

IBM PC & PCjr

DRAW "TA n" causes rotation of the figure to be drawn by subsequent DRAW commands, where **n** is the number of degrees for the figure to be turned. Range is −360-360.

COMMODORE 64

Cannot easily be simulated on the Commodore 64 and is beyond the scope of this book.

ROW

APPLE IIe & II+

Simulate it with this routine:

```
10 R=PEEK(37)+1
```

where **R** is the variable name denoting the screen line number—range 1-24.

IBM PC & PCjr

CSRLIN returns the value of the line of the active screen on which the cursor is positioned—range 1-25. It may be used to simulate ROW.

COMMODORE 64

Simulate it with the following routine, where **R** is the variable name denoting the line number—range 1-25:

```
10 R=PEEK(214)+1
```

TRS-80 Models IV & III

RND(n) returns a pseudo-random number, where n is a numeric argument—range 0-32767. If parameter n=0, a number between 0 and 1 will be returned. If n is greater than 0, RND will return a number between 1 and the integer value of the parameter n.

TRS-80 Color Computer

RND(n) returns a pseudo-random number, where n is a numeric argument with a value of 1 or greater, RND will return a random number between 1 and the specified value of parameter n.

COMMENTS

TRS-80 Models IV & III

Cannot easily be simulated on the TRS-80 Models IV and III because they do not have graphics screens.

TRS-80 Color Computer

DRAW "Ax" causes subsequent figures to be DRAWn with the angular displacement specified by x. Possible values for parameter x follow:

x=0	0° (default)
x=1	90°
x=2	180°
x=3	270°

COMMENTS

TRS-80 Models IV & III

ROW(Ø) returns the row location of the cursor on the Model IV. Note that the Ø is a dummy argument that should not be changed.

Simulate it on the Model III with

TRS-80 Color Computer

Neither ROW nor the address where the cursor location is kept is documented for the COCO by Radio Shack.

COMMENTS

```
10 DEF FNR(d)=INT((PEEK
   (16416)+(PEEK(16417)
   AND 3)*256)/64)+1
20 X=FNR(Ø)
```

FNR(0) will return the vertical position of the cursor.

RSET (See LSET)

RUN

APPLE IIe & II+

RUN
RUN [n]
RUN [filename]

In the first form, RUN will begin executing the program currently in memory, starting at the lowest line number. In the second form, RUN will begin executing the program currently in memory, starting at the line number specified by parameter **n**. In the final form, RUN will LOAD the program specified by **filename** from disk, and begin execution at the lowest line number. However used, the RUN command will reset all numeric variables to zero and all string variables to null.

IBM PC & PCjr

RUN
RUN [n]
RUN [filename][,R]

In the first form, RUN will begin executing the program currently in memory, starting at the lowest line number. In the second form, RUN will begin executing the program currently in memory, starting at the line number specified by parameter **n**. In the final form, RUN will LOAD the program specified by **filename** from disk, and begin execution at the lowest line number. If the **R** option is included, all data files remain open. Otherwise, all data files will be closed. However used, the RUN command will reset all numeric variables to zero and all string variables to null.

COMMODORE 64

RUN
RUN [n]

In the first form, RUN will begin executing the program currently in memory, starting at the lowest line number. In the second form, RUN will begin executing the program currently in memory, starting at the line number specified by parameter **n**.

The Commodore 64 does not have a RUN[filename] command, but its effect can be simulated in one of two ways. First, you can use

LOAD "filename",8

which will automatically load and run the BASIC program specified by **filename**, if **filename** is shorter than the program calling it. Second, you can use the dynamic keyboard technique. For more details on that technique, see **LOAD**.

SAVE

APPLE IIe & II+

SAVE filename [,Ss][,Dd][,Vv] where **filename** specifies a file. SAVE will place a copy of the program currently in memory onto the specified diskette. Parameters **s**, **d** and **v** are optional, with **s** specifying the slot, **d** specifying the drive, and **v** specifying the volume of the diskette to receive the SAVEd file. This command must be preceded by PRINT CHR$(4);.

IBM PC & PCjr

SAVE "filename"[,A][,P] where **filename** specifies a file. SAVE will place a copy of the program currently in memory onto diskette. If switch **A** is appended, the program will be saved in ASCII format. If switch **P** is appended, the program will be saved in an encoded binary format. This prevents subsequent LISTing or EDITing of the program, which is useful for code protection.

COMMODORE 64

SAVE[filename][,device] places a copy of the BASIC program currently in memory onto a storage device, where **filename** is the name of the file to be saved, and **device** is the storage device. The **filename** may be a maximum of 16 characters long. Values for **device** may be 1 (cassette) or 8 (disk). The **filename** is not optional for a disk save, and the **filename** selected must not already be on the disk being saved to.

If you wish to replace a program already on disk with the program in memory—and also call the new program on disk **filename**—there are two different ways to do it:

100 SAVE"@0:filename",8

This first saves a copy of your new program to disk, then changes the pointers to this new program rather than the old program. There are sporadic references in magazines to the occasional failure of this command, although that may be due to the misalignment of disk drives or

TRS-80 Models IV & III

RUN
RUN [n]
RUN [filename][,R]
In the first form, RUN will begin executing the program currently in memory, starting at the lowest line number. In the second form, RUN will begin executing the program currently in memory, starting at the line number specified by parameter **n**. In the final form, RUN will LOAD the program specified by **filename** from disk, and begin execution at the lowest line number. If the **R** option is included, all data files remain open. Otherwise, all data files will be closed. However used, the RUN command will reset all numeric variables to zero and all string variables to null.

TRS-80 Color Computer

RUN
RUN [n]
RUN [filename][,R]
In the first form, RUN will begin executing the program currently in memory, starting at the lowest line number. In the second form, RUN will begin executing the program currently in memory, starting at the line number specified by parameter **n** In the final form, RUN will LOAD the program specified by **filename** from disk, and begin execution at the lowest line number. If the **R** option is included, all data files remain open. Otherwise, all data files will be closed. However used, the RUN command will reset all numeric variables to zero and all string variables to null.

COMMENTS

TRS-80 Models IV & III

SAVE "filename"[,A][,P] where **filename** specifies a file. SAVE will place a copy of the program currently in memory onto diskette. Switches **A** and **P** are optional. If switch **A** is appended, the program will be saved in ASCII format. If switch **P** is appended (Model IV only), the program will be saved in an encoded binary format that prevents subsequent LISTing or EDITing of the program. This is useful for code protection.

TRS-80 Color Computer

SAVE "filename"[,A] where **filename** specifies a file. SAVE will place a copy of the program currently in memory onto diskette. Switch **A** is optional. If switch **A** is appended, the program will be saved in ASCII format.

COMMENTS

---

the non-uniqueness of disk IDs. See **NEW**.

The second method is safer and requires the following program lines:

```
100 OPEN15,8,15 "S0:
    bufilename"
110 PRINT#15,
    "R0:bufilename=
    filename"
120 CLOSE15
130 SAVE"filename",8:
    VERIFY"filename",8
```

Line 100 deletes the back-up copy of filename, here called **bufilename**. Line 110 renames the old **filename** on the disk to **bufilename**. Line 130 SAVEs and VERIFIES the latest version of the program in the computer to the disk under the name **filename**. The disk finally contains two programs—**filename**, which is your latest version, and **bufilename**, which was the version immediately preceding the latest modification. The pri-

mary use for the latter code is while constructing a program, in which case the following lines are usually inserted into the above routine.

```
10 GOTO 200
140 END
200 REM MAIN PROGRAM STARTS
    HERE
```

Now, whenever the latest version of your modified program needs to be saved, you merely type

RUN 100

SCALE =

APPLE IIe & II +

SCALE=n sets the scale factor for subsequent shapes drawn from the high-resolution shape table, where **n** is an integer in the range 1-255. The shape will be drawn **n** times the original size.

IBM PC & PCjr

DRAW "S n" causes all objects subsequently DRAWn to be DRAWn to the scale specified by **n**—default is 4, range 1-255. The actual scale factor is **n** divided by 4, thus the default scale factor is 1. This accomplishes scaling by affecting the distances traveled by the U, D, L, R, E, F, G, H and M parameters of the DRAW command.

COMMODORE 64

Simulating SCALE on the Commodore 64 is not easily accomplished in BASIC without machine-language routines. It is beyond the scope of this book.

SCRATCH

APPLE IIe & II +

Simulate it with the following program lines:

```
10 PRINT CHR$(4);"OPEN
   filename"
20 PRINT CHR$(4);"DELETE
   filename"
```

IBM PC & PCjr

KILL "filename" erases the file **filename** from the disk. The file must have been previously CLOSEd. **Filename** can include a disk drive specification, and must include the extension. For example:

KILL]b:file.bas]

COMMODORE 64

Killing a file is called "SCRATCHing" by Commodore. It is usually abbreviated "S" and is accomplished with these lines:

```
10 OPEN 15,8,15,"S0:
   filename"
20 CLOSE 15
```

TRS-80 Models IV & III

You cannot simulate SCALE on the Model IV or Model III because they do not provide graphics capabilities.

TRS-80 Color Computer

DRAW "S n" causes all objects subsequently DRAWn to be DRAWn to the scale specified by **n**—default is 4, range 1-255. The actual scale factor is **n** divided by 4, thus the default scale factor is 1. This accomplishes scaling by affecting the distances traveled by the U, D, L, R, E, F, G, H and M parameters of the DRAW command.

COMMENTS

TRS-80 Models IV & III

KILL "filename" erases the file **filename** from the disk. The file must have been previously CLOSEd. **Filename** can include a disk drive specification, and must include the extension. For example:

```
KILL "file/bas:2"
```

If no disk drive is specified, the **file** is deleted from the first drive that has it.

TRS-80 Color Computer

KILL "filename:d" erases the file **filename** on disk drive number **d**. If **d** is omitted, drive 0 is assumed. Files can be KILLed on the cassette-based COCO by simply recording over them.

COMMENTS

SCREEN

APPLE IIe & II+

See **HGR**, **GR** and **TEXT**. They're used on the Apple to control screen attributes.

IBM PC & PCjr

SCREEN [m] [,[c] [,[a][,v]] [,e]] (Statement) sets the screen attributes to be used. Parameter **m** represents the mode to be used—default is current mode.

Possible values for **m** are 0-6. Their significances follow:

SCREEN 0 is the text mode at current WIDTH (40 or 80). In Cartridge BASIC, WIDTH 80 is only available if you have 128K RAM.

SCREEN 1 is the four-color, medium-resolution graphics mode (320x200).

SCREEN 2 is the two-color, high-resolution graphics mode (640x200).

SCREEN 3 (Cartridge BASIC Only) is the 16-color, low-resolution graphics mode (160x200).

SCREEN 4 (Cartridge BASIC Only) is the four-color, medium-resolution graphics mode (320x200).

SCREEN 5 (Cartridge BASIC Only) is the 16-color, medium-resolution graphics mode (320x200). Requires 128K RAM.

SCREEN 6 (Cartridge BASIC Only) is the four-color, high-resolution graphics mode (640x200). Requires 128K RAM.

Parameter **c** enables or disables color, depending on the value of **m**. Parameter **a** specifies the active page—default is the current page. The active page is the one that will be addressed by output statements to the screen. Parameter **v** specifies the page that is displayed—the visual page. The default visual page is the active page.

Ranges available for **a** and **v**, and the result of **c**=0, are given in the table below:

m Value	WIDTH Value	Range For a And v	Result of c=0
0	40	0-7	Color disabled
0	80	0-3	Color disabled
1*		Not available	Color enabled
2*		Not available	c has no effect
1**		Depends on RAM	Color enabled
2**		Depends on RAM	c has no effect
3**		Depends on RAM	c has no effect
4**		Depends on RAM	Color enabled
5**		Depends on RAM	c has no effect
6**		Depends on RAM	c has no effect

* Other than Cartridge BASIC
**Cartridge BASIC

COMMODORE 64

The following program lines sets the Commodore 64 into high-resolution mode with a 320 column by 200 row display screen, having two colors available. Colors are determined by parameters **P** and **B** in line 140. Parameter **P** represents the pixel color, and **B** the background. Parameters **P** and **B** are in the range 0-15. For the actual color values, see the list of colors under **COLOR**. In this example, the background is blue and the pixels are black.

```
100 POKE 53272, PEEK(53272)
    OR 8
110 POKE 53265, PEEK(53265)
    OR 32
120 FOR I=8192 TO 16191
130 POKE I,0: NEXT
140 P=0: B=6
150 FOR I=1024 TO 2032
160 POKE I,P*16+B: NEXT
```

Lines 120 through 130, which clear the high-resolution screen, take about 45 seconds to execute. If desired, they could be replaced by the single line:

```
120 SYS 2024
```

which executes almost immediately. However, prior to calling this line, the following lines are required:

```
10 FOR I=2024 TO 2047: READ
   A: POKE I,A: NEXT
20 DATA 169, 0, 168, 132,
   251, 162, 32, 134
30 DATA 252, 145, 251, 200,
   208, 251, 232, 224
40 DATA 64, 240, 4, 134,
   252, 208, 242, 96
```

Other high-resolution screens are available on the Commodore 64, but require extensive knowledge of bit mapping. A discussion of them is beyond the scope of this book.

To return to low-resolution mode, the following lines may be used:

```
200 POKE 53265, PEEK(53265)
    AND 223
210 POKE 53272, 21
```

For more information on graphics, see *Commodore 64 Graphics & Sound Programming* by Stan Krute or *How to Program Your Commodore 64* by Carl Shipman.

TRS-80 Models IV & III

Cannot be simulated on the Model IV or Model III because they are always in the text mode.

Parameter **e** is used in Cartridge BASIC only. It specifies the amount of video memory to erase if **m** or **c** is changed. The range is 0-2 with the following significance:

> 0 does not erase video memory even if **m** or **c** changes.
>
> 1 erases the union of the new page and the old page if **m** or **c** changes—default.
>
> 2 erases all of video memory if **m** or **c** changes.

If all parameters are valid, the screen is erased, the new mode takes effect, the background and border are set to black, and the foreground is set to white. Don't forget to reset the COLOR after using SCREEN.

SCREEN (r,c[,z]) (Function) returns the ASCII code—range 0-255—for the character on the active screen at the specified row and column. Parameter **r** must be in the range 1-25. Parameter **z** is valid only in text mode, and is an expression that evaluates to a true or false value. If the expression **z** evaluates as true, the color attribute for the character is returned instead of the code for the character—range 0-255. This color attribute may be deciphered as follows:

1) (z MOD 16) is the foreground color.

2) (((z-foreground)/16) MOD 128) is the background color.

3) The expression (z>127) is True (−1) if the character is blinking, False (0) if not.

In graphics mode, if the specified location contains graphic information, then the SCREEN function returns zero.

TRS-80 Color Computer

SCREEN m,c selects the screen type and color. If **m**=0, the text mode is set. If **m**=1, the graphics mode is set. Parameter **c** may be either 1 or 0. It selects the color combination, or palette, that will be used. The colors in the palette are determined by PMODE.

PMODE [m][,p] sets the graphics mode, where **m** specifies the mode—range 0-4. Parameter **p** specifies the memory graphics page you wish to start on. Possible modes are listed below:

PMODE	Grid Size	Color Mode	Pages Required
0	128x96	Two color	1
1	128x96	Four color	2
2	128x192	Two color	2
3	128x192	Four color	4
4	256x192	Two color	4

If **m** is omitted, the most recently assigned value is used. If PMODE has not been previously used, parameter **m** defaults to 2. If **p** is omitted, the most recent value is used. If PMODE has not been previously used, **p** defaults to 1.

COMMENTS

SCRN

APPLE IIe & II+

SCRN (c,r) returns the color currently displayed on the low-resolution graphics screen at column **c** and row **r**. SCRN is not designed to be used in high-resolution mode.

IBM PC & PCjr

POINT(x,y) returns the attribute of the specified point on the screen, where parameters **x** and **y** specify legal absolute horizontal and vertical coordinates. This command will return a value of −1 if the specified coordinates are out of range. See COLOR for a listing of valid attribute numbers for the various SCREEN modes.

COMMODORE 64

Different models of the Commodore 64 deal with the color screen in various ways because of the different chips installed in various production series. Therefore, no attempt will be made here to simulate SCRN.

SET

APPLE IIe & II+

PLOT x,y will place a block at the specified coordinates on the low-resolution screen, where **x** specifies the horizontal coordinate—range 0-39—and **y** specifies the vertical coordinate—range 0-39 with text window, 0-47 with full screen graphics. This command will use the current low-resolution display color, and may be used to simulate SET.

HPLOT x,y will set a point on the high-resolution screen, where **x** is the horizontal coordinate—range 0-279—and **y** is the vertical coordinate—range 0-159 with text window or 0-191 without text window. HPLOT may be used to simulate SET.

IBM PC & PCjr

PSET (x,y) [,c] (Graphics Modes Only) may be used to simulate SET, and causes the point specified by coordinates **x** and **y** to be set to attribute **c**. The actual color specified by **c** will vary, depending on the SCREEN in use. See COLOR and PSET. If **c** is omitted, the current foreground attribute is used. The range for **x** is 0-199. The range for **y** depends on the SCREEN in use. See SCREEN.

COMMODORE 64

Can be simulated by the following routine, which will print the letter **A** at row 20, column 30. Of course, any character could be printed in place of **A**, including any graphics character.

```
10 R=20:C=30
20 POKE 783,0:POKE 781,R:
   POKE 782,C
30 SYS 65520:PRINT "A";
```

Here, parameter **R** must be in the range 0-24, and **C** must be in the range 0-39. If an attempt is made to PRINT in the lower-right corner of the screen, the screen will scroll up.

SGN

APPLE IIe & II+

SGN(x) where **x** is any numeric expression or variable. SGN returns −1 if **x** is negative, 0 if **x** is 0, and 1 if **x** is positive.

IBM PC & PCjr

Same.

COMMODORE 64

Same.

TRS-80 Models IV & III

Cannot be simulated on the Model IV or Model III because they do not have color capabilities. See **POINT** for a similar function.

TRS-80 Color Computer

PPOINT (x,y) returns the color code of the graphics point at coordinates **x**—range 0-255—and **y**—range 0-191. Note that the value returned by PPOINT may be misleading if you SET the point while in a different PMODE than the current PMODE.

COMMENTS

TRS-80 Models IV & III

PRINT @ (x,y),CHR$(191) (Model IV) may be used to simulate SET, where **x** specifies the vertical coordinate, and **y** specifies the horizontal coordinate. PRINT @ places a graphics block (CHR$(191)) at the specified screen location. Parameter **y** may be in the range 0-23, and parameter **x** may be in the range 0-79.

SET (x,y) (Model III) will place a graphics block at the specified screen location, where **x** specifies the horizontal coordinate, and **y** specifies the vertical coordinate. Parameter **x** may be in the range 0-127, and parameter **y** may be in the range 0-47.

TRS-80 Color Computer

SET (x,y,c) will place a graphics block at the specified screen location, where **x** specifies the horizontal coordinate, **y** specifies the vertical coordinate, and **c** specifies the color to be SET. Parameter **x** may be in the range 0-63. Parameter **y** may be in the range 0-31. Parameter **c** may be in the range 0-8. See **COLOR** for a list of the actual colors returned by the various values of **c**.

COMMENTS

TRS-80 Models IV & III

Same.

TRS-80 Color Computer

Same.

COMMENTS

SHELL

is an undocumented IBM reserved word.

SHLOAD

APPLE IIe & II+

SHLOAD loads a shape table from cassette. It loads the table into the highest available memory, then sets HIMEM: just below it. Shapes can then be called from the shape table by shape number using **DRAW x** or **XDRAW x**, where **x** is the shape number.

IBM PC & PCjr

Though IBM does not utilize shape tables, they can be simulated using GET and PUT to manipulate shapes on the screen. PRINT# and INPUT# can then be used to save and load arrays of shapes to disk or tape.

COMMODORE 64

Shape tables are not easily accomplished on the Commodore without extensive machine language. Therefore, it is beyond the scope of this book. You may wish to investigate the use of sprites if you need to move shapes around the screen. See the *Commodore 64 Programmer's Reference Guide,* pages 131 to 182.

SIN

APPLE IIe & II+

SIN (a) where parameter **a** is an argument expressed in radians. SIN (a) will return the trigonometric sine of the argument.

IBM PC & PCjr

Same.

COMMODORE 64

Same.

SKIPF

APPLE IIé & II+

PRINT CHR$(4);"LOAD **filename**" will cause the computer to search for the specified file on cassette if you do not have DOS loaded. If you have DOS loaded, you omit the **filename**, and the next program is loaded. There is no way to skip to a specified data file. Therefore, you should be sure your data files are saved on cassette immediately after the program file that calls them. Otherwise, you will have to search the cassette manually.

IBM PC & PCjr

LOAD "CAS1:filename" will cause the computer to search for and load the specified **filename** on cassette. There is no way to skip to a specified data file. Therefore, you should be sure your data files are saved on cassette immediately after the program file that calls them. Otherwise, you will have to search the cassette manually.

COMMODORE 64

Can be simulated with VERIFY on the Commodore 64. Although not actually intended for this purpose, VERIFY without any parameters will cause the program to skip over the next program on cassette. It will display a ?VERIFY ERROR if the program on cassette is not the same as that in memory. But it will position the tape at the end of that program. If used in the program mode, execution will stop after the error message. To avoid this, use the following dynamic keyboard technique:

```
100 PRINT CHR$(147) "RUN
    130"
110 POKE 198,2: POKE 631,19:
    POKE 632,13
120 VERIFY
130 PRINT CHR$(147); :REM
    PROGRAM CONTINUES HERE
```

TRS-80 Models IV & III

INPUT#−1 will load values from cassette tape, and **PRINT#−1** will write values to cassette tape. There is no easy way to simulate shape tables in BASIC on the TRS-80 because it lacks extensive graphics capabilities.

TRS-80 Color Computer

Though COCO does not utilize shape tables, they can be simulated using GET and PUT to manipulate shapes on the screen. PRINT# and INPUT# can then be used to save and load arrays of shapes to disk or tape.

COMMENTS

TRS-80 Models IV & III

Same.

TRS-80 Color Computer

Same.

COMMENTS

To convert degrees (D) to radians (R), use the following formula:

$R=D*3.141593/180$

TRS-80 Models IV & III

Though there is no way to skip a specified program on cassette with the TRS-80, you may skip to and load a program by specifying the program name after CLOAD. There is no way to skip to a specified data file. Therefore, you should be sure that data files are saved on cassette immediately after the program file calling them. Otherwise, you will have to search the cassette manually.

If this code is renumbered, then the number 130 in quotation marks in line 100 should be changed to refer to the new line number.

TRS-80 Color Computer

SKIPF ["name"] where **name** is a program to be skipped. Default is the next program. SKIPF skips to the end of the specified program on cassette. This may be useful for moving to a specific data file.

COMMENTS

SOUND

APPLE IIe & II+

Cannot be simulated on the Apple without extensive machine-language routines. They are beyond the scope of this book.

IBM PC & PCjr

SOUND f,d
SOUND f, d, [,[volume] [,[voice]]] (Cartridge BASIC Only) generates sound, where **f** is the frequency of the note to be SOUNDed through the speaker—range 37-32767—measured in cycles per second. In Cartridge BASIC, any value for **f** less than 110 will be interpreted as 110. Parameter **d** is the duration of the sound measured in "clock ticks." There are 18.2 clock ticks per second—range is 0-65535 (.0015-65535 for Cartridge BASIC). If **d**=0, the current sound is turned off. If **f**=32767, the "sound" is silence.

Volume is defined by a numeric expression in the range 0-15 —default=15. **Voice** is either 0, 1 or 2, and specifies which voice is being addressed. SOUND must be ON when you use **voice** or **volume**. Otherwise, you will get an ILLEGAL FUNCTION CALL.

A new sound turns an old sound off unless you have used a PLAY "MB" statement. In that case the new sound is buffered, awaiting the end of the old sound before it begins. For an extended discussion of the relationship of SOUND to the notes of the keyboard and to tempo, see the *BASIC Reference Manual,* pages 4-262 through 4-264, or the Cartridge *BASIC Reference Manual,* page 4-341. The main difference between SOUND and PLAY is that SOUND is oriented to a decimal system. PLAY is oriented to an octave system.

SOUND ON (Cartridge BASIC Only) enables the external speaker and disables the internal speaker.

SOUND OFF (Cartridge BASIC Only) disables the external speaker and enables the internal speaker.

SOUND ON and SOUND OFF used in conjunction with BEEP ON and BEEP OFF have the following effects:

SOUND OFF: BEEP OFF selects the internal speaker only.
SOUND ON: BEEP OFF selects the external speaker only.
SOUND OFF: BEEP ON selects both speakers—default setting.

COMMODORE 64

Though the Commodore 64 supports extensive sound capabilities, there is no SOUND command. Its simulation is beyond the scope of this book. Machine-language sound utilities are commercially available for this function. Also see *Your Commodore 64* by Heilborn and Talbott, Chapter 7.

TRS-80 Models IV & III

Cannot be simulated on the TRS-80 Models IV and III without extensive machine-language routines. They are beyond the scope of this book.

TRS-80 Color Computer

SOUND **f,d** generates sound through the speaker, where **f** is the pitch of the note to be SOUNDed and **d** is the duration of the sound. Parameters **f** and **d** have a range of 1-255.

COMMENTS

SPACE$, SPC

APPLE IIe & II+

SPC(n) prints **n** spaces, where **n** is any numeric expression that will be truncated to an integer. SPC can be used only with a PRINT statement. If SPC(n) is the last item in a PRINT statement, it will be assumed to be followed by a semicolon and therefore does not cause a carriage return.

IBM PC & PCjr

SPACE$(n) returns a string consisting of **n** spaces, where **n** is an integer numeric expression in the range 0-255.

SPC(n) prints **n** spaces, where **n** is any numeric expression. Parameter **n** will be truncated to an integer. SPC can be used only with a PRINT, LPRINT or PRINT# statement. If SPC(n) is the last item in a PRINT statement, it will be assumed to be followed by a semicolon and will not cause a carriage return. If **n** is greater than the width of the device being printed to, the value used for **n** is N MOD WIDTH.

COMMODORE 64

SPC(n) prints **n** spaces, where **n** is any numeric expression. Parameter **n** will be truncated to an integer. SPC can be used only with a PRINT or PRINT# statement. If SPC(n) is the last item in a print statement, it will be assumed to be followed by a semicolon and will not cause a carriage return.

SPEED=

APPLE IIe & II+

SPEED=n sets the speed of execution of the program, where **n** is an integer numeric expression in the range 0-255, default=255. If n<255, program execution slows down.

IBM PC & PCjr

You can slow the execution of a program on the IBM by specifying event trapping—ON COM, ON PLAY, ON STRIG, ON PEN, ON KEY, ON TIMER. These commands cause BASIC to check for the event before the execution of each line, thus slowing program execution for each statement included. You can further slow execution by putting in timer loops, such as the one below. These will slow execution only of that particular portion of the program.

10 FOR X=1 TO 100 : NEXT X

COMMODORE 64

You can slow program execution by putting in timer loops, such as the following. These will slow execution only of that particular portion of the program.

10 FOR X=1 TO 100 : NEXT X

SQR

APPLE IIe & II+

SQR(n) returns the square root of **n**, where **n** is greater than or equal to 0.

IBM PC & PCjr

Same.

COMMODORE 64

Same.

TRS-80 Models IV & III

SPACE$(n) returns a string consisting of **n** spaces, where **n** is an integer numeric expression in the range 0-255.

SPC(n) prints **n** spaces, where **n** is any numeric expression. Parameter **n** will be truncated to an integer. SPC can be used only with a PRINT, LPRINT or PRINT# statement. If SPC(n) is the last item in a PRINT statement, it will be assumed to be followed by a semicolon and will not cause a carriage return. SPC is useful in that it does not use string space.

TRS-80 Color Computer

PRINT STRING$(n,32) prints a string of **n** spaces, and can be used to simulate SPC(n).

COMMENTS

TRS-80 Models IV & III

You can slow program execution by putting in timer loops, such as the following. These will slow execution only of that particular portion of the program.

```
10 FOR X=1 TO 100 : NEXT X
```

TRS-80 Color Computer

You can slow execution of a program by putting in timer loops, such as the following. These will slow execution only of that particular portion of the program.

```
10 FOR X=1 TO 100 : NEXT X
```

COMMENTS

TRS-80 Models IV & III

Same.

TRS-80 Color Computer

Same.

COMMENTS

ST

APPLE IIe & II+

There is no need to simulate ST on the Apple because it has built-in error messages, as well as the more powerful ONERR GOTO error-handling routines.

IBM PC & PCjr

There is no need to simulate ST on the IBM because it has built-in error messages, as well as the more powerful ERL, ERR, ERROR and ON ERROR GOTO error-handling routines.

COMMODORE 64

ST is used to return an eight-bit status report on how the last input or output operation occurred. The values returned by **ST** can indicate I/O errors for cassette, disk, printer, or serial bus peripheral devices. For example, if **ST**=64, the end of the file was encountered. And if **ST**=−128, the device requested was not present. For a detailed explanation see the *Commodore 64 Programmer's Reference Guide,* pages 84 and 85. For an example of its usage see **EOF**.

STEP

APPLE IIe & II+

STEP n sets the incremental value of a loop, where **n** is any numeric expression—default=1. It is used only within a FOR-NEXT loop, such as

```
10 FOR A=1 TO 10 STEP 2.
    NEXT A
```

If **n** is 0, the loop is infinite. If **n** is negative, and the number the loop is going TO is greater than the number where it starts, or vice-versa, then only the first iteration will be executed. No error condition will occur, and program execution will continue.

IBM PC & PCjr

Same.

COMMODORE 64

Same.

STICK

APPLE IIe & II+

PDL(n) tests the game paddles, where **n** is an integer in the range 0-225. If values other than 0, 1, 2 or 3 are used, the PDL function will give erratic and unpredictable results! Values of 0-3 will return a "resistance variable" for the respective paddle between 0 and 150K ohms. This value must then be interpreted to produce the desired results. Note that this will require extensive programming changes when converting to or from other computers.

IBM PC & PCjr

STICK(n) where **n** is an integer in the range 0-3. STICK returns the coordinates of the joysticks. STICK(0) obtains the values of both joysticks, but returns the x coordinate of joystick A. STICK(1), STICK(2) and STICK(3) do not sample the joystick, but return the coordinates retrieved by the most recent STICK(0). STICK(1) returns the y coordinate of joystick A. STICK(2) returns the x coordinate of joystick B. STICK(3) returns the y coordinate of joystick B.

COMMODORE 64

The Commodore 64 supports two game ports, 1 and 2. The joystick in port 1 is read by PEEKing 56321. Port 2 is read by PEEKing 56320. The number returned by the PEEK is logically ANDed with 15 to indicate the direction according to the chart below:

NW=10	North=14	NE=6
West=11	Home=15	East=7
SW=9	South=13	SE=5

To read the "fire" button, the number returned is logically ANDed with 16. If the value resulting is 16,

TRS-80 Models IV & III

There is no need to simulate ST on the Models IV and III because they have built-in error messages, as well as the more powerful ERL, ERR, ERROR, ERR$ and ON ERROR GOTO error-handling routines.

TRS-80 Color Computer

Not available and cannot be simulated on the COCO without extensive machine-language programming.

COMMENTS

TRS-80 Models IV & III

Same.

TRS-80 Color Computer

Same.

COMMENTS

TRS-80 Models IV & III

Joysticks and paddles are not currently supported on the Model IV or Model III. Even so, some independent companies have devised joysticks that work through the cassette port.

the button is not pressed. If the value is 0, the button is pressed.

The following program lines demonstrate how to read Port 2:

```
10 FOR I=0 TO 10: READ
   D$(I): NEXT
```

TRS-80 Color Computer

JOYSTK(n) returns a coordinate from the joystick, where n is an integer from 0-3. If n=0, it returns the horizontal coordinate of the right joystick. If n=1, it returns the vertical coordinate of the right joystick. If n=2, it returns the horizontal coordinate of the left joystick. If n=3, it returns the vertical coordinate of the left joystick.

COMMENTS

```
20 DATA SE,NE,E,,SW,NW,
   W,,S,N,H,
30 F$(0)="FIRE":
   F$(1)="SAFE"
40 PRINT CHR$(147);
50 PRINT
   CHR$(19)D$((PEEK(56320
   )AND 15)-5)
60 PRINT F$
   ((PEEK(56320)AND
   16)/16)
70 GOTO 50
```

STOP

APPLE IIe & II+

STOP causes program execution to halt and returns to the command level. The following message is printed:

BREAK IN X

where **X** is the line number containing the STOP command. Files are not closed and variables are not lost. The program may be restarted with a CONT command.

IBM PC & PCjr

Same.

COMMODORE 64

Same.

STORE

APPLE IIe & II+

STORE **n** where **n** is any valid numeric array name. STORE will cause the values of the array, such as **n**(1), **n**(2), **n**(3), ..., to be stored on the cassette tape. No prompt will be given, so the proper buttons on the cassette must be previously pressed. Note that the subscripts of the array are not indicated in the command, and that the array itself is not affected by the storage. STORE is the complement to RECALL.

IBM PC & PCjr

Simulate it by PRINTing the data elements to a cassette, or disk, data file. One method would be to use a loop that repeats itself as long as there are array elements left.

COMMODORE 64

Simulate it by PRINTing the data elements to a cassette, or disk, data file. One method would be to use a loop that repeats itself as long as there are array elements left.

STR$

APPLE IIe & II+

STR$(n) returns a string representation of **n**, where **n** is any numeric expression. That is, the digits in the numbers will be treated as individual characters rather than as a number. If the number is negative, the minus sign is included. This is the complement to VAL, which returns a numeric expression when given a string argument.

IBM PC & PCjr

STR$(n) returns a string representation of **n**, where **n** is any numeric expression. That is, the digits in the numbers will be treated as individual characters rather than as a number. If the number is negative, the minus sign is included. If the number is positive or zero, a leading blank will be returned in the string. This is the complement to VAL, which returns a numeric expression when given a string argument.

COMMODORE 64

STR$(n) returns a string representation of **n**, where **n** is any numeric expression. That is, the digits in the numbers will be treated as individual characters rather than as a number. If the number is negative, the minus sign is included. If the number is positive or zero, a leading blank will be returned in the string. This is the complement to VAL, which returns a numeric expression when given a string argument.

TRS-80 Models IV & III

Same.

TRS-80 Color Computer

Same.

COMMENTS

TRS-80 Models IV & III

Simulate it by PRINTing the data elements to a cassette, or disk, data file. One method would be to use a loop that repeats itself as long as there are array elements left.

TRS-80 Color Computer

Simulate it by PRINTing the data elements to a cassette, or disk, data file. One method would be to use a loop that repeats itself as long as there are array elements left.

COMMENTS

TRS-80 Models IV & III

STR$(n) returns a string representation of **n**, where **n** is any numeric expression. That is, the digits in the numbers will be treated as individual characters rather than as a number. If the number is negative, the minus sign is included. If the number is positive or zero, a leading blank will be returned in the string. This is the complement to VAL, which returns a numeric expression when given a string argument.

TRS-80 Color Computer

STR$(n) returns a string representation of **n**, where **n** is any numeric expression. That is, the digits in the numbers will be treated as individual characters rather than as a number. If the number is negative, the minus sign is included. If the number is positive or zero, a leading blank will be returned in the string. This is the complement to VAL, which returns a numeric expression when given a string argument.

COMMENTS

STRIG

APPLE IIe & II+

Although it can handle four paddles, the Apple can read the status of only three paddle buttons. This is accomplished with PEEK(−16287) for the value of the button on paddle 0, PEEK(−16286) for paddle 1, and PEEK(−16285) for paddle 2. If the value returned is greater than 127, then the button is being pressed.

IBM PC & PCjr

STRIG ON
STRIG(n)

STRIG OFF controls status checking on the joystick buttons, where **n** is an integer from 0-3 in BASIC, or 0-7 in Advanced, Cartridge or Compiler BASIC. STRIG ON causes the program to begin checking the status of the joystick buttons at the beginning of execution of each program line.

n Value	Button Number	Value If Button Has Been Pressed	Value If Button Is Being Pressed	Default
0	A1	−1		0
1	A1		−1	0
2	B1	−1		0
3	B1		−1	0

The following apply to Advanced BASIC and Compiler BASIC only.

4	A2	−1		0
5	A2		−1	0
6	B2	−1		0
7	B2		−1	0

STRIG(n) ON
ON STRIG(n) GOSUB line
STRIG(n) STOP
STRIG(n) OFF

These commands enable or disable trapping for the specified joystick button **n**, with the value of **n** determined by the chart below. The parameter **line**—range 1-65535—specifies a line to GOSUB to if the specified button has been pressed.

n	Button
0	A1
2	B1
4	A2
6	B2

When STRIG(n) ON has been specified and the ON STRIG(n) GOSUB line command is in effect, BASIC checks at the beginning of execution of each line to see if the button has been pressed. If it has, the GOSUB is executed. If not, then program execution continues uninterrupted. STRIG(n) STOP causes trapping to cease, but the computer remembers whether the button was pressed. If so, when a STRIG(n) ON is executed, then the GOSUB is executed immediately. STRIG(n) OFF causes trapping to cease, and even if the button is pressed it will not be remembered.

COMMODORE 64

The Commodore 64 supports two game ports, 1 and 2. The joystick in port 1 is read by PEEKing 56321, while port 2 is read by PEEKing 56320. The number returned by the PEEK is logically ANDed with 15 to indicate the direction according to the chart below:

NW=10	North=14	NE=6
West=11	Home=15	East=7
SW=9	South=13	SE=5

To read the "fire" button, the number returned is logically ANDed with 16. If the value resulting is 16, the button is not pressed. If the value is 0, the button is pressed.

The following program lines demonstrate how to read Port 2:

```
10 FOR I=0 TO 10:READ
   D$(I):NEXT
20 DATA SE,NE,E,,SW,NW,
   W,,S,N,H,
30 F$(0)="FIRE":
   F$(1)="SAFE"
40 PRINT CHR$(147);
50 PRINT CHR$(19)D$((PEEK
   (56320)AND 15)-5)
60 PRINT F$((PEEK(56320)
   AND 16)/16)
70 GOTO 50
```

TRS-80 Models IV & III

Joysticks and paddles, and their buttons, are not currently supported by Radio Shack on the Model IV or Model III. Even so, some independent companies have devised joysticks that work through the cassette port.

TRS-80 Color Computer

Joystick buttons are accessed by PEEKing memory location 65280. PEEK(65280) will return 127 or 255 if no button is pressed. It will return 126 or 254 if the right button is pressed, or 125 or 253 if the left button is pressed.

COMMENTS

STRING$

APPLE IIe & II+

Simulate it with the following line, where **C$** specifies a character to be repeated, and **NMB** is the number of characters desired. The following line will return, in variable **T$**, the specified number of characters:

```
100 T$="": FOR I=1 TO NMB:
    T$=T$+C$: NEXT I
```

IBM PC & PCjr

STRING$(n,m) or **STRING$(n,x$)** where **n** specifies the number of characters, **m** specifies an ASCII code representing a character (range 0-255), and **x$** specifies a character. This function will return a string of the specified number of characters.

COMMODORE 64

Simulate it with the following line, where **C$** specifies a character to be repeated, and **NMB** is the number of characters desired. The following line will return, in variable **T$**, the specified number of characters:

```
100 T$="": FOR I=1 TO NMB:
    T$=T$+C$: NEXT I
```

SUB

is a TRS-80 Color Computer undocumented reserved word.

SWAP

APPLE IIe & II+

Simulate it with the following routine, where **S1** and **S2** are the variables to be SWAPped. They could also be **S1$** and **S2$**. In that case, use **T$** instead of **T**.

```
1000 T=S1: S1=S2: S2=T
```

IBM PC & PCjr

SWAP n,m exchanges the values of variables **n** and **m**. The variables may be any type—numeric, string or array—but must both be of the same type. Thus if **n**=1 and **m**=2,

```
10 SWAP n,m
```

would cause **m**=1 and **n**=2.

COMMODORE 64

Simulate it with the following routine, where **S1** and **S2** are the variables to be SWAPped. They could also be **S1$** and **S2$**. In that case, use **T$** instead of **T**.

```
1000 T=S1: S1=S2: S2=T
```

SYS

APPLE IIe & II+

CALL n causes execution of the machine-language routine at memory location **n**, where **n** is a decimal numeric expression in the range −65535-65535, representing a memory location.

IBM PC & PCjr

CALL n[(x1 [,x2]...)] executes a machine-language subroutine at the location specified by the most recent DEF SEG and the offset defined by variable **n**, where **n** is a numeric expression and **x1, x2...,** are names of variables that are to be passed as arguments to a machine-language routine.

COMMODORE 64

SYS n causes execution of the machine-language routine starting at memory location **n**, where **n** is decimal numeric expression in the range 0-65535, representing a memory location. You cannot pass parameters to a machine-language program on the Commodore 64 without POKEing the information into a memory address and subsequently retrieving it within the machine-language routine.

TRS-80 Models IV & III

STRING$(n,m) or **STRING$(n,x$)** where **n** specifies the number of characters, **m** specifies an ASCII code representing a character (range 0-255), and **x$** specifies a character. This function will return a string of the specified number of characters.

TRS-80 Color Computer

STRING$(n,m) or **STRING$(n,x$)** where **n** specifies the number of characters, **m** specifies an ASCII code representing a character (range 0-255), and **x$** specifies a character. This function will return a string of the specified number of characters.

COMMENTS

Simulation on the Apple and Commodore 64 can also be done by direct assignment, such as:

```
20 T$="**********"
```

This would create a string of 10 asterisks.

The advantage of using STRING$ is that it does not use up string storage space unless you assign a variable name to it. Simulating it uses string storage space.

TRS-80 Models IV & III

SWAP n,m (Model IV) exchanges the values of variables **n** and **m**. The variables may be any type—numeric, string or array—but must both be of the same type. Thus if **n**=1 and **m**=2,

```
10 SWAP n,m
```

would cause **m**=1 and **n**=2.

Simulate SWAP on the Model III with the following routine, where **S1** and **S2** are the variables to be SWAPped. They could also be **S1$** and **S2$**. In that case, use **T$** instead of **T**.

```
1000 T=S1: S1=S2: S2=T
```

TRS-80 Color Computer

Simulate it with the following routine, where **S1** and **S2** are the variables to be SWAPped. They could also be **S1$** and **S2$**. In that case, use **T$** instead of **T**.

```
1000 T=S1: S1=S2: S2=T
```

COMMENTS

TRS-80 Models IV & III

CALL n [,a [,b...]] causes execution of the machine-language routine starting at memory location **n**, where **n** is a non-array variable specifying the beginning address of the machine-language subroutine being called, and **a,b,...** are variables representing parameters being passed to the machine-language routine.

TRS-80 Color Computer

EXEC [n] transfers control to the machine-language program at memory location **n**. If **n** is omitted, it assumes the address specified at the last CLOAD.

COMMENTS

Also see **USR** and **VARPTR**. The primary differences between USR and CALL are that multiple arguments or parameters can be passed to the machine-language routine using CALL, and that CALL does not require POKEing the address of the routine, but rather specifies it in the CALL statement. The method of passing parameters to the machine-language routine varies machine. IBM passes parameters through its stack, Radio Shack uses registers HL, DE and BC. See the manuals.

SYSTEM

APPLE IIe & II+

Because the BASIC command mode and the system command mode are indistinguishable to the user, SYSTEM is not used on the Apple. There is no need to simulate it.

IBM PC & PCjr

SYSTEM closes all files and takes the computer to DOS. The program in memory is lost. This command is not available in cassette BASIC. If you are using Cartridge BASIC, DOS 2.1 must be present or an ILLEGAL FUNCTION CALL error will result.

COMMODORE 64

Because the BASIC command mode and the system command mode are indistinguishable to the user, SYSTEM is not used on the Commodore 64. There is no need to simulate it.

TAB

APPLE IIe & II+

TAB(n) tabs to position **n**, where **n** is an integer numeric expression in the range 1-255, or 1 to the WIDTH of the device. If **n** is greater than the WIDTH of the device, TAB goes to position **n** on the next line. If TAB is the last item in a list, a semicolon is assumed to follow it. TAB can be used only in the context of PRINT statements.

IBM PC & PCjr

TAB(n) tabs to position **n**, where **n** is an integer numeric expression in the range 1-255, or 1 to the WIDTH of the device. If **n** is greater than the WIDTH of the device, TAB goes to position **n** on the next line. If TAB is the last item in a list, a semicolon is assumed to follow it. TAB can be used only in the context of PRINT, LPRINT or PRINT# statements.

COMMODORE 64

TAB(n) tabs to position **n**, where **n** is in the range 0-255, from the left margin of the cursor's line. If parameter **n** is not an integer, **n** is truncated. If **n** does not exceed the current cursor position on the line, then no tabbing is performed. Because the screen is only 40 characters wide, if **n** exceeds 39 then **n**=40 will take you to the left margin of the following line, etc. If TAB is the last item in a list, a semicolon is assumed to follow it. TAB should be used only in the context of PRINTing

TRS-80 Models IV & III

SYSTEM [command] (Model IV) executes the specified **command**, where **command** is any valid DOS command. If **command** is omitted, you are returned to DOS, and the program in memory is lost. If **command** is included and is a valid DOS library command, then **command** is executed and you are returned to BASIC with the program in memory intact.

SYSTEM (Model III) places you in the system mode for the sole purpose of loading a machine-language program from cassette. It should not be used within a program.

CMD"S" (Model III) returns you to DOS. You can re-enter BASIC with your program intact if you have not done anything that would alter the memory space occupied by the program or BASIC. To re-enter, type

```
BASIC *
```

The space between the word and the asterisk is required.

CMD"I" command (Model III) returns you to DOS and executes the specified **command**, where **command** is any valid DOS command or valid program name. You automatically re-enter BASIC if the BASIC memory area is intact after **command** is executed.

For a more detailed explanation of how CMD may be used, see **CMD**.

TRS-80 Color Computer

Because the BASIC command mode and the system command mode are indistinguishable to the user, SYSTEM is not used on the COCO. There is no need to simulate it.

COMMENTS

TRS-80 Models IV & III

TAB(n) tabs to position **n**, where **n** is an integer numeric expression in the range 1-255, or 1 to the WIDTH of the device. If **n** is greater than the WIDTH of the device, TAB goes to position **n** on the next line. If TAB is the last item in a list, a semicolon is assumed to follow it. TAB can be used only in the context of PRINT, LPRINT or PRINT# statements.

to the screen. Using it to format output to the printer may lead to unpredictable effects.

TRS-80 Color Computer

TAB(n) tabs to position **n**, where **n** is an integer numeric expression in the range 1-255, or 1 to the WIDTH of the device. If **n** is greater than the WIDTH of the device, TAB goes to position **n** on the next line. If TAB is the last item in a list, a semicolon is assumed to follow it. TAB can be used only in the context of PRINT, LPRINT or PRINT# statements.

COMMENTS

TAN

APPLE IIe & II+

TAN(n) returns the trigonometric tangent of **n**, where **n** is an angle measured in radians.

IBM PC & PCjr

Same.

COMMODORE 64

Same.

TERM

APPLE IIe & II+

Not available. Cannot be easily simulated. Some commercial communications programs give similar capabilities.

IBM PC & PCjr

TERM (Cartridge BASIC Only) loads and runs a Terminal Emulator program. All OPEN files are CLOSEd and any BASIC program in memory is lost. See the Cartridge *BASIC Reference Manual,* pages 4-360 through 4-367 for complete details on TERM.

COMMODORE 64

Not available. Cannot be easily simulated. Some commercial communications programs give similar capabilities.

TEXT

APPLE IIe & II+

TEXT converts the display screen to 40 columns by 24 lines of text display. This is the normal text mode.

IBM PC & PCjr

Simulate it with the following:

```
100 SCREEN 0,0
```

COMMODORE 64

To return to low-resolution mode—after using the high-resolution mode discussed under HGR—use the following program lines:

```
200 POKE 53265,PEEK(53265)
    AND 223
210 POKE 53272,21
```

THEN (See IF-THEN-ELSE)

TI, TIMER

APPLE IIe & II+

Apple does not provide a built-in timer, so there is no way to simulate interval timing without extensive machine-language programming or installing a clock card.

IBM PC & PCjr

TIMER (BASIC 2.0 and Cartridge BASIC Only) returns the number of seconds since midnight, according to the system clock. TIMER returns a single-precision number accurate to about 1/100th of a second. It is a read-only function. Not available in cassette BASIC. Cartridge BASIC requires the presence of DOS 2.1 to use TIMER.

COMMODORE 64

TI reads the interval timer, a "jiffy clock." The value returned represents the number of 1/60 seconds elapsed since the computer was turned on. Maximum value is 5,184,000, or 24 hours. It is a read-only function, equivalent to

```
256*256*PEEK(160)+256*PEEK
(161)+PEEK(162)
```

Timer accuracy is affected by I/O operations, such as the use of the cassette or disk drive, as well as other operations, such as disabling the RUNSTOP/RESTORE keys.

TRS-80 Models IV & III

Same.

TRS-80 Color Computer

Same.

COMMENTS

To convert degrees (D) to radians (R), use the following formula:

```
R=D*3.141593/180
```

TRS-80 Models IV & III

Not available. Cannot be easily simulated. Some commercial communications programs give similar capabilities.

TRS-80 Color Computer

Not available. Cannot be easily simulated. Some commercial communications programs give similar capabilities.

COMMENTS

TRS-80 Models IV & III

Because there is no graphics screen on the TRS-80, there is no need to simulate TEXT.

TRS-80 Color Computer

Simulate it with the following:

```
100 SCREEN 0,0
```

COMMENTS

TRS-80 Models IV & III

If you set the TRS-80's internal time clock to 00:00:00—see **TIME$**—you can simulate Commodore's TI function with the following:

For the Model IV:

```
200 T$=TIME$
210 S=VAL(RIGHT$(T$,2)):
    M=VAL(MID$(T$,4,2)):
    H=VAL(LEFT$(T$,2))
220 S=S+(M*60)+(H*360)
230 T=S*60
```

For the Model III:

```
200 T$=RIGHT$(TIME$,8)
210 S=VAL(RIGHT$(T$,2)):
    M=VAL(MID$(T$,4,2)):
    H=VAL(LEFT$(T$,2))
220 S=S+(M*60)+(H*360)
230 T=S*60
```

TRS-80 Color Computer

TIMER reads the interval timer. The value returned represents the approximate number of 1/60 seconds elapsed since the computer was turned on. When the timer reaches 65535, it resets to 0. This takes about 18 minutes. The timer can be set with the command

```
10 TIMER=n
```

where **n** is in the range 0-65535. Note that cassette I/O may cause erroneous TIMER readings.

Elapsed time—in terms of the number of 1/60 seconds elapsed since initialization—will be returned in variable **T**.

COMMENTS

TI$, TIME$

APPLE IIe & II+

Apple does not provide a built-in clock, so there is no way to simulate one without extensive machine-language programming or installing a clock card.

IBM PC & PCjr

TIME$=n$ sets the clock, where **n$** is a variable or constant with the form hh[:mm][:ss]. Parameter **hh** is hour—range 0-23. Parameter **mm** is minutes—range=0-59. Parameter **ss** is seconds—range 0-59. If **mm** or **ss** is omitted, the default is 0.

n$=TIME$ assigns the current value of the clock to **n$**. The string assigned to **n$** takes the form hh:mm:ss, where **hh** represents the hour, **mm** represents the minutes, and **ss** represents the seconds. Ranges are as described above. Note that the clock may have been set using TIME$ or may have been set before entering BASIC.

COMMODORE 64

TI$=n$ sets the clock, where **n$** is a variable or constant with the format of "hhmmss". All six parameters are necessary. Anything in **ss** that exceeds 59 seconds is automatically converted to minutes and seconds. Similarly, a value for **mm** in excess of 60 is converted to hours and minutes. However, if the final entry translates to a time in excess of 24 hours, TI$ is set to 000000. For example:

112233 is interpreted as 11 hours, 22 minutes, and 33 seconds.
112293 is interpreted as 112333—11 hours, 23 minutes, and 33 seconds.
118293 is interpreted as 122333—12 hours, 23 minutes, and 33 seconds.
238233 is interpreted as 240233—which is converted to 000000.

Note that this may be set during the program or before the program is RUN. Its accuracy is affected by I/O operations, such as the use of the cassette or disk drive, as well as other operations, such as disabling the RUNSTOP/RESTORE keys.

n$=TI$ assigns the current value of the clock to **n$**. String assignment to **n$** takes the form of "hhmmss". Parameter **hh** represents the hour—range 0-23. Parameter **mm** represents the minutes—range 0-59. Parameter **ss** represents the seconds—range 0-59.

TO (See FOR-TO)

TRACE, TROFF, TRON

APPLE IIe & II+

TRACE turns the trace utility on. This causes the line number of the line in execution to be printed on the screen, following a # symbol, at the cursor position as the line begins execution.

NOTRACE turns the trace utility off.

IBM PC & PCjr

TRON turns the trace utility on. This causes the line number of the line in execution to be printed on the screen—inside a pair of square brackets—at the cursor position as the line begins execution.

TROFF turns the trace utility off.

COMMODORE 64

Simulating **TRACE** on the Commodore 64 is not easily accomplished in BASIC. It is beyond the scope of this book.

TRS-80 Models IV & III

TIME$ (Model IV) returns the time of day in the format hh:mm:ss. The time may be set during initial power-up by answering the TIME question in TRS-DOS, or from BASIC by using the statement:

```
SYSTEM "TIME hh:mm:ss"
```

where **hh** specifies two digits for hours, **mm** specifies two digits for minutes, and **ss** specifies two digits for seconds.

TIME$ (Model III) returns the date and time of day in the format dd/mm/yy hh:mm:ss. The time may be set during initial power-up by answering the TIME question in TRS-DOS. Time may be obtained by using the statement:

```
T$=RIGHT$(TIME$,8)
```

TRS-80 Color Computer

COCO does not provide TIME$, and it cannot be simulated in BASIC.

COMMENTS

TRS-80 Models IV & III

TRON turns the trace utility on. This causes the line number of the line in execution to be printed on the screen—inside a pair of brackets—at the cursor position as the line begins execution.

TROFF turns the trace utility off.

TRS-80 Color Computer

TRON turns the trace utility on. This causes the line number of the line in execution to be printed on the screen—inside a pair of square brackets—at the cursor position as the line begins execution.

TROFF turns the trace utility off.

COMMENTS

TRACE functions are usually used at the programming level, while debugging a program. These commands are normally removed from the final version of a working program.

UNLOAD

APPLE IIe & II+
Simulate it with the CLOSE statement.

IBM PC & PCjr
Simulate it with the CLOSE statement.

COMMODORE 64
Simulate it with the CLOSEn statement, where parameter **n** is the previously OPENed file. To close all files, execute

SYS 65511

USING

is used by some machines to format PRINTed output. See **PRINT USING**.

USR

APPLE IIe & II+
USR(**a**) calls a machine-language routine and passes argument **a** to it. Argument **a** is any numeric or string variable or expression that will be passed to the routine. Also see **CALL**.

IBM PC & PCjr
USR[n](**a**) calls machine-language routine **n**, and passes argument **a** to it. Parameter **n** is the number of the routine as defined with DEF USR **n**—range 0-9, default 0. Argument **a** is any numeric or string variable or expression that will be passed to routine **n**. Also see **CALL**.

COMMODORE 64
USR(**a**) calls a previously written machine-language subroutine, where argument **a** is an arithmetic expression in the range 0-65535. The subroutine's address must have been previously poked to addresses 785 and 786—in low byte, high byte order. This function passes the argument **a** to the subroutine via address 97. Returned to this address is the new value for **a**.

VAL

APPLE IIe & II+
VAL(**x$**) converts **x$** to a numeric expression, where **x$** is any string expression. Leading blanks, tabs and line feeds are stripped from **x$** before the conversion is made. If the first character of **x$** is not numeric, the value returned is 0. Thus, only that left portion of **x$** consisting of numeric characters is converted to a numeric expression.

IBM PC & PCjr
VAL(**x$**) converts **x$** to a numeric expression, where **x$** is any string expression. Leading blanks, tabs and line feeds are stripped from **x$** before the conversion is made. If the first character of **x$** is not numeric, the value returned is 0. Thus, only that left portion of **x$** consisting of numeric characters is converted to a numeric expression.

COMMODORE 64
VAL(**x$**) converts **x$** to a numeric expression, where **x$** is any string expression. Leading blanks and embedded spaces are stripped from **x$** before the conversion is made. If the first character of **x$** is not numeric, the value returned is 0. Thus, only that left portion of **x$** consisting of numeric characters is converted to a numeric expression.

VALIDATE

APPLE IIe & II+
Not available. Cannot be simulated.

IBM PC & PCjr
Cannot be simulated in BASIC, but with DOS procedure CHKDSK, similar results are possible.

COMMODORE 64
VALIDATE deletes all improperly CLOSEd files and creates a new block-availability map of the disk. This effect is obtained with the following program lines, where 8 is the number of the disk drive. Also note that

TRS-80 Models IV & III	TRS-80 Color Computer	COMMENTS
Simulate it with the CLOSE statement.	UNLOAD **d** where **d** specifies a disk drive number. This command will close all OPENed files on the specified drive. UNLOAD does not close cassette files.	

TRS-80 Models IV & III	TRS-80 Color Computer	COMMENTS
USR[n](a) calls machine-language routine **n**, and passes argument **a** to it. Parameter **n** is the number of the routine as defined with DEF USR **n**—range 0-9, default 0. Parameter **a** is an integer expression—range −32768-32767. It will be passed to routine **n**. Also see **CALL** for the Model IV.	USR[n](a) calls machine-language routine **n**, and passes argument **a** to it. Parameter **n** is the number of the routine as defined with DEF USR **n**—range 0-9, default 0. Parameter **a** is any numeric or string variable or expression that will be passed to routine **n**.	

TRS-80 Models IV & III	TRS-80 Color Computer	COMMENTS
VAL(x$) converts **x$** to a numeric expression, where **x$** is any string expression. Leading blanks, tabs and line feeds are stripped from **x$** before the conversion is made. If the first character of **x$** is not numeric, the value returned is 0. Thus, only that left portion of **x$** consisting of numeric characters is converted to a numeric expression.	VAL(x$) converts **x$** to a numeric expression, where **x$** is any string expression. Leading blanks, tabs and line feeds are stripped from **x$** before the conversion is made. If the first character of **x$** is not numeric, the value returned is 0. Thus, only that left portion of **x$** consisting of numeric characters is converted to a numeric expression.	

TRS-80 Models IV & III	TRS-80 Color Computer	COMMENTS
Not available. Cannot be simulated.	Not available. Cannot be simulated.	

VALIDATE may be abbreviated to just **V**:

```
10 OPEN 15,8,15:
   PRINT#15,"VALIDATE":
   CLOSE 15
```

VARPTR, VARPTR$

APPLE IIe & II+

Cannot be simulated in BASIC on the Apple without machine-language programming. You can, however, find the address of the first byte of data about the most recently used variable by PEEKing locations 131 and 132. You must multiply the value found at 132 by 256, then add it to the value found at 131. The result will be the address of the data about the most recently used variable.

IBM PC & PCjr

VARPTR(n) returns the address of the first byte of data associated with variable **n**, which may be a string, numeric or array variable. The address returned will be an integer in the range 0 to 65535, which is an offset from BASIC's data segment. Consequently, it is not affected by DEF SEG. You should assign all simple variables before calling VARPTR for an array because the address of an array changes each time a simple variable is assigned. VARPTR is usually used to get an address to be passed to a USR machine-language routine.

VARPTR (#n) returns the starting address of the file control block for file number **n**, where **n** is the file number named when the file was OPENed. This is not the same as the DOS file control block. The address returned will be an integer in the range 0-65535, which is an offset from BASIC's data segment. Consequently, it is not affected by DEF SEG. This command has no meaning for cassette files.

VARPTR$(n) returns the address of the variable **n** in the form of a three-byte string. The first byte of the string specifies the type of the variable. If the first byte—byte 0—is 2, **n** is an integer. If it is 3, **n** is a string. If it is 4, **n** is a single-precision number. If it is 8, **n** is a double-precision number.

The second byte—byte 1—is the low byte of the variable address. The third byte—byte 2—is the high byte of the variable address. You should assign all simple variables before calling VARPTR$ for an array because the address of an array changes each time a simple variable is assigned. VARPTR$ is most commonly used to indicate a variable name in a command string for PLAY or DRAW in programs to be compiled, but it may be found in interpretive BASIC programs as well.

COMMODORE 64

Cannot be simulated without extensive machine language, which is beyond the scope of this book.

TRS-80 Models IV & III

VARPTR(n) returns the address of the first byte of data associated with variable **n**, which may be a string, numeric or array variable. The value returned will be an integer that is the absolute memory address of the data, unless the value is negative. If the value returned is negative, add 65536 to it to obtain the absolute memory address. VARPTR is usually used to get an address to be passed to a USR machine-language routine.

VARPTR (#n) (Model IV) returns the starting address of the file data buffer for file number **n**, where **n** is the file number named when the file was OPENed. The value returned will be an integer that is the absolute memory address of the data, unless the value is negative. If the value returned is negative, add 65536 to it to obtain the absolute memory address. VARPTR is usually used to get an address to be passed to a USR machine-language routine.

Simulate VARPTR$ by using VARPTR to get an address. Then add a value to that address. The value you add depends upon what information you need. You then PEEK the location represented by the address plus the value. There are complex rules for determining what value to add to the address. They depend on the information you are seeking and the type of variable you are using. For a detailed discussion, refer to the Model IV *Disk System Owner's Manual*, pages 2-183 to 2-186 or the *Model III Operation and BASIC Language Reference Manual*, pages 193 to 194.

TRS-80 Color Computer

VARPTR(n) returns the address of the first byte of data associated with variable **n**, which may be a string, numeric or array variable. The value returned will be the absolute memory address of the data about the variable. The data does not contain any information about the type of variable. The programmer is responsible for passing that to any USR routines. The actual information found at the memory address returned by VARPTR depends on the variable type. For a discussion of the format of the information found at the memory address, see *Going Ahead With Extended Color Basic,* pages 148 to 150. VARPTR is usually used to get an address to be passed to a USR machine-language routine.

VARPTR$ cannot be simulated on the COCO.

COMMENTS

VERIFY

APPLE IIe & II+

Cannot be easily simulated on the Apple. Some independent vendors have published extensive programs that can simulate it.

IBM PC & PCjr

The VERIFY option can be specified only from DOS before entering BASIC. Once specified, this option causes all data written to disk to be verified.

COMMODORE 64

VERIFY [filename][,device] checks the file **filename** against the BASIC program in memory. If **filename** is omitted and **device** is 1 (cassette), the next program on cassette is assumed. If **device** is 8 (disk), **filename** is not optional. If **device** is omitted, the cassette is assumed. If the programs are not the same, a VERIFY ERROR message is displayed and program execution stops. VERIFY can also be used as a convenient means of skipping over a program on cassette to get to the next program, or the next free area on the tape. See **SKIPF**.

VIEW

APPLE IIe & II+

Not available. Cannot be simulated.

IBM PC & PCjr

VIEW [SCREEN] [(x1,y1)-(x2,y2) [,[attribute][,[boundary]]]] (BASIC 2.0 and Cartridge BASIC Only) defines subsets of the viewing screen—called **viewports.** Although several viewports may be displayed at a time, only one may be active. Used in conjunction with WINDOW, it may also accomplish scaling of objects. VIEW is used only in the graphics modes. If no parameters are included, VIEW defines the entire screen as the viewport and cancels any other viewports in use. If the x and y coordinate parameters are included, they define the location of the viewport on the screen.

Note that VIEW will sort the coordinates correctly, so it does not matter whether you specify the smaller value of x as **x1** or **x2**, or the smaller value of y as **y1** or **y2**. The only restriction is that **x1** cannot equal **x2**, and **y1** cannot equal **y2**. They must be valid screen coordinates—i.e., they must lie within the actual screen.

The color attribute parameter will fill the viewport with the specified color. See the **COLOR** command for specific colors and an explanation of the relationship between colors and attributes.

The parameter boundary causes a border line to be drawn around the

COMMODORE 64

Not available. Cannot be simulated.

viewport in the specified color from the current palette. See **COLOR** for a list of valid color numbers. If you do not include SCREEN, the characters you subsequently draw will be within the viewport. That is, the upper-left corner of the viewport becomes coordinate 0,0. If you do include SCREEN, the upper-left corner of the screen remains coordinate 0,0. Those portions of the figures that you subsequently draw outside the viewport will not be drawn. This is known as *clipping.*

You can accomplish scaling of objects by defining WINDOW SCREEN as the size of the actual screen. See **WINDOW.** Then vary the size of the viewport before drawing objects. In this case you should not use SCREEN within the VIEW command.

When you use VIEW, CLS will not clear the whole screen. It will clear only the current viewport. To clear the entire screen, use VIEW without any parameters, then CLS. Any RUN command or SCREEN command— i.e., not SCREEN as a parameter for a VIEW or WINDOW command—will disable the viewports.

TRS-80 Models IV & III

The VERIFY option (Model IV) can be specified only from DOS before entering BASIC. Once specified, this option causes all data written to disk to be verified.

CLOAD?["filename"] (Model III) compares the file **filename** from the tape to the program in memory. If **filename** is omitted, the next program on cassette is compared.

TRS-80 Color Computer

VERIFY ON causes all disk output to be verified.

VERIFY OFF causes cancellation of verification.

COMMENTS

TRS-80 Models IV & III

Not available. Cannot be simulated.

TRS-80 Color Computer

Not available. Cannot be simulated.

COMMENTS

VLIN

APPLE IIe & II+

VLIN y1,y2 AT x draws a vertical line from row **y1** to row **y2** at column **x** on the low-resolution color display, using the current color.

IBM PC & PCjr

LINE [(x1,y1)]-(x2,y2)[,[a][,B[F]] [,style]] (Graphics Modes Only) draws a line, where **x1** is the beginning horizontal coordinate, **y1** is the beginning vertical coordinate, **x2** is the ending horizontal coordinate, and **y2** is the ending vertical coordinate. The ranges for x and y depend on the current value of SCREEN. See **SCREEN**.

The optional value **a** is the attribute used for drawing. See **COLOR** for an explanation of the possible values for **a**. Specifying **B** will cause a box to be displayed, with its opposite corners at **x1,y1** and **x2,y2**. **BF** will display a filled box.

The **style** is used to determine whether to draw a solid line or some sort of a dotted line. The placement of the dots is determined by the bit pattern of the number used. For example, if &HCCCC is used, it will display a dashed line with the pattern 1100110011001100. Here, 1 represents a dot and 0 represents a space because &HCCCC hexadecimal= 1100110011001100 binary.

COMMODORE 64

Although there is no VLIN command on the Commodore, the following program lines produce a similar effect:

```
100 R=1: COL=3: LN=5: LI=165
110 POKE 783,0: POKE 781,R:
    POKE 782,COL
120 SYS 65520
130 FOR I=1 TO LN: PRINT
    CHR$(LI)CHR$(17)CHR$(1
    57);
140 NEXT: PRINT
```

This produces a vertical line of length **LN**, starting at row **R**, column **COL**. In this case, the line is positioned at the left edge of the cursor. To move the position of the line within the cursor, change **LI** from 165 to 116, 103, 98, 125, 104, 121 or 167. **LI** equal to 167 will position the line on the right edge of the cursor.

VTAB

APPLE IIe & II+

VTAB n moves the cursor to line **n**, where **n** is a numeric expression between 1 and 24. The column position remains unchanged and only the row position changes.

IBM PC & PCjr

LOCATE [r] [,[c] [,[v] [,[start] [,stop]]]] places the cursor and specifies several options for cursor display. Parameter **r** specifies the row—range 1-25. Parameter **c** specifies the column—range 1-40 or 1-80, depending on the current WIDTH. If **v**=0 the cursor is invisible. If **v**=1, the cursor is visible. Variables **start** and **stop** indicate the cursor scan start and stop lines—range 0-31. **Start**, **stop** and **v** do not apply in graphics modes. If **r** is 25, then you must use the KEY OFF command prior to the LOCATE command.

COMMODORE 64

Simulate it with the following program lines. They will place the cursor on line **R** at column **COL**. Of course, you must assign values to **R** and **COL** before calling the subroutine.

```
1000 POKE 783,0: POKE 781,R:
     POKE 782,COL
1010 SYS 65520
1020 RETURN
```

TRS-80 Models IV & III

To simulate a vertical line drawn from **y1** to **y2** with VLIN, use

```
10 X=0: FOR Y=Y1 TO Y2:REM
   RANGE x=0-47, RANGE
   y=0-127
20 SET (X,Y)
30 NEXT Y
```

TRS-80 Color Computer

LINE   [(x1,y1)]-(x2,y2),a,[b]   will draw a line, where **x1** is the beginning horizontal coordinate, **y1** is the beginning vertical coordinate, **x2** is the ending horizontal coordinate, and **y2** is the ending vertical coordinate. If **(x1,y1)** is omitted, the end point from the previous LINE statement is used. Parameters **x1** and **x2** may have a range of 0-255, while **y1** and **y2** may have a range of 0-191. Parameter **a** is either PSET or PRESET, one of which is required. PSET sets the line in the foreground color, while PRESET sets the line in the background color. Parameter **b** is either B or BF, both of which are optional. Specifying B will cause a box to be displayed, while BF will display a filled box.

COMMENTS

TRS-80 Models IV & III

PRINT @ **n** (Model IV) or **PRINT** @ **(r,c)** places the cursor at the specified position, where **n** is a screen position in the range 0-1919, and **(r,c)** is a pair of coordinates specifying the row—range 0-23—and the column—range 0-79.

PRINT @ **n** (Model III) places the cursor at the specified position, where **n** is a screen position in the range 0-1023.

TRS-80 Color Computer

PRINT @ **n** places the cursor at the specified position, where **n** is a screen position in the range 0-511.

COMMENTS

WAIT

APPLE IIe & II +

WAIT addr,n[,m] halts program execution while monitoring the condition of a memory location for a change in status. Parameter **addr** is an integer—range −65535-65535—but not practical outside legal memory addresses. It specifies which address is to be monitored. The bit value read at the address is first XORed with **m**—default 0. This tests for the value of each position. The resulting bit value is then ANDed with **n**, thus determining which bit positions are tested. If the result of these operations is 0, BASIC loops back and tests again.

This command is usually used for communications. It is possible to enter an infinite loop with this command. The loop can be exited only by resetting the machine.

Use of ports on the Apple is not accomplished without the use of machine-language routines or extensive PEEKs and POKEs. This is beyond the scope of this book. A good reference on the subject is *The Apple Connection* by James W. Coffron.

IBM PC & PCjr

WAIT port,n[,m] halts program execution while monitoring the condition of a machine-input port for a change in status. Parameter **port** is an integer—range 0-65535—specifying which port is to be monitored. The bit value read at the port is first XORed with **m**—default 0. This tests for the value of each position. The resulting bit value is then ANDed with **n**, determining which bit positions are tested. If the result of these operations is 0, BASIC loops back and tests again.

This command is usually used for communications. It is possible to enter an infinite loop with this command. The loop can be exited only by resetting the machine.

COMMODORE 64

WAIT n,m[,p] halts program execution while awaiting a change in a bit at a memory location, where **n** is a memory location—range 0-65535—**m** and **p** are in the range 0-255 with the optional **p** defaulting to 0. WAIT causes program execution to halt until the value of the bit at memory location **n** changes in a specific way dictated by the other two parameters. Parameter **n** is exclusively ORed with **p**, then the result is ANDed with **m**, continuing until the final result is non-zero. The command is seldom used.

WEND, WHILE

APPLE IIe & II +

Apple does not recognize the WHILE-WEND commands, but they may be simulated by IF-THEN loops. The loops could be structured as in the example below. The test in line 140 could be any test relevant to your algorithm:

```
140 IF X < > 5 THEN 160 : REM
    TEST EXPRESSION
150 GOTO 190 : REM TEST FAILED
160 REM OTHER STATEMENTS
    HERE EXECUTED IF LINE 140
    TEST SUCCESSFUL
180 GOTO 140 : REM TEST AGAIN
190 REM PROGRAM EXECUTION
    CONTINUES HERE
```

IBM PC & PCjr

WHILE test (Program lines to be executed while test is true.)
WEND (Program lines to be executed when test fails.)

These commands are used to structure a program so that a series of commands is executed as long as a particular expression tests true. WHILEs may be nested, as with FOR-NEXT loops. Parameter **test** may be any logical, Boolean, string or mathematical expression that can return a True (non-zero) or False (0) value. For example:

```
10 WHILE INKEY$ = " "
20 LOCATE 1 , 1 : PRINT "PRESS
   ANY KEY"
30 WEND
40 CLS : PRINT "THANK YOU FOR
   PRESSING MY KEY"
```

COMMODORE 64

Commodore does not recognize the WHILE-WEND commands, but they may be simulated by IF-THEN loops. The loops could be structured as in the example below. The test in line 140 could be any test relevant to your algorithm:

```
140 IF X < > 5 THEN 160 : REM
    TEST EXPRESSION
150 GOTO 190 : REM TEST FAILED
160 REM OTHER STATEMENTS
    HERE EXECUTED IF LINE 140
    TEST SUCCESSFUL
180 GOTO 140 : REM TEST AGAIN
190 REM PROGRAM EXECUTION
    CONTINUES HERE
```

TRS-80 Models IV & III

WAIT port,n[,m] (Model IV) halts program execution while monitoring the condition of a machine-input port for a change in status. Parameter **port** is an integer—range 0-255—specifying which port is to be monitored. The bit value read at the port is first XORed with **m**—default 0. This tests for the value of each position. The resulting bit value is then ANDed with **n**, determining which bit positions are tested. If the result of these operations is 0, BASIC loops back and tests again.

This command is usually used for communications. It is possible to enter an infinite loop with this command. The loop can be exited only by resetting the machine.

Not available. Cannot be simulated on the Model III.

TRS-80 Color Computer

The COCO requires machine-language routines or extensive PEEKs and POKEs to allow use of a port. This is beyond the scope of this book.

COMMENTS

Also see **INP**, **COM** and **TERM**.

TRS-80 Models IV & III

WHILE test (Program lines to be executed while test is true.)
WEND (Program lines to be executed when test fails.)

With the Model IV, these commands are used to structure a program so that a series of commands is executed as long as a particular expression tests true. WHILEs may be nested, as with FOR-NEXT loops. Parameter **test** may be any logical, Boolean, string or mathematical expression that can return a True (non-zero) or False (0) value. For example:

```
10 WHILE INKEY$=""
20 PRINT@1, "PRESS ANY KEY"
30 WEND
40 PRINT "THANK YOU FOR
   PRESSING MY KEY"
```

The Model III does not recognize the WHILE-WEND commands, but they

TRS-80 Color Computer

The COCO does not recognize the WHILE-WEND commands, but they may be simulated by IF-THEN loops. The loops could be structured as in the example below. The test in line 140 could be any test relevant to your algorithm:

```
140 IF X<>5 THEN 160 ELSE
    190: REM TEST EXPRESSION
160 REM OTHER STATEMENTS
    HERE EXECUTED IF LINE 140
    TEST SUCCESSFUL
180 GOTO 140: REM TEST AGAIN
190 REM PROGRAM EXECUTION
    CONTINUES HERE
```

may be simulated by IF-THEN loops. The loops could be structured as in the example below. The test in line 140 could be any test relevant to your algorithm:

COMMENTS

```
140 IF X<>5 THEN 160 ELSE
    190: REM TEST EXPRESSION
160 REM OTHER STATEMENTS
    HERE EXECUTED IF LINE 140
    TEST SUCCESSFUL
180 GOTO 140: REM TEST AGAIN
190 REM PROGRAM EXECUTION
    CONTINUES HERE
```

WIDTH

APPLE IIe & II+

Changing the width of the text screen on the Apple depends on the monitor card installed. If an 80-column card is installed, you can normally switch between 40 and 80 columns under software control. However, the commands that do this vary with the card you use. If you wish to have the screen narrower than the maximum width normally available, use the following program lines:

```
10 POKE 33,w
```

where **w** is the width you desire for the text window. Parameter **w** must be less than 40 when in 40-column mode, and less than 80 when in 80-column mode.

The following routine will cause a carriage return to be inserted every **w** characters in a PRINT statement. You must define the string you wish to be printed as **T$** before entering the subroutine. You can vary **w** to be whatever width you want. For output to go to the printer or to a sequential file, use the proper routine before calling this subroutine.

```
1000 W=40: P=1
1010 O$=MID$(T$,P,W): IF
     LEN(O$)=0 THEN 1030
1020 PRINT O$: P=P+W: GOTO
     1010
1030 RETURN
```

IBM PC & PCjr

WIDTH [d,]s sets the width of output for PRINT statements—the number of characters after which BASIC will insert a carriage return. Parameter **d** is either a file number—range 1-15—or a device name such as SCRN:, LPT1: or COM1:. Parameter **s** specifies the width—default 80 for screen and printers, 255 for COM: devices. If **d** is omitted then SCRN: is assumed and only 20, 40 or 80 columns are valid, depending on the machine configuration and version of BASIC used. The screen will be cleared and the border set to black. If you specify a device, the current width is not changed until you open the device at a later time. If you specify a file number, the current width is changed immediately, affecting the currently OPENed file number.

COMMODORE 64

The following routine will cause a carriage return to be inserted every **W** characters in a PRINT statement. You must define the string you wish to be printed as **T$** before entering the subroutine. You can vary **W** to be whatever width you want. To cause output to go to the printer or to a sequential file, you must use the proper routine before calling this subroutine.

```
1000 W=40: P=1
1010 O$=MID$(T$,P,W): IF
     LEN(O$)=0 THEN 1030
1020 PRINT O$: P=P+W: GOTO
     1010
1030 RETURN
```

Changing the width of the display screen on the Commodore 64 is beyond the scope of this book. It requires machine language and extensive knowledge of the graphics chips in the computer.

WINDOW

APPLE IIe & II+

Not available. Cannot be simulated.

IBM PC & PCjr

WINDOW [[SCREEN] (x1,y1)-(x2,y2)] (BASIC 2.0 or Cartridge BASIC Only) redefines the graphic screen coordinates. You can define the "world coordinates," which may actually define an area larger than the screen or may cause the screen to be much smaller on a coordinate system. Thus, you are not bound by the physical borders of the screen. The x and y coordinates can be any single-precision, floating-point number. The only restriction is that **x1** cannot equal **x2**, and **y1** cannot equal **y2**.

WINDOW sorts the x and y coordinates so that the smallest values of x

COMMODORE 64

Not available. Cannot be simulated.

and y will always be considered first. If the x and y coordinates are not specified, the world coordinates equal the normal graphic screen coordinates.

If SCREEN is omitted, the screen is given in true Cartesian coordinates—**x1,y1** is the lower-left coordinate. If SCREEN is included, the screen is given in inverted Cartesian coordinates—**x1,y1** is the upper-left coordinate. This is the normal convention for computer-graphics screens.

TRS-80 Models IV & III

You can switch to large screen type—32 columns on the Model III, 40 columns on the Model IV—and back by using PRINT CHR$ statements.

```
10 PRINT CHR$(23): REM
   SWITCH TO LARGE TYPE
20 PRINT CHR$(28): REM
   SWITCH TO SMALL TYPE
```

The following routine will cause a carriage return to be inserted every **W** characters in a PRINT statement. You must define the string you wish to be printed as **T$** before entering the subroutine. You can vary **W** to be whatever width you want up to 255. For output to go to the printer, use LPRINT instead of PRINT in line 1020. To send the output to a sequential file, use PRINT# n in line 1020, where **n** is the file number that was used to open the file.

```
1000 W=40: P=1
1010 O$=MID$(T$,P,W): IF
     LEN(O$)=0 THEN 1030
1020 PRINT O$: P=P+W: GOTO
     1010
1030 RETURN
```

TRS-80 Color Computer

The following routine causes a carriage return to be inserted every **W** characters in a PRINT statement. You must define the string you wish to be printed as **T$** before entering the subroutine. You can vary **W** to be whatever width you want up to 255. For output to go to the printer, use LPRINT instead of PRINT in line 1020. To send the output to a sequential file, use PRINT# n in line 1020, where **n** is the file number that was used to open the file.

```
1000 W=40: P=1
1010 O$=MID$(T$,P,W): IF
     LEN(O$)=0 THEN 1030
1020 PRINT O$: P=P+W: GOTO
     1010
1030 RETURN
```

COMMENTS

TRS-80 Models IV & III

Not available. Cannot be simulated.

If you DRAW a figure outside the screen coordinates, but within the world coordinates, line clipping will occur. You can use WINDOW in conjunction with the VIEW statement to look at several portions of the world coordinates at a time. You can also use WINDOW—with or without VIEW—to zoom and pan images. Using RUN, SCREEN or WINDOW commands, without parameters, cancels any previous WINDOW commands.

TRS-80 Color Computer

Not available. Cannot be simulated.

COMMENTS

WRITE, WRITE#

APPLE IIe & II+

WRITE redirects output to a specific file, as in

```
10 PRINT CHR$(4); "OPEN
   filename"
20 PRINT CHR$(4); "WRITE
   filename"
```

where **filename** is the name of the file to be written to. For more details, see **OPEN**.

You can simulate the IBM command WRITE on the Apple by PRINTing a CHR$(44) between each item in the list of items to be printed, and by PRINTing CHR$(34) before and after each string in the list. The items should be separated by semicolons to print them on the same line. Stripping leading blanks from positive numbers would require too much program overhead for the intended benefit.

To simulate WRITE#, simply redirect output to the specified file before the PRINT statement, as discussed above.

IBM PC & PCjr

WRITE list outputs a **list** of expressions to the screen. The list can consist of any variables or expressions separated by commas or semicolons.

WRITE# n, list outputs a **list** of expressions to a sequential file, where **n** is the number assigned to the file when it was OPENed. The list can consist of any variables or expressions separated by commas or semicolons.

The differences between WRITE and PRINT are as follows: 1) WRITE delimits each item with a comma. 2) WRITE delimits strings with quotation marks. 3) WRITE follows the last item in a list with a carriage return/line feed. 4) WRITE does not precede positive numbers with a blank space.

To simulate the Apple word WRITE, see **OPEN**.

COMMODORE 64

You can simulate the IBM word WRITE on the Commodore by PRINTing a CHR$(44) between each item in the list of items to be printed, and by PRINTing a CHR$(34) before and after each string in the list. The items should be separated by semicolons to PRINT them on the same line. Stripping leading blanks from a positive number X is accomplished by PRINTing X$, where X$=RIGHT$(STR$(X),LEN(STR$(X)-1))

To simulate WRITE#, simply use PRINT# n, in place of PRINT, after a sequential file, **n**, has been OPENed.

To simulate the Apple word WRITE, see **OPEN**.

TRS-80 Models IV & III

WRITE list (Model IV) outputs a **list** of expressions to the screen. The list can consist of any variables or expressions separated by commas.

WRITE# n, list (Model IV) outputs a **list** of expressions to a sequential file, where **n** is the number assigned to the file when it was OPENed. The list can consist of any variables or expressions separated by commas.

The differences between WRITE and PRINT are as follows: 1) WRITE delimits each item with a comma. 2) WRITE delimits strings with quotation marks. 3) WRITE follows the last item in a list with a carriage return/line feed. 4) WRITE does not precede positive numbers with a blank space.

To simulate the Apple word WRITE, see **OPEN**.

You can simulate the IBM word WRITE on the Model III by PRINTing a CHR$(44) between each item in the list of items to be printed, and by PRINTing CHR$(34) before and after each string in the list. The items should be separated by semicolons to print them on the same line. Stripping leading blanks from positive numbers would require too much programming overhead for the intended benefit.

You can simulate WRITE# on the Model III in the same manner by using PRINT#.

To simulate the Apple word WRITE, see **OPEN**.

TRS-80 Color Computer

WRITE list outputs a **list** of expressions to the screen. The list can consist of any variables or expressions separated by commas.

WRITE# n, list outputs a **list** of expressions to a sequential file, where **n** is the number assigned to the file when it was OPENed. The list can consist of any variables or expressions separated by commas.

The differences between WRITE and PRINT are as follows: 1) WRITE delimits each item with a comma. 2) WRITE delimits strings with quotation marks. 3) WRITE follows the last item in a list with a carriage return/line feed.

To simulate the Apple word WRITE, see **OPEN**.

COMMENTS

XDRAW

APPLE IIe & II +

XDRAW n [AT c,r] draws the shape n from the shape table currently in use. Parameter c specifies the row for XDRAWing on the high-resolution screen, while r specifies the row. If c and r are omitted, the most recently specified location will be used. XDRAW differs from DRAW in that XDRAW draws in the inverse of the colors currently displayed under where the shape will be. Thus the shape n will be reversed out of the existing screen. XDRAW also differs from DRAW in that if a shape is XDRAWn to the same location twice, the screen under it will be restored to its original state.

IBM PC & PCjr

PUT (x,y),n,[XOR] causes the graphics array n to be PUT on the screen at coordinates (x,y). Because XOR is the default action for PUT, it does not have to be explicitly stated. PUT with the XOR option simulates Apple's XDRAW in that it inverts an image onto the existing graphics in the area it is to occupy, and PUTting a shape to the same location twice will return the screen area occupied by it undisturbed. See PUT.

COMMODORE 64

Simulating XDRAW on the Commodore is not easily accomplished without machine-language programming. This is beyond the scope of this book. If you need this capability, you may wish to investigate the use of sprites. See the *Commodore 64 Programmer's Reference Manual,* pages 131 to 182.

XOR

APPLE IIe & II +

Simulate it with ((x AND NOT y) OR (NOT x AND y))

The truth table for this expression is below:

x	y	((x AND NOT y) OR (NOT x AND y))
T	T	F
T	F	T
F	T	T
F	F	F

IBM PC & PCjr

XOR is a logical and bitwise operator that exclusively ORs two values. The truth table for XOR is below:

x	y	x XOR y
T	T	F
T	F	T
F	T	T
F	F	F

COMMODORE 64

Simulate it with ((x AND NOT y) OR (NOT x AND y))

The truth table for this expression is below:

x	y	((x AND NOT y) OR (NOT x AND y))
T	T	F
T	F	T
F	T	T
F	F	F

XPLOT

is an undocumented reserve word for Apple. No command has been assigned to it.

TRS-80 Models IV & III

Cannot be simulated on the Models IV or III because they lack graphics.

TRS-80 Color Computer

PUT **(x1,y1)-(x2,y2),n** draws a graphics rectangle with the upper-left corner at coordinates **(x1,y1)** and the lower-right corner at coordinates **(x2,y2)**. The contents of the rectangle are determined by the values in the array **n**. The array **n** must have been previously created using the GET statement. The COCO does not have the capability to erase the rectangle back to its previous state, so if this is desired, you must first GET the original values of the rectangle and store them in another array. Then you can PUT that rectangle back with the PUT command. See **GET** and **PUT**.

COMMENTS

TRS-80 Models IV & III

XOR (Model IV) is a logical and bitwise operator that exclusively ORs two values. The truth table for XOR is below:

x	y	x XOR y
T	T	F
T	F	T
F	T	T
F	F	F

Simulate it on the Model III with **((x AND NOT y) OR (NOT x AND y))**

The truth table for this expression is below:

x	y	((x AND NOT y) OR (NOT x AND y))
T	T	F
T	F	T
F	T	T
F	F	F

TRS-80 Color Computer

Simulate it with **((x AND NOT y) OR (NOT x AND y))**

The truth table for this expression is below:

x	y	((x AND NOT y) OR (NOT x AND y))
T	T	F
T	F	T
F	T	T
F	F	F

COMMENTS

Index